Vehicle of Influence

Michigan Studies in International Political Economy

SERIES EDITORS: Edward Mansfield and Lisa Martin

Vehicle of Influence

Building a European Car Market

Roland Stephen

Ann Arbor

THE UNIVERSITY OF MICHIGAN PRESS

Copyright © by the University of Michigan 2000
All rights reserved
Published in the United States of America by
The University of Michigan Press
Manufactured in the United States of America
⊗ Printed on acid-free paper

2003   2002   2001   2000   4   3   2   1

*A CIP catalog record for this book is available
from the British Library.*

Library of Congress Cataloging-in-Publication Data

Stephen, Roland Francis, 1957–
      Vehicle of influence : building a European car market / Roland
Stephen.
          p.   cm. — (Michigan studies in international political economy)
      Includes bibliographical references and index.
      ISBN 0-472-11121-3 (cloth : alk. paper)
      1. Automobile industry and trade—European Union countries.
      2. Automobile industry and trade—Government policy—Europe.
      3. Competition, International.   I. Title.   II. Series.
      HD9710.E82 S74   2000
      380.1′456292′094—dc21   00-008328

For Holly

Contents

Figures

Tables

Preface

The European Union (EU) poses the same kind of problem for social scientists as the bumblebee does for aerospace engineers. Scrutiny of the bumblebee suggests that anything with such a large body in comparison with its wings cannot possibly fly—yet fly it does. By the same token, the complex forces pushing and pulling the EU in every direction are so powerful and contradictory that death by paralysis (or "eurosclerosis") is often expected. Yet so far the Union has contrived to inch forward, both thwarting its critics and disappointing its supporters. Of course, the EU is not propelled onward by some grand historical or material imperative. It is the product of numerous political bargains, great and small, that serve prosaic purposes. That is why its uncertain progress seems so difficult to chart.

To understand this trajectory, it is necessary to understand the complex political processes behind these various bargains. No single, parsimonious theory is adequate to the task. The goal of this book is to tie together an appropriate bundle of analytical tools that in combination can make sense of EU policy outcomes—both the successes and the failures. The larger goal, at least by implication, is to cast new light on a global process. Economic and political integration advances by fits and starts throughout the world, and the forces at work seem to be as prosaic as any discovered in Brussels. If the details of policy-making reported below appear highly specific, the patterns observed and analyzed, I believe, recur in other regions. The outcomes touch the lives of millions far removed from Europe.

In an effort to keep a complicated task as simple as possible, I chose to concentrate my analysis on the European automobile industry during a period of increased economic and political integration. The interests at stake were significant, the political battles highly visible. This made analysis tractable. More important than that, however, is the suspicion that any program such as the EU should be judged by its consequences for core economic sectors, and, like it or not, the auto industry remains the largest manufacturing activity on earth. I believe that this focus will allow readers to judge for themselves both the value of my analytical approach and the degree to which the consumers, voters, and workers of Europe are likely to realize all the benefits of regional political and economic integration.

Any project such as this one owes much to others. In particular, Jeffry Frieden was, and remains, a constant source of wisdom, encouragement, and good humor. I also owe a great debt of gratitude to Miriam Golden, Ron Rogowski, and George Tsebelis, who have helped me with the project from the beginning, at once anxious about the many signs of confusion I have exhibited while remaining strangely confident in my future progress. In addition, I would like to acknowledge the help of Jean-Laurent Rosenthal, Gary Marks, Thomas Oately, and Kathleen McNamara, and the very useful contributions of two anonymous reviewers. Needless to say, what errors remain are my own. Finally, I am especially grateful to Charles Myers, who has been a thoughtful and helpful editor throughout.

This kind of research would have been impossible without financial support at vital moments. I gratefully acknowledge the assistance of the Center for German and European Affairs at the University of California, Berkeley; the Center for International Business Education and Research at the University of California, Los Angeles; the Institute on Global Conflict and Cooperation at the University of California, San Diego; and the Department of Political Science, University of California, Los Angeles.

In my fieldwork I was often forced to seek long answers from busy people. Everyone I encountered proved to be incredibly helpful. I would single out for thanks Dr. Hans-Viggo von Hülsen, Volkswagen AG; Dr. Stephen Wilks, Exeter University; and especially Madame Béatrice de Castlenau, Comité des Constructeurs Français d'Automobile. I would also like to thank the Groupe d'Étude et de Recherche Permanent sur l'Industrie et les Salariés d'Automobile for the immense amount of material they have produced on the European auto industry. I would also like to thank Gwen Brewer who helped with the bibliography, and Helen Lodge who helped edit the final version. Last I would thank my friend, partner, and wife, Holly Brewer.

CHAPTER I

Completing Europe's Internal Market: The Single European Act in Perspective

The Puzzle of European Integration

In 1991 the European auto industry seemed to be in deep trouble. A controversial trade agreement between the European Union (EU) and Japan restricting Japanese imports had just been completed, and Raymond Levy, chairman of the French automaker Renault, was defending the agreement before a committee of the European Parliament. His comments were defensive, reflecting the views of many at that time.

> We are told that we must make adjustments . . . but my enterprise [Renault] has already laid off 40,000 employees over the last five years. Europeans . . . are subject to social exigencies. We have a debt to our workers . . . especially older workers; the social environment matters. For this reason the agreement is indispensable. The European auto industry needs eight years to adjust.[1]

The fear in the industry was palpable. It wasn't just fear of the Japanese, but more generally of the changes being forced on this privileged industrial sector by a program of accelerated market liberalization. How had the industrial champions of Europe been brought to such a pass? What was this program of market liberalization, and what had brought it about?

In 1987 the member states of the EU signed the Single European Act (SEA). It was a public commitment by each government to eliminate the barriers that continued to obstruct trade among them, and to open up Europe's markets by the end of 1992. This ambitious goal attracted plenty of press coverage, on both sides of the Atlantic, and seemed to give a dramatic new impetus to the process of European integration. However, upon reflection, there was good reason to wonder whether the public rhetoric could be matched by the necessary, wide-ranging policy changes required of each national government and of the institutions of the EU. If the past history of the EU was any guide, these countries were going to find it very difficult to implement the terms of this bargain. Although the agreement was the first significant institutional modification of the Treaty of Rome (which established the EU), it was seen by many as a minor, incremental change.

In the event, much of the "1992" project was accomplished. At the same time, Raymond Levy's fears proved to be exaggerated. Even the powerful automobile industry, which employed hundreds of thousands of people and faced an uncertain economic future, had to swallow a dose of market liberalization. Market segmentation was reduced, subsidies were subject to increased control, and a variety of other regulations were harmonized. In other words, the results of the SEA exceeded past practices and expectations. On the other hand, old habits died hard. While subsidies were reduced, they were by no means eliminated, and external trade remained subject to a costly regime of voluntary restraint on the part of Japanese automakers. Overall, outcomes across the four issue areas examined by this study ranged widely, from a significant change over the status quo to little or no change. Specifically, there was a dramatic increase in harmonization in the case of emissions control, increased transparency but limited reductions in the case of national subsidies, the development of a clearly defined if producer-friendly antitrust regime, but changes in external trade policies that could be construed as positively retrograde. What was the constellation of political and institutional factors that explains these mixed outcomes?

There are good substantive and analytical reasons why these complex changes in policy warrant closer scrutiny. At the time, of course, many people in the United States had reservations about the prospect of "Fortress Europe." There was a fear that Europe's integration would be accomplished at the expense of its trading partners—in other words, that internal trade creation would be offset by the diversion away from Europe of U.S. and Japanese products. This proved to be an exaggerated danger, but the willingness of the EU to play a liberalizing role in international trade has remained uncertain. For example, the consequences of the EU's mixed economic policies are most acutely felt in the economies in the East struggling to make the transition from Soviet central planning. German leaders may promise Poland and others rapid membership in the European club, but Polish pigs cannot be exported to the EU, while Polish steel piping has been subject to anti-dumping suits brought by the EU Commission. This book develops a refined analytical framework that captures the interaction of special interests, national governments, and the institutions of the EU that explains these contradictory policies.

The objective of this book is to move beyond broad-scale discussions of globalization and interdependence and develop the tools with which to analyze the actual policy outcomes that shape economic integration. I begin with the role of national and private interests: the governing elites of the member states stood to reap political benefits if the SEA delivered economic gains, and many large and medium-sized corporations trading in the European market would benefit from the elimination of barriers. Other firms and their employees, however, would face acute adjustment difficulties and served as a significant check on the political process of integration. In my research I show how variation in the costs and benefits from integration across issue areas resulted in variation in the ability of governments and firms to combine in their efforts to shape the future of the European economy.

This account of firm and government preferences is then incorporated into an analysis of the heterogeneous institutional environment of the EU. The institutional environment varied across issue areas, and as a consequence the independent effect of institutions varied. Furthermore, I also discover that the member states, on occasion, were able to refine the institutional environment in order to realize superior political and economic outcomes. In short, the explanation for the policy outcomes combines an analysis of preference formation and collective action problems with an analysis of political institutions. This approach gives new understanding to issues at the core of political economy: the way economic interdependence shapes the formation of transnational interests, and how institutional design—under certain circumstances—may foster policy-making that serves a general interest over the particular.

In this introductory chapter I place the research reported in this book in historical context. Specifically, I sketch the background to the SEA and establish its significance in the light of the previous history of European integration. I go on to map the degree to which economic theory is a useful guide to expected outcomes. I then offer a brief summary of existing approaches commonly used to understand EU policy and compare them with the salient elements of my own analytical framework. I finish by presenting a telegraphic account of my findings. Simply stated, they are as follows: the interests of firms and governments were determined by their exposure to economic adjustment. They were often able to act collectively in shaping outcomes, in ways occasionally structured by the institutional environment of the EU. I argue that this interaction between more or less well-articulated interests and various institutional arenas accounts for the observed variation in the level of integration and harmonization accomplished.

The Single European Act in Historical Perspective

It was in July 1987 that the member states of the EU finally ratified the SEA. This was the first modification of the institutional architecture originally put in place by the Treaty of Rome, the treaty that founded the EU in 1957.[2] In the SEA, and in conjunction with the accompanying "White Paper" published in 1985, these governments committed themselves to full economic integration (defined here as economic openness and regulatory harmonization). This commitment had always been the fundamental objective of the EU, but over the years it had remained elusive. The member states now set themselves the ambitious goal of finally eliminating the remaining barriers to trade, and harmonizing regulations across a range of economic sectors and issue areas before the end of 1992. This agreement was to be the cornerstone of a concerted effort to revitalize the European economy and close the gap in productivity, innovation, and growth that seemed to divide European firms from their U.S. and Japanese competitors. It was hoped that the aggregate economic gains from increased openness would act as a spur to the sluggish economy and promote a beneficial cycle of income growth and investment. (On the SEA see De Ruyt 1989; Taylor 1989; Moravcsik 1991; and Garrett 1992.)

But the ability to realize mutual economic gains through international cooperation is always problematic. While cooperation might be sure to yield such gains *in the aggregate*, the adjustment imposed on privileged domestic interests is often the source of insurmountable political difficulties. For example, although it was understood at the founding of the EU that economic intervention by national governments distorted free competition, all too often in the past the member states had shown themselves willing to protect and subsidize large industrial and commercial enterprises. Even in the years between 1986 and 1988, long after the recession of 1982–83 was over, the average annual expenditures by European governments on state aid represented 2.2 percent of the European Union's gross domestic product (GDP) (CEC [Commission of the European Community] 1991a, 13). Like secret drinkers, they publicly embraced the virtues of sobriety, yet all the while they clung to the bottle in order to dull the political pain that would come from shaking off the claims of powerful clients.

The telegraphic account that follows of the first 25 years of European economic and political integration highlights its many past difficulties. In particular it will serve to emphasize three important points: (a) the uncertain path of European integration—the way in which it has always been episodic, a function of political bargains rather than of some relentless economic logic; (b) the role of divergent national interests and policies in giving rise to this unsteady progress; and (c) (as a result of the first two factors) the significant limitations on European integration that persisted up until the passage of the SEA. Taken together, these elements highlight the distinctiveness of the SEA and its central place in the puzzle that motivates my research project. Given the political character of the integration process, the forces often arrayed against it, and its unsatisfactory record of accomplishments, it is hardly to be wondered that the accomplishments of the SEA were mixed, even if it did move the process of European integration forward further and faster than skeptics initially imagined. The explanation for these mixed outcomes that forms the core of this book will also increase our understanding of the many dilemmas and obstacles that the EU has faced in the past.

The First Twenty-five Years

In the years immediately following the end of the Second World War the international community, under the leadership of the United States, actively sought to establish international institutions that would foster economic stability and political security. Since interstate rivalry and economic instability in Europe had been the source of both world wars, it was there that the search for appropriate international institutions was most energetic. Experiments with a wide range of regional institutions culminated in the establishment of the European Economic Community (EEC), for which an agreement was signed by six European countries, but not the United Kingdom, in 1957. The Treaty of Rome was formally aimed at establishing a free-trade area, but it is important to remember that it was, fundamentally, an economic means to a political end—that of amity and political cooperation. (On the origins and early history of the EEC see Milward 1984, 1992; Pinder 1991; and Moravcsik 1998.)

In its early years the EEC, or EU, as it later became, succeeded in meeting many of the high expectations its founders had for it. Under the energetic leadership of Walter Hallstein, the first president of the European Commission (the supranational body established to forward the purposes of the treaty), progress toward the reduction of tariffs and the expansion of the authority of European institutions seemed impressive. The generally favorable economic conditions of the postwar period no doubt played an important part in lowering the political costs, while magnifying the economic gains associated with these developments.

This halcyon period was disrupted by the policies of the French leader General Charles de Gaulle in the 1960s, who sought to protect French sovereignty. He was responsible for the de facto institutionalization of national vetoes in the Council of Ministers, the governing body of European institutions. He was also responsible for the exclusion of the United Kingdom from EU membership. Earlier progress seemed, as a result, to suffer a political check. However, with the fall from power of de Gaulle and the admission of the United Kingdom, together with Ireland and Denmark, at the beginning of the 1970s, the pace of change seemed to pick up again. The last tariff barriers were eliminated at the end of the 1960s, and in an effort to minimize the consequences of a profligate U.S. monetary policy, the member states began to coordinate their exchange rates within an exchange rate mechanism known as the "snake."

But the 1970s was a period in which the industrial economies endured numerous economic shocks, beginning with the oil embargo in 1973. These occurred in the context of slow rates of growth and widely divergent national economic policies. As a result the level of coordination of policies across Europe actually declined as the decade wore on. The member states proved, for the most part, to be unable to maintain stable exchange rates. At the same time, they resorted to divergent fiscal policies, state interventions, and other strategies that carried with them all kinds of negative collective consequences. In particular this was the era of the "national champion," a state-sanctioned and subsidized firm in a key sector that was to act as an industrial and technological leader. Several auto companies were thought of in these terms (see chapter 3). The result was that by the end of the decade not only was cooperation within the context of the EU paralyzed, but economic performance had begun to sag. Europe seemed trapped by a combination of low growth, high inflation, and increasing unemployment. It was at this time that people began to speak of both "stagflation" and "eurosclerosis" or "europessimism."

The shortcomings of the European economy became even clearer following the recovery in the West after the recession of 1981–82. While the United States and Japan recovered quickly, the EU's return to health was slow. Worse, it proved to be, by comparison, a "jobless" recovery. While the EU grew at an average annual rate of 1.9 percent between 1981 and 1986, the United States grew at 2.9 percent, and Japan at 3.6 percent (CEC 1988a, 42). At the same time, unemployment in the EU remained stubbornly above 10 percent up until 1986 (as a percentage of the civilian labor force), while in the United States it fell below 7 percent (CEC 1988a, 126).

At this point the preferences of the member states, which had diverged in the 1970s as each sought to solve its economic difficulties autonomously, now began to converge. Keynesian management of the economy had failed, and inflation was now perceived as more of a threat than unemployment; as a result monetary policies with a deflationary bias became widely accepted (McNamara 1998; see also Oatley 1997). At the same time, European business had become much more regionally integrated and so found the existing barriers to regional trade increasingly burdensome. Finally, and partly as a consequence of the foregoing, the political balance in many European countries shifted to the right. Taken together, all this led to the focus on a neoliberal strategy of economic openness in the region. That is to say, the SEA and the White Paper were part of a general set of supply-side measures designed to stimulate demand and investment and therefore economic growth. Indeed, the agreement was one of the most important elements in a comprehensive European recovery (inasmuch as external liberalization was more politically acceptable than, for example, eliminating rigidities in domestic labor markets). However, it was also an enterprise that was likely to be very difficult to accomplish.

The Single European Act

The SEA was, therefore, a political project from which the governments of the member states anticipated political payoffs of some kind. Nevertheless, in spite of the shift in political and economic strategies in Europe in the 1980s, this project's success should not be thought of as inevitable. Its success is what makes it an interesting object of inquiry: a favorable (Pareto-superior) outcome was not preordained; it had to be realized by a process of political bargaining over numerous details that cut across issue areas and sectors and that was subject to the institutional structures of the EU.

Significantly, these structures were deliberately modified by the SEA in order to foster rapid political progress. Indeed, these institutional changes were the most important aspect of the SEA, rather than the particular policies it embraced, which were notable for their specificity rather than for their overall purpose (which was no more than the completion of the project envisaged by the original treaty). The crucial institutional change was that, in issues relating to the internal market (which was the focus of the action program), supermajority decision making was adopted. This was called "qualified majority" voting, under which the small states enjoyed voting power in the Council of Ministers somewhat greater than would be warranted by a strictly proportionate rule.[3]

Clearly, qualified majority voting was a less demanding form of self-rule than unanimity and would lead to more decisions being taken more quickly (but see Golub 1999 for an empirical challenge to this view). The adoption of qualified majority voting would make it easier to realize the mutual gains associated with international cooperation. However, what of the costs inevitably commingled with those gains? Perhaps other aspects of the institutional arena could help overcome these political costs. The discussion will return to the question of institutional innovation in the conclusion and will examine these characteristics of the SEA with reference to the specific policy outcomes it fostered. For the moment all that I wish to observe is this: to the extent that the political costs of integration were ameliorated by an appropriate institutional technology, so the set of politically possible outcomes—in this case, liberalization and harmonization—was enlarged.

In conclusion, the puzzle posed at the beginning is a significant one: what explains the mixed success enjoyed by the member states in their effort to increase regional openness and regulatory harmonization? The difficulties were significant, notwithstanding the underlying structural changes that had occurred by the middle of the 1980s that may have made regional integration more politically viable. As noted, progress in European integration had encountered numerous stumbling blocks in the past—the old habits of tending to domestic political clients would be hard to break, even in good economic times. Yet much was accomplished, even if outcomes across issue areas varied. The chapters that follow will show how weighty domestic interests responded to the adjustment that was imposed on them, how the governments of the member states coalesced around specific policy outcomes, and how the institutional environment framed—and directed—the political process.

The Economics of European Integration

Before discussing the political economy of regional integration, it is necessary to establish the economic background. What does economics reveal about the winners and losers from integration? The degree to which economic outcomes are indeterminate will define the role to be played by politics.

Economic Theory

The basic insight is that the formation of a customs union leads to trade diversion and trade creation; if the former outweighs the latter, then the welfare effects of such a union would be negative (Viner 1950). A simple guide to the consequences of a customs union is the level of the common external tariff and the complementarities between the economies of the member countries. If the common external tariff is as low as, or lower than, the tariff of that member of the union that had the lowest upon joining, then trade creation is likely to predominate (see Krugman 1995). This would also be likely where countries specialized in, and protected, different economic activities prior to joining (Lipsey 1960). These effects are static effects, depending as they do upon the superior allocation of resources from the lowering of barriers—they represent, therefore, a one-time gain. Another static effect is the reduction in market power and increase in efficiency for firms. At the same time, given monopolistic competition, joining a customs union may allow firms specializing in specific niches to reap greater economies of scale, fostering intra-industry trade (Krugman and Obstfeld 1994, 124–33).

More interesting effects, albeit ones that are much harder to identify, are so-called dynamic effects. Integration may also stimulate investment, provoking a virtuous circle in which the expectations of future profit are self-fulfilling as businessmen invest in order to make the most of improved prospects. (On dynamic gains see Molle 1990, 103–11; on the investment effect see Pinder 1988, 40–41; and Baldwin 1989.) The formation of a customs union may also divert investment into it from other areas, investment being a substitute for trade flows. (On investment diversion see Mendes 1987, 85–90; Molle 1990, 231–37; and Yannopoulos 1990; on investment as a substitute for trade see Mundell 1957; as a complement, Markusen 1983.)

Econometric Findings

The empirical record is reasonably clear: Davenport (1982) and Mendes (1987) suggest that there were measurable, if modest, gains for all the original member states; however, gains were greatest in the early years, as tariff barriers were eliminated. As for trade diversion, the results are encouraging—mutual openness led also to greater openness to third parties (Frankel and Wei 1994). There seem to have been two reasons for this, one of which helps explain the other. The deepening of the EU was accompanied by the series of multilateral tariff reductions under the General Agreement on Tariffs and Trade (GATT). Frankel and Wei suggest an interesting explanation that may account for the EU's willingness to participate in the GATT rounds:

> Leaders might not be able to obtain a majority vote in favor of multilateral liberalization . . . yet might be able to obtain a majority vote in favor of regional liberalization which, when completed, then shifts the economic incentive so as to [subsequently] produce a majority in favor of wider liberalization. (1994, 23)

The effect on investment flows is less certain (Krause 1968; Yannopoulos 1990). The European Free Trade Association (EFTA) member states, those who held back from joining the EU in the beginning, may have been penalized as U.S. investment was diverted into the EU, but the matter is not settled.

Taken all together, aggregate gains were realized by the member states of the EU—from static and dynamic effects, even if the latter were hard to disentangle. However, so much uncertainty exists about the models used to evaluate past performance that making predictions about the consequences of the SEA was very difficult (Tsoukalis 1993, 92). The Commission, in its now legendary study of the "costs of non-Europe," took a very optimistic view, even though its model relied largely on estimating the static effects of increased economies of scale (CEC 1988d, 1988b; for a review of other estimates see Hufbauer 1990, 7–8; on unrealized economies of scale in the auto sector see Owen 1983). There was an economic glow associated with the internal market program, but investment and the rationalization of production seem to have played the largest part (on investment see Tsoukalis 1993, 68; on the rationalization of multinational business see Dunning and Robson 1987).

The crucial political question, of course, was how the economic gains were distributed, both across and within countries. It is a core premise of neoclassical trade theory that greater economic openness everywhere yields increased aggregate economic gains. However, trade theory gives few guides to the *distribution* of gains in the absence of closely specified models of the economies of the respective countries. This uncertainty is especially pronounced in the case of intra-industry trade, which is the characteristic form of exchange between advanced industrial economies, in particular the economies of Western Europe (on intra-industry trade see Grubel and Lloyd 1975; in the case of the EU see Greenaway 1987; Belassa and Bauwens 1988; and Krugman 1989).

The "new" trade theory is well adapted to address this phenomenon, as it accepts that traded goods are produced by large firms enjoying economies of scale subject to imperfect competition (Krugman 1979, 1986, 1987; Dixit 1983; Helpman and Krugman 1985; Helpman and Razin 1991). This approach does not usually call into question the presence of aggregate economic gains, but it does highlight the uncertainty over the distribution of those gains.[4] It is this uncertainty that can lead to strategic behavior, economic and political, by which firms and governments might try to ensure distributional outcomes in their favor.

In summary, the discussion of the economics of EU integration yields two general points. First, the member states have enjoyed measurable, if modest, economic gains in the past from the EU; and the SEA was likely to yield more of the same in the future, although how much exactly and through what economic processes remained unclear. All would gain from the move to economic open-ness.[5] Second, how the gains were to be distributed was uncertain ex ante, and subject to manipulation through strategic behavior. This behavior is at the core of the political story to follow. Not only did the member states of the EU have to overcome the cooperation problem inherent in the process of integration, but they had to do so under circumstances in which the costs of adjustment were *endogenous* to the political process. The costs of adjustment were to be determined by the policy outcomes produced by political cooperation—for example, by the use of side-payments (structural funds, in EU parlance).

Explaining EU Policy Outcomes

My explanation for the outcomes identified at the beginning of this project relies on a combination of analytical approaches. In order to develop a systematic account of the preferences of states and firms, and of the manner in which they interact, I rely on the insights available from well-known theories of regulation and endogenous policy formation. This general account of the political marketplace is then situated within a systematic explanation for the way political institutions shape outcomes. Here I rely on the eclectic set of insights generated by the political science literature on institutions, which shows how they overcome transaction costs and yield stable political equilibria but present monitoring problems for their principals.[6] However, I begin by quickly reviewing existing approaches to European integration and EU policy-making, in order to highlight the analytical framework I have adopted.

Other Approaches

Existing approaches suffer from various deficiencies. For example, standard approaches do not, except by implication, deal adequately with the issue of interest formation and aggregation. "Neofunctionalism" is a long-established analytical approach for explaining the process of integration (Haas 1958, 1961). To be sure, it privileges the role of transnational coalitions of interests in this process. But as an explanation, it focuses on the relevant political mechanism and takes for granted the preferences of actors and their ability to articulate them. In Haas's words:

> A system of demands may develop in the programme of a national elite, seeking the support of kindred elites in other . . . countries, designed to establish a far-reaching series of policies realisable only in the framework of supranational institutions. (1958, 287)

He goes on to argue that, once granted powers in one area or sector, supranational institutions constantly expand their authority and influence through a process of "spill-over," a process associated not only with attitudinal change (although Haas argued that this was important) but also with practical necessities. It is constantly necessary to harmonize other, separate, national policies in order to make it possible for already integrated sectors to function (Haas 1958, 297).

This model is echoed in more recent accounts of the process of European integration (Taylor 1983; Sandholtz and Zysman 1989; Peters 1991; Lodge 1994). Sandholtz and Zysman, for example, in discussing the SEA, highlight the role of an inter-elite bargain, in which government, business, and "Eurocrats" all played a part. But no clear micro-foundations for the origins of various interests, or simple account of the structures of the political marketplace, are offered.

Alternative explanations tend to be pitched at the level of the nation-state and privilege interstate—that is, intergovernmental—bargains (see the reply to neofunctionalism from Hoffmann 1966; see also Keohane and Hoffmann 1991; Moravcsik 1991, 1998; and Garrett 1992). However, they too do not give a sufficiently elaborate account of the formation and articulation of interests. In the case of the SEA, for example, it is not enough to merely identify some group of interests who would profit from a particular interstate bargain and with whom government leaders must negotiate as part of some two-level game. Moravcsik (1993, 1998) indicates the way forward by insisting on the theoretical priority of an interest-based account of state preferences, before any analysis of an intergovernmental bargain can begin. The project that follows takes this as a starting point and then goes on to show how national, and transnational, interest-based politics takes over after the intergovernmental bargain is complete.

The existing approaches to institutions have until recently also been subject to numerous objections. In spite of the fact that neofunctionalist explanations for the process of EU integration place a considerable emphasis on institutions, they tend not to distinguish systematically between the roles played by different institutional actors within the EU. Nor do they show the way in which various actors, institutional or otherwise, interact, and what the consequences of the rules governing that interaction might be. For example, what is likely to be the systematic effect on outcomes when the rules governing the relationship between the member states and the Commission are changed? Neofunctionalists tend to neglect these kinds of questions, as do those who adopt an intergovernmental perspective.

Explanations pitched at the level of the member state add value to our understanding of the major political bargains that punctuate the development of the EU. However, this approach also has trouble accounting for the way power is exercised on a day-to-day basis within the institutions of the EU. (For an example of the application of power indices to EU policy-making see Hosli 1993; for an institutionalist critique see Garrett and Tsebelis 1996.) Yet, in the execution of the ambitious plan to complete the internal market, it was "day-to-day" politics that determined outcomes, and the approach proposed here will be well adapted to account for the intricacies of this kind of political process.

Theories of Regulation and Endogenous Policy Formation

In assembling the building blocks of my analytical framework I begin with individual preference formation and aggregation. Ray (1991), following Peltzman (1976) and Stigler (1971) (see also Becker 1983), has proposed an analytical framework to explain which domestic interests become mobilized and how their efforts fit into the political marketplace. It nicely accounts for the behavior of political leaders who seek to maximize some combination of voter and special interest support. What follows owes much to this framework. Let me begin with the preferences of firms over increased economic integration.

The literature on the domestic political economy of foreign economic policy-making (specifically on tariffs and tariff formation), consistent with the Stigler/Peltzman approach, offers a fully developed set of variables to account for preferences, preference intensities, and the organizational capacities of firms, such as geography, labor and/or capital intensity, asset specificity, industry concentration, and competitive efficiency. The structure of any particular industry can be evaluated in these terms and specific predictions about its political performance generated (among many others, see Caves 1976; and Cassing, McKeown, and Ochs 1986; for an overview see Nelson 1988; see also Magee, Brock, and Young 1989). Likewise, in this project, I derive firm preferences and their ability to organize from the following elements: their exposure to adjustment costs, industry concentration, shared cost structures, and technological capacities.

The Ray/Stigler/Peltzman approach gives a simple account of the ability of firms to organize, which is derived from group size and the benefits to be had from organizing. Small, organized interests seeking concentrated benefits are able to obtain protection or advantageous regulation from compliant politicians, who transfer wealth to them at the expense of large, diffuse, and poorly organized groups. The most valuable insight is that this is not a simple story of regulatory capture. Politicians must weigh the benefits to themselves of trade restrictions, which come in the form of campaign contributions or bribes or whatever, against the costs in lost votes from the exploited majority. Furthermore, the effective size of a successful rent-seeking group is limited by the costs of organizing and the exposure to free riders (see, of course, Olsen 1965). In short, within a constraint set by their ability to organize, an industry is able to obtain protection up to that point at which the marginal benefits to politicians equal the marginal costs of granting the favor (information asymmetries generated by a noisy political process will tend to favor narrower, better-organized groups).

For my purposes the story runs in reverse, so to speak. An exogenous shift in the set of possible policy outcomes (that is, the new opportunity to realize mutual gains represented by the SEA) made a preferred political equilibrium available to the political leadership of the member states. They could now increase their political "maximum," if only slightly, by tending to the interests of the exploited majority through the economic gains from increased economic integration, and by imposing some costs (but not too many!) on narrow, organized interests (such as the automakers) by eroding their rents. This would be accomplished by dismantling national barriers to trade and harmonizing regulations.

The virtue of the Stigler/Peltzman approach is that it specifies a political market in which political coalitions are in balance, rather than a crude adding machine model, in which winners take all. As a result, outcomes are not a set of binary choices, favoring one coalition or another, but are more or less "weighted" in a world in which political outputs can be finely allocated between competing groups. This kind of approach is a good starting point for showing how the preferences of firms and the member states over increased integration interact. However, for private interests such as firms the strategic environment of the EU was significantly more complicated than that commonly supposed by this literature. There existed potential transnational allies, with whom cooperation might be fruitful, and supranational institutions, from which desired political objectives might be directly or indirectly obtained. It is necessary, therefore, to develop a theoretically informed account of when interests seek transnational allies. Here the literature on cooperation problems and strategic interaction (or game theory) is of some help (see Olsen 1965; and Rasmusen 1989).

Another complication is that policy outputs varied across issue areas. The "endogenous policy" literature tends to suppose that the particular political goals of group action have the constant characteristic of a "public" good for the interest group in question. The attributes of the group and its members determine whether cooperation is accomplished or not. However, in the context of economic integration a range of different regulatory and policy issues must be addressed. As a result different policies, or political goods, will be pursued. Some may be public goods, but some may be excludable, or private in character. This will surely lead to variation in firm preferences, and so in their ability to cooperate. This variation in potential policy outputs must be distinguished from, or perhaps explained by, the institutional environment.

Institutional Analysis

The literature on institutions generated in the study of American politics can add to the analysis of the EU in two general ways: it can suggest how they induce outcomes (see, for example, Shepsle 1979); and, reasoning backward from that, it can suggest why institutions are adopted (see, for example, McCubbins 1985). After all, institutions are surely chosen with a view to the outcomes that they generate. The discussion of why the institutions of the EU take the form that they do will be reserved for the conclusion of this project—relying on the insights generated by the empirical findings reported below. The question is likely to have a purely empirical answer as much as an analytical one. Here are addressed the ways in which institutions foster particular outcomes (for a good review of the issues that follow as they apply to the EU see Pollack 1997).

An increasingly well understood characteristic of rules and institutions is the way in which they grant to a particular actor, perhaps a transnational institution, a privileged position by giving it the ability to make proposals and so set the agenda (Shepsle and Weingast 1984; Ordeshook and Schwartz 1987; Tsebelis 1994a). Those outcomes preferred by the agenda setter may then enjoy a strategic advantage.[7] If it is an institutional actor who sets the agenda (for example, the Commission), then a systematic account of the origins of its institutional preferences must be developed. If the institution is an agent for others (as is the Commission), and its preferences are different from the preferences of its principals (the member states who established it in the first place), then agency drift will lead to the institution promoting outcomes at odds with those preferred by its principals. Public choice offers an appropriate framework, in which government institutions displace the formal goals assigned to them with the private goals of institutional power and growth, from which the functionaries of the institution in question derive greater satisfaction. The principals respond by attempting to create effective and economical monitoring devices (see, among others, Niskanen 1971; for a corrective, Miller and Moe 1983).[8]

Institutions may also shape outcomes because they privilege certain actors. The rules of the game, whether de facto or de jure, may only grant standing or access to certain interests, and so only (or mainly) their preferences are considered when bargaining over proposals. This privileging could have nothing to do with an institution pursuing its own private preferences; the deck could be stacked in favor of private interests outside government as a result of the administrative rules written by the principals who established the institutions in the first place (see McCubbins, Noll, and Weingast 1987).

Institutions also lower transaction costs and increase the efficiency of outcomes. As a result of Williamson's work (1985) political scientists now better understand how institutions solve the problems associated with making contracts (see Weingast and Marshall 1988; and Milgrom, North, and Weingast 1990; on the role of international institutions in resolving these problems see Keohane 1984; and Yarborough and Yarborough 1987; for a realist critique see Grieco 1988). It is very often difficult, and in the context of the EU surely impossible, to write a contract that specifies all outcomes, foresees all contingencies, and effortlessly regulates the behavior of all the parties to it. In effect the Treaty of Rome was, of necessity, incomplete. As a result the problem became one of governing the contract after the fact. Institutions help solve this problem: they increase transparency by obtaining and circulating information, they monitor compliance, and they sanction the recalcitrant. These practices increase the ability of all parties to an agreement to make credible promises about future behavior.

Furthermore, because institutions may be perceived to be impartial, the solutions they propose for the resolution of coordination problems have credibility and so are generally acceptable. Such acceptance is often suggested to be the case for the institutions of the EU, especially the Commission (see Majone 1994).[9] This credibility also helps the Commission to administer complicated political exchanges, in which side-payments are used to accomplish agreement across multiple issue areas, and through time.

One final property of international institutions is that they are convenient scapegoats for national governments—notwithstanding the fact that they were chosen by, and are supervised by, those same governments. Delegating power may help deflect blame and so permit the member states, for example, to accept greater adjustment costs than would otherwise be possible (see Fiorina 1982; and Weaver 1989).

In summary, the literature on institutions directs attention toward the power of agenda setters, differences in access, the interests of institutional actors, and the ability of institutions to lower transaction costs and political costs.

In the context of the EU these characteristics may foster various kinds of outcomes: efficient outcomes, outcomes tending to the interests of powerful groups or particular actors, and outcomes that expand the level of integration. In the analysis that follows in chapter 2 the institutions of the EU will be evaluated for the way in which they share in some of the political properties identified above.

Interests and Institutions

The discussion of how interests could be accounted for in this project, how governments might respond to them, and the variety of ways in which institutions mediate outcomes has not emphasized the most important analytical element in the explanatory framework offered below. This project does not simply add a model of interest formation and aggregation to a set of institutional variables. The crucial point, revealed by the empirical episodes I examine, is the way in which interests and institutions interact. This interaction is the most important element missing from existing approaches that seek to explain EU policy outcomes, for good reason. In a complex policy space with a variety of actors such interaction is very difficult to analyze in a systematic way. My objective will be to sift out the interaction between the institutional elements identified by Tsebelis (1994a) and Pollack (1997) and the interests and political leadership analyzed by Peltzman (1976) and Ray (1991). Such an approach will supply a rigorous explanation for the complex policy outcomes that extended the boundaries of political and economic integration.

Overview of the Framework

In summary, the analytical framework I have developed, based on the material reviewed above, isolates the variables identified in table 1 and yields a discrete set of expectations about the way in which they shaped outcomes (the framework is fully developed in chapter 2).

TABLE 1.   Issue Areas, Variables, and Outcomes

Issue Area	Firms	Member States	Institutional Arena	Level of Integration
Emissions control	Divided	Divided	Legislative	High harmonization
State aid	Divided	Mixed	Bureaucratic	Limited reductions
Antitrust	United	United	Legal	Limited restrictions
External trade	United	Divided	Informal	Persistent barriers

The preferences of governments represented the political balance between the interests of firms in sheltered sectors on the one hand, and the interests of consumers and voters on the other hand. Firms were influenced by, among other things, their competitive strength, market location, and technological orientation, all of which determined their exposure to adjustment. The costs and benefits of integration were therefore asymmetrically distributed between governments and firms in ways that varied across issue areas, creating a variety of different strategic environments for the actors involved. This, in turn, led to variation in the ability of governments and firms to cooperate in shaping EU policy outcomes.

This general picture of firm and government preferences and their ability to cooperate played out in each specific issue area in a predictable way. In the case of auto emissions, because firms specialized in different technologies and different products, the costs of regulation fell heavily on only a few of them. National governments were also divided in their exposure to environmental sentiment among their voters. Both groups were divided and unable to act in a concerted fashion. In the case of state aid, firms were again divided, for some had stronger claims on public patrons than others. Governments had mixed motives. On the one hand, they all shared an interest in shaking off the economic claims of poorly performing "national champions"; however, each feared that others might snatch economic activity by offering subsidies if they practiced restraint. In antitrust, firms were united in their interest in the collective good of tacit collusion at the expense of voters. Governments were also interested in a common antitrust regime but were willing to set the rules of the regime at a low level. Finally, on the question of external trade (specifically Japanese imports), mass-market automakers were all equally exposed and therefore strongly united in their desire for continued trade barriers, while governments were divided between free trade and protection—some, such as France and Italy, responding to the demands of exposed producers; others, such as Germany, responding to the interests of successful specialist producers.

This map of preferences, and the level of cooperation they fostered, occurred in an institutional arena where rules restricted the set of possible outcomes (in particular by excluding the status quo) and favored some coalitions over others, and some agenda setters over others. Specifically, in the case of emissions control, agenda setting shifted from producers and governments to the institutions of the EU, in particular the Parliament, a shift which helps to account for the significant increases in the level of harmonization accomplished. In state aid, the governments of the member states agreed to rule changes that increased transparency and so increased their ability to overcome the strategic dilemma they faced. However, actual reductions were modest. In antitrust, producers would have pursued, and governments would have allowed, even more exploitation of consumers through anticompetitive practices had it not been for the effectiveness of the rule-integrity regime in this issue area. Finally, such were the political forces opposed to external openness that formal institutional arenas played no part in this issue area—an antiliberal outcome was informally imposed on consumers and importers.

In keeping with the emphasis placed on the interaction of interests and institutions, an inspection of table 1 reveals that outcomes cannot be inferred in a direct manner from the variables that I argue matter. To discover whether firms and governments behave in the way I anticipate, and whether institutions exhibit the properties claimed, a detailed analysis of each case is required, in which outcomes are inevitably the product of a partly contingent interaction among the various elements.

The Automobile Industry

Finally, it is necessary to justify more fully why the auto industry itself is an appropriate object of inquiry.

The auto industry has always been a politically sensitive issue in trade among all the industrial countries, and the subject of extensive and painfully protracted bargaining (Cowhey and Long 1983; Dunn 1987).[10] For example, the "auto pact" between the United States and Canada represented a prominent example of managed trade between two very interdependent developed economies. It was ultimately transformed into the North American Free Trade Agreement (Keeley 1983; Hufbauer and Schott 1993). It is an industry typically characterized by segmented markets and protection, which has attracted many econometric studies (see, for example, Smith and Venables 1991; Kirman and Schueller 1990; Bourdet 1988; Dixit 1988; and Mertens and Ginsburgh 1985). Nowhere is it a likely candidate for a sudden move toward economic openness.

This political sensitivity is especially true in the European case. Roughly 8 percent of the EU's manufacturing workforce was employed in the auto industry in 1987 (CCFA [Comité des Constructeurs Français d'Automobile] 1990, 11). These employees were mainly to be found in six producing countries—the United Kingdom, France, Italy, Germany, Spain, and Belgium. The industry was one of the most concentrated in Europe, in this respect similar to aerospace. Six mass-market producers controlled over 70 percent of the market by the late 1980s (CEC 1989e, 41; 1990a, 54). In the 10-year period between 1977 and 1987 the industry received over ECU (European currency units) 15 billion in subsidies

($22 billion), roughly ECU 1,000 per person employed in the industry in 1987 (CEC 1990a, 57).

In summary, the industry was politically sensitive because of the number of jobs at stake, easy to organize because of its concentration, and clearly favored by national governments in the past, judging by its impressive track record in extracting direct transfer payments. Furthermore, nontariff barriers and other distortions imposed additional welfare losses on consumers and yielded rents to producers of more than ECU 3 billion a year (Smith and Venables 1991). Since giving up these rents was sure to be painful, clearly the auto industry was one of the economic sectors most likely to block the single-market program. In this sector the dilemma faced by the member states was acute: here the trade-off between the general interest and particularistic claims was at its sharpest. If they could pull it off here, the EU should be able to realize its goals everywhere else.

This view of the industry as a crucial test case was shared by many commentators at the time. The passage of the SEA prompted many published studies, by academics, representatives of industry, and national governments, which constantly emphasized the importance for the industry of economic integration and the importance of success in this sector to the political program of the SEA (see, for example, Sadler 1992; Salvadori 1991; Smith and Venables 1990; Diekmann 1992b; Glatz 1989; Perrin-Pelletier 1988; Commissariat Général du Plan 1992; Assemblée Nationale 1992; and House of Lords 1990). In the minds of many across the member states the automobile industry occupied a central place in the politics of integration.

Finally, there are good analytical reasons to examine the auto industry. It is possible to capture the interaction of interests and institutions in this case because the constellation of political forces at work was relatively clear. It was an industry in which a few well-organized, intensely strategic interests were fully mobilized in a well-defined (if complex) institutional environment. This clarity makes it possible to compare the expectations generated by my analytical approach with observed political activity as well as the actual policy outcomes, thus subjecting the approach to a clear test. In other words, it is an "easy" case from the point of view of analytical transparency, unusual for an area of research made opaque by the variety of possible actors and the complexity of their interactions.

Explaining Liberalization in the European Auto Industry

The whole history of the EU shows how international agreements that realize mutual gains are always subject to collective action problems and so have been undersupplied. The purpose of the SEA was to overcome these kinds of problems and bring an end to political and economic stagnation and to the divergent (and collectively inefficient) policy-making that sustained it. In the case of the politically powerful auto industry this ambitious program of political and economic cooperation was only partly successful. What accounts for this mixed success?

The chapters that follow are organized in a straightforward manner with a view to supplying a comprehensive, analytically informed answer to this question. Chapter 2 develops the analytical approach in a way that yields a series of expectations about firm and state behavior and the role of institutions. This is followed by a thoroughgoing examination of the history and character of the European auto industry, as it stood on the eve of the SEA. In particular I distinguish those elements that tended to help or hinder firm cooperation. I also define the policy objectives that were likely to be the focus of collective action by the automakers and the governments of the member states. The existing (and formerly stable) pattern of firm-state relationships is also described, as well as the cross-national variation in private industry associations. Finally, the expectations derived by my analytical framework, given the economic and political geography of the sector, are scrutinized in the context of four case studies of EU policy-making: environmental regulation, external trade, state aid, and antitrust.

Automobile Emissions

Automobile emissions were finally harmonized across Europe in December 1987, after protracted and divisive bargaining. The outcome appeared to reflect the interests of the mass-market automakers because standards, while uniform for the first time, were low by comparison with U.S. practice. This agreement was soon followed by another dealing with small autos. However, that outcome was much more favorable to those wanting high environmental standards and imposed significant adjustment costs on the automakers. This change in outcome is nicely explained by the interaction of divided interests in the context of a changing institutional environment.

There was a lack of cooperation between firms on the level of regulation because of the way in which it imposed different costs on each. This proved to be crucial. Change in the institutional arena favored a coalition of governments, firms, and others that preferred harmonized regulation at any level rather than low but regionally fragmented regulation. It is especially worth noting how environmental interests in the European Parliament were given the power to set the agenda by rule changes incorporated into the SEA.

External Trade

The EU-Japanese agreement on trade in autos, which was adopted in July 1991, was a very irregular international economic agreement, clearly contrary to the spirit and letter of the EU's obligations under the General Agreement on Tariffs and Trade (GATT) and at odds with the liberal purpose of the SEA. Why did the establishment of a common external trade regime fall so short of free-trade principles? The explanation is that mass-market auto producers, in direct contrast to the policy outcome in emissions control described above, were united by a very strong interest in the outcome. This political weight was decisive.

The issues of external trade and transplant production were closely linked. While there existed a common interest among producers in limiting imports, there existed a powerful coalition among some governments of the member states for a liberal foreign investment regime. This balance of competing interests was reflected in the outcome. The passage of the SEA meant an end to the patchwork of existing national practice and forced the issue of external trade onto the agenda, giving the Commission a significant role in international bargaining for the first time. This also meant that industry interests were privileged, due to their cohesion and influence over the Commission. The auto producers' transnational industry association, renewed after the defeat over emissions control, further increased the political effectiveness of the industry (the forces that fostered interfirm cooperation predominated in this case). Imports were capped for 10 years and a regional market-sharing arrangement established, while foreign investment remained unfettered.

Antitrust

The single-market program meant increased economic openness, leading to increased competitive pressures, with increased efficiency, lower prices, increased growth, and a variety of other beneficial effects as a consequence. However, the persistence of cartels and other anticompetitive practices would, of course, thwart the project no matter how many formal regulatory barriers were eliminated. But it was sure to be hard for the member states to agree on a common antitrust policy. They may have wished for a single policy (the rapid rise of cross-border mergers and acquisitions following the SEA made multiple national practices an increasing burden), but choosing between, for example, the very different practices of Germany and the United Kingdom would be politically very sensitive. What is more, the auto industry appears to have been generously treated where it might have expected significant constraints placed upon it by an EU-wide regulatory regime.

The member states delegated some power to the Commission, which enjoyed considerable discretion. Nevertheless, the interests of member states were not overlooked by the policy choices of the Commission. On the other hand, firms shared an interest in tacit collusion if it could be accomplished, which was partly allowed them by escape clauses in the regulatory framework. I also discover that the Commission, due to a degree of legal autonomy, was able to check the influence of the industry upon occasion.

State Aid

In the case of state aid, the member states faced a more complicated strategic environment because of the fear that others might cheat. Industry rationalization was a likely consequence of the SEA, and a government could be tempted to subsidize a "champion" in order to ensure its survival in the event of a shakeout. Of course, if all governments did that then the benefits of the 1992 project would be lost. In the event, the institutions of the EU were adapted by the member states so as to mitigate this dilemma by increasing transparency. Another problem was that while all the automakers fed at the public trough in one way or another, some were better fed than others. This meant that state aid from national patrons was a divisive issue for firms, while for governments restraint would save them money, although injure established favorites.

As it turned out, policy outcomes were in keeping with the interest of the member states in reducing state aid. Constraints were placed on the level of state aid, but only slowly, in order to keep the political costs of imposing these constraints as low as possible. By contrast, automakers persisted in making separate claims on individual national governments, rather than presenting a collective demand for the resources needed to help them adjust. The issue area kept them divided. However, the Commission proved to be less autonomous in this issue area; governments lobbied for their favorites, and improvements over past practice were only incremental.

Conclusions

In the final chapter I conclude by showing how the elements in the case studies were consistent with the analytical framework presented in chapter 2. I go on to draw out the implications of my findings for our understanding of institutional innovation and adaptation. To the extent that this research shows the consequences for policy outcomes of political institutions, so it should be possible to make inferences about the political struggles I expect to observe over their control and their adaptation. I find in general that the institutions of the EU were closely circumscribed by the interests of the governments and firms that acted on them and through them. I also suggest that a subset of the important players in the auto industry—VW and the U.S. multinational producers—were better prepared to take advantage of regional integration because they were less enmeshed in long-standing client relationships with national governments.

CHAPTER 2

Understanding the Role of Governments, Firms, and Institutions

Building an Analytical Framework

How did the member states of the European Union overcome a variety of political obstacles and execute the program of radical economic integration represented by the Single European Act and the White Paper proposals of 1985? A common interest in economic openness is often vitiated by the opposition of small but politically influential groups, yet in the case of the European auto industry, although the level of integration and liberalization accomplished varied across issue areas, the member states had some success in overcoming this classic dilemma. As a result, significant, if incomplete, economic adjustment was accomplished by a crucial economic sector.

In order to obtain a general understanding of these changes, this book focuses on policy outcomes in four important issue areas, in the period between 1985 and the beginning of 1993: environmental regulation, external trade, antitrust, and state aid. This was the period during which the so-called 1992 program—the complete integration of the internal European market—was to be realized. The analysis reveals the constellation of political forces, within the relevant institutional context, that was responsible for the level of integration and regulatory harmonization accomplished in each case. As a result, the analysis yields a clear picture of the changes that took place at a crucial time in Europe's economic development and reveals the role played by the complex institutions of the EU.

To conduct this analysis, a parsimonious and flexible framework is required. The approach adopted here combines a political economy explanation

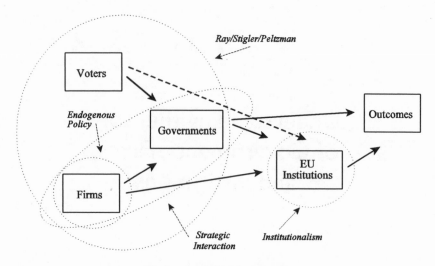

Fig. I. Analytical framework

for preferences and political action with an institutionalist account of the political arena: preferences were a function of economic exposure, while the ability to shape policy was a function of collective action problems in a variety of strategic environments. Outcomes were then shaped in systematic ways by the rules and institutions of the EU. A simple overview of the framework is presented in figure 1.

The propositions that make up this approach form three groups. First, I argue that the main purpose of international cooperation in Europe over economic integration was to obtain previously unrealized joint economic gains. Therefore the preferences of governments and firms were a function of these anticipated gains. Consider the situation facing governments. A crude adding machine model of the costs and benefits does not do justice to the political constraints and opportunities they faced. Each sought to maximize the political gains to be had (in terms of votes) from a move to openness that increased economic activity. However, integration imposed costs on various narrow interests. Those states that harbored firms most likely to suffer from integration found such a move politically more costly than those states with firms less likely to face adjustment costs. In short, as discussed in the introductory chapter, different governments had different political maxima corresponding to different levels of integration. This approach is in the tradition of what I have called the Ray/Stigler/Peltzman framework in figure 1. Below is a tentative map of the preferences of the member states of the EU based on this line of reasoning. The preferences of firms may be mapped in a more straightforward manner, based on their competitive position in regional and global markets, their cost structures, product lines, and technological orientation. This is in keeping with what I call the endogenous policy approach.

Second, I examine the cooperation problems faced by governments and firms as they devised strategies to shape policy outcomes. Forging coalitions yielded significant rewards to the governments of the member states as they sought to control outcomes. Interfirm cooperation (across national boundaries) increased the influence of firms over policy. This cohesion among actors was fostered, or obstructed, by a variety of elements in the strategic environment. Among such elements were the spatial distribution of preferences of governments and firms over specific outcomes, the character of the cooperation problem (for example, whether it was a variable or zero-sum situation), and the ability of states to give and receive side-payments. This discussion is firmly in the tradition of what can be called the "cooperation" literature.

In the third set of propositions, I examine the role of institutions as mediating and independent variables, influencing outcomes.[1] The level of cooperation accomplished by states was also a function of the rules governing each issue area—where unanimity was required, for example, member state control would be difficult. Firm cooperation was a function of the relative importance of the relevant EU institutions, and the character of the good they could obtain from any political enterprise (for example, whether it was a public good or not). Beyond this, the institutions of the EU may have shaped outcomes by giving power to agenda setters, by tilting the political playing field toward actors with privileged access, by distorting the policies desired by the principals (the member states), or by helping governments by lowering political costs. The role actually played by the institutions of the EU is an empirical question. The goal at this stage is to simply show how different characteristics might determine the role played by institutions, and to link these possibilities to the overarching framework presented here. Taken together, these make up an eclectic group of "institutionalist" theories.

The Preferences of Governments and Firms

The analysis begins by suggesting more precisely why the member states had different preferences over the general move to integration, differences that accounted for the character of the pre-commitment embodied in the SEA. Crucially, the SEA included institutional changes that reflected the fact that cooperation was desired in issues over which preferences varied. The analysis then goes on to suggest how the preferences of states and firms were shaped within the automobile industry, and within each issue area. As is shown below, the preferences over individual policies, for both states and firms, varied in systematic ways, depending on the character of the policy output. The intuition is that while the political payoffs to the member states from the *overall* move to integration account for the commitment to the SEA (a commitment that embraced a range of outcomes), the variation in preferences among states and firms on matters relating specifically to the auto industry helps to account for the variation in policy outcomes across issue areas.

It might be imagined that commitment ex ante ought to preclude subsequent alteration or evasion of the terms agreed upon, but of course such alterations and evasions are the stuff of international economic cooperation. The puzzles to be solved are why the larger agreement was only partly implemented, what consequences this had, and what role was played in all of it by the institutions of the EU (in particular their role in restricting evasion and alteration). That is the purpose of the research reported here. This book shows how much by way of economic integration was actually accomplished in the European auto industry at a crucial juncture in its history.

Choosing Integration

Whatever the political purposes behind the establishment and growth of the European Community, they could only be realized in conjunction with economic objectives. For example, if a purpose of the EU was to create a geopolitical "home" for the nation-states of Europe, designed to give them greater weight in a world of superpowers and new trading states, such an association would be valuable if it fostered not only concerted political action but also the economic vitality to back it up. Or if, for example, the Community is seen more simply as the fruit of a grand bargain between the French and the Germans, who were determined to choose economic cooperation over political and military competition, it is sure that for such a bargain to work, mutual economic gains would have to play some part. In general, the political foundations of the EU were economic and social similarities, and its purpose the opportunity for improvement in these areas afforded by integration (Milward 1992, 436).

There is reasonably solid empirical evidence that economic gains have flowed from the growth of the EU. Such gains are not easily measured (see chapter 1) and have often been exaggerated, but there are good grounds for thinking that they were substantial in the early postwar period and have persisted to the present (Mendes 1987; Pinder 1988; Molle 1990, 175–200). It is, of course, a core premise of neoclassical trade theory that greater economic openness always yields increased aggregate economic gains. Therefore, without making claims about the distributional consequences of integration, it seems safe to say that the pursuit of such gains was attractive to all the governments of the member states.

But it is not enough to show why the member states might choose economic integration. While the SEA credibly committed each to the goal of greater integration, it was a commitment that allowed for a *range* of possible outcomes in each issue area, more or less equitably distributed across the member states. Furthermore, it was a commitment that included significant institutional adaptation. This kind of bargain reflected variation in the political costs radical economic integration would impose on each government.

Put at its most abstract, it is likely that different preferences among the member states over the level of integration reflected the fact that the *net* political benefits to one government were less than, or at least rose less rapidly than, the *net* political benefits to some other government. I argued above that the realization of mutual economic gains was an important reason why member states pursued radical economic integration. This implies that there was political benefit attached to these economic gains. However, since economic theory generally does not predict a systematic bias in the distribution of the aggregate economic gains from integration, the fact that one member state preferred less integration than another indicates, instead, some asymmetry in the political costs.[2]

What follows is a sketch of the way the governments of the member states optimized their response to the political gains to be had from integration, given the existence of political costs. On the one hand, those who enjoyed the economic benefits of integration—consumers and economically successful interests—were likely to be politically grateful. On the other hand, integration was subject to political costs as rents were surrendered by formerly sheltered domestic interests. The intuition here is that it was relatively easy, politically, to impose a moderate loss in rents on certain influential constituents in exchange for greater integration, but that as the dislocation became more severe so would opposition to integration. In short, the political costs of integration rose more rapidly (and asymmetrically across countries) in comparison to the rise in aggregate economic and political benefits.[3]

From this it follows that the politically acceptable level of integration varied across the member states. Certainly there existed increased opportunities for collective neoliberal reforms in the early 1980s in response to a new policy consensus on a variety of issues. For example, it was becoming clear that it was ineffective to continue to shelter clients who showed no gains in performance.

This all helped to make the governments of the member states generally willing to choose international economic cooperation and endure some of the associated political costs. The point is that there were significant differences in the degree of openness desired.

Is this sketch plausible? The speed and intensity of the reaction by the domestic interests involved were governed by a variety of factors. Among them, as identified by work on endogenous policy formation, would be labor intensivity, asset specificity and diversification, and competitive position. Another, possibly more important factor, of course, was the ability of these interests to overcome their collective action problem, which would be influenced by such elements as firm size, industry concentration, and geographic dispersion. The central point is that those seeking protection from the costs of adjustment were more willing to trade in the political marketplace than those seeking openness and its benefits. There could be several reasons why. A manager's time might be better spent on economic effort when the prospects are good, whereas the *relative* return on political effort is greater when economic prospects are poor. Declining industries are more likely to keep political rents than new industries subject to competitive entry, raising the return to them of lobbying (Cassing, McKeown, and Ochs 1986).[4] The fear of loss may be a greater motivator than the prospect of gain (Quattrone and Tversky 1988).

On the other hand, Milner (1988) has argued that winners from liberalization are just as likely to mobilize, and that this helps to explain why poor economic performance in the West after 1973 was not matched by a return to protectionism. However, this is not inconsistent with the discussion above. In the case of the auto industry, conveniently enough, one or two firms determined national sectoral competitiveness. There is no question of winners being pitted against losers within member states (with the exception of Germany and the division between specialist and mass-market manufacturers). The question then becomes whether firms in *other* sectors in the same country would take issue with illiberal auto-related outcomes. No evidence of that was found. Where Milner's work is very relevant is in understanding firms on a Europe-wide basis, in issue areas where the industry was divided (emissions control being a prominent case). There the leading, internationally orientated and competitive firms were able to impose a costly outcome on less competitive firms.

The Preferences of Governments for Integration

In what ways was the bargain represented by the SEA consistent with this bundle of propositions? Bargaining ultimately revolved around two issues: the extent of internal market liberalization and the changes to EU decision making believed necessary in order to make such liberalization possible. In the past the efforts of the member states to harmonize regulations had been subject to the severe constraint imposed by the "joint decision trap" (Scharpf 1988), that is, the limits imposed by decision making based on unanimity. Many of the member states, and the European Commission under its newly appointed president Jacques Delors, believed that any program of market liberalization required the introduction of qualified majority voting.

The negotiating history of the SEA has been reported elsewhere (see Moravcsik 1991 and Taylor 1989). The crucial point was reached under the Italian presidency in 1985 when an Intergovernmental Conference (IGC) was called for, by use of a majority vote, in order to draft the necessary institutional changes. Few member states were ready to yield sovereignty over foreign affairs or monetary issues, and the role of majority voting was limited to matters dealing with the internal market. However, that in itself was a significant institutional innovation that would make the proposed radical economic integration possible.

Overall, following the discussion in Garrett (1992, 545–48), the preferences of the member states over institutional changes, the level of integration, and the role of side-payments can be conveniently depicted as running along one continuum, presented in figure 2.

Spain and the other less developed countries are located on the right. They preferred minimal economic integration unless they were granted side-payments to limit the costs of adjustment. From that it followed that they preferred rule changes that favored simple majority voting, in order to increase their power over side-payments dispensed by the EU and limit the power of net contributors to the Community budget who might wish to block such payments.

On the left is the United Kingdom (and Denmark), which opposed formal changes in Council of Ministers procedures (even qualified majority voting) but favored market liberalization. As a net contributor Britain was also opposed to side-payments. The Danes have been placed with the British; while they opposed a surrender of sovereignty, they were probably content with the side-payments

High integration *Low institutionalization*		*Low Integration* *High institutionalization*	
◄───────────			──────────►
United Kingdom Denmark	Germany France Belgium/Lux. Netherlands	Italy	Spain Ireland Portugal Greece

Fig. 2. Government preferences over the Single European Act

adopted. In the center are clustered a core of countries about a Franco-German axis, which preferred qualified majority voting and modest side-payments. The Italians are set off slightly to the right of the French and Germans because they preferred to have greater powers conferred on the European Parliament and had an interest in the supply of structural funds to help develop the Mezzogiorno.

The French and Germans, and others, had a strong interest in completing the single market. This is shown by an EU report on the relative competitive position of all the member states in those 40 sectors most sensitive to the effects of the SEA (CEC 1990b, 30–39). The report calculated the employment share of each member state in "strong" and "weak" sectors (based on static measures of competitiveness); based on this, the member states can be easily divided into two groups: those with employment concentrated in strong sectors—Germany, Italy, France, Denmark, Ireland, and Benelux—and those with employment concentrated in weakly situated sectors—the United Kingdom, Spain, Portugal, and Greece. This picture is somewhat arbitrary. For example, a dynamic analysis gives a more encouraging picture of the opportunities available to the United Kingdom. In many ways the completion of the single market, especially in financial services, was very much in keeping with the United Kingdom's strategy of radical economic liberalization and was "the issue which could entice the U.K." (Corbett 1987, 245). On the other hand, the French and Italians (at the least) did not share the British Conservative party's taste for pure, free-market capitalism, but rather for a European model of liberalization in which governments, rather than individuals and firms, carried many of the costs of adjustment. To make this possible at the level of EU policy-making required a supermajority voting rule that favored those who wanted managed change over those who wanted little and those who wanted too much.

In short, a core group of governments wished for increased liberalization, under an institutional arrangement that prevented blocking by any individual country but allowed for political control by a majority over the degree of liberalization and integration accomplished. This agreement, therefore, is clearly consistent with the propositions advanced in the previous section. Some new range of political maxima was desired, but the details were to be subject to political bargains in which the political costs in each particular issue area could be separately managed.

The Preferences of Governments over Auto Industry Liberalization

Just as there were general economic gains available from market integration as a whole, so were there general economic gains to be had from liberalizing the

European auto industry. The SEA would result in increased demand, and the automakers would, as they say, move more metal. These gains were estimated by Smith and Venables (1990). They showed that the auto producers had to give up ECU 2 billion in rents under integration (or about $2.5 billion), but that this yielded aggregate net gains to consumers of ECU 10 billion. A subsequent elimination of the European voluntary export restraints (VERs) imposed on Japanese imports would yield a further net gain of ECU 3 billion in aggregate welfare, while producers would lose ECU 1.5 billion more in rents. The governments and consumers of the member states had much to gain from integrating the market for autos in the EU, which surely helps to explain the commitments by leaders to accomplish such a goal. But some firms would suffer, which would inevitably moderate the enthusiasm of some of the governments of the member states.[5]

A historical and comparative analysis of the European auto industry is presented in chapter 3, which will supply a detailed picture of the comparative advantages enjoyed by the major producing nations and the competitive situation of the major auto assemblers and their suppliers. Here the purpose will be merely to suggest the basic elements that determined the competitive position of firms and states in this sector and so show more precisely how the costs and benefits of integration would be distributed.[6]

The member states may first be divided between those that had long-established, fully integrated auto industries and the rest. This division is determined by size; prior to integration small national markets, with the exception of Belgium, were unable to support locally an industry subject to such pronounced economies of scale. Belgium and the five largest member states—France, Germany, Italy, Spain, and the United Kingdom—had between 5 and 8 percent of their industrial labor force engaged in motor vehicle production (CEC 1990b, xvi). All the other member states had less than 1 percent, with the exception of the Netherlands with less than 2 percent. The preferences of the small states on trade, therefore, can be easily imagined: free trade in autos, both internally and externally. In other areas, such as environmental regulation and taxation, small states felt free to pursue goals without regard to the impact on producers, although they were presumably constrained by the costs such choices might impose on consumers.

A plausible measure of exposure to adjustment for the larger states, following an approach adopted by the Commission of the European Communities (1990b), would be to compare their export performance in intra-EU trade in autos. An illustrative map is presented in figure 3. The data upon which it draws are presented in table 2. Germany, with a strong overall export performance, would surely gain from increased economic integration, along with the

34   Vehicle of Influence

High exposure   *Low exposure*

◄───►

United Kingdom   France   Spain   Germany
Italy   Belgium/Lux.   Small states

Fig. 3.   National adjustment and industry liberalization

small states (see figure 7 in chapter 3 for a time series of the balance of trade in autos for the major producing states). Spain and Belgium as net exporters also stood to gain from integration, although as sites for the multinational production of low-end mass-market vehicles they could be threatened by new capacity in other, low-cost regions. France, as the second-largest producer, enjoyed a rough trade balance, but any significant decline would impose serious adjustments on an industry that was heavily concentrated in one national market. Italy and the United Kingdom had a poor balance of trade in autos in the 1980s. While the Italian market was still dominated by one producer, FIAT, which might hope to use that as a base from which to renew exports, in the United Kingdom the situation was much more problematic. The severe contraction of Rover, formerly British Leyland, and the reduction of U.K.-based capacity by the multinational producers Ford and General Motors (GM) had resulted in a steady decline in export performance. In 1965 the United Kingdom was the second-largest producing country in the EU; by 1985 it was only the fifth-largest.

This map of exposure to adjustment must then be considered in the context of the framework suggested above for understanding a government's preferences. It was true, of course, that the large producing member states had a long history of sheltering firms in this sector—the manner and degree to which they

TABLE 2.   Auto Industry Trade and Employment

Country	Balance of Trade[a]	Employment in Autos[b]
Belgium/Luxembourg	1.19	8.2
Germany	8.52	8.0
France	−0.02	6.6
Italy	−2.39	5.0
U.K.	−4.86	6.3
Spain	1.47	4.9

[a]Balance of Trade, 1985, in Automobiles, Six Largest Producers: Figures drawn from the COMTAP data base, OECD (1987), SITC category 3843 (motor vehicles), in billions of nominal U.S. dollars.

[b]Employment in Auto Sector as a Percentage of Employment in Manufacturing Industry, Average, 1985–87: Data from CEC 1990b, xvi.

were able to break with that past, in the context of the SEA, are at the core of this research project. What is more, a significant percentage of industrial employment in the producing countries was engaged in auto-making—a good measure of its political sensitivity. These workers were fully unionized and earning at or above the average manufacturing wage (SAF [Swedish Employers Federation] 1992, 20, 44). In other words, they shared in the rents estimated above by Smith and Venables (1990), in the form of "good jobs at good wages"—jobs that structural changes in the economies of the developed countries were making harder and harder to replace. However, not to accomplish the goals of the White Paper, the EU's program for market integration, would be to put the whole project into doubt and so risk losing the aggregate economic gains identified above.

While this map of exposure to adjustment is a good place to start in deriving the preferences of the member states over policy, it cannot be the whole story. The British case is instructive. The Conservative British government was in favor of regional integration of the auto industry, not only because this was consistent with its overall belief in the efficacy of liberal policies but also, I argue, because the United Kingdom had already paid the costs of adjustment. Greater market integration, under conditions that favored inward investment, could only have beneficial consequences for a sector largely reduced to only foreign manufacturers. Specifically, the British government hoped that a wave of investment from Japan would save the day (this is examined in detail in chapter 5). On the other hand, Spain, although it made great gains in this sector in the 1980s, ultimately became anxious that low-wage sites elsewhere (in Eastern Europe) under conditions of heightened competition would result in production facilities moving away. In other words, past performance must be integrated with the set of future opportunities, as governments understood them, in order to derive policy preferences. The standard political economy account of the political forces shaping government choices is inevitably mediated by contingent elements in the strategic environment.

The crucial point was that the payoffs in any particular sector were, in principle, bundled together into one "grand bargain," that is, the SEA, in which the overall gains outweighed the losses for each. The question was whether, when the time came to bargain over specific policies at the level of the sector, the member states and the firms involved were likely to have lost sight of this "grand bargain." On the one hand, they were sure to become preoccupied by the distribution of costs and benefits within the sector. On the other hand, defection from the larger bargain in an area as politically sensitive as the auto industry would be costly. Given the political costs to some countries, when the rubber hit the road and the SEA had to be implemented, breakdown and defection should have been likely. However, the adjustment costs firms were likely to experience, and the institutional environment, varied across issue areas, so leading to variation in outcomes. It is firm preferences, therefore, that are addressed next.

The Preferences of Firms over Auto Industry Liberalization

The firms in this sector may be divided between specialist and mass-market producers. The specialist producers had interests very distinct from those of the mass-market producers (Camerra-Rowe 1993). They faced only moderate external competition and traded highly differentiated products throughout regional and global markets. They already met global best practice on environmental standards (California) and regarded trade barriers, especially those directed at the Japanese, as a danger, not a benefit (see chapter 5). The mass-market producers were subject to a variety of influences. Many elements of the internal market appealed to them (for example, the liberalization of capital markets); however, the breakdown of existing market segmentation would undoubtedly impose adjustment costs on several of them. In other words, I argue that such costs were a function of the degree to which the sales of any particular producer were concentrated in any one national market, as opposed to being evenly spread over the whole of the EU—the logic being that greater concentration implied potentially greater adjustment costs.

In figure 4 the exposure of the automakers to adjustment is illustrated, based on this idea; the figure draws on the data presented in table 3. As a measure of the degree to which each producer's output is skewed across markets, I calculate the standard deviation in the percentage share of the sales of each producer in each of the five main EU markets. The larger the figure, the greater the

TABLE 3.   Firm Market Shares

Producer	STD
FIAT	18.7
Peugeot	10.4
Renault	9.4
VW	7.4
Ford	6.4
GM	5.6

Source: CCFA 1990, 13.

Note: Standard deviation in percentage of market share of the mass-market producers in the 5 largest national markets.

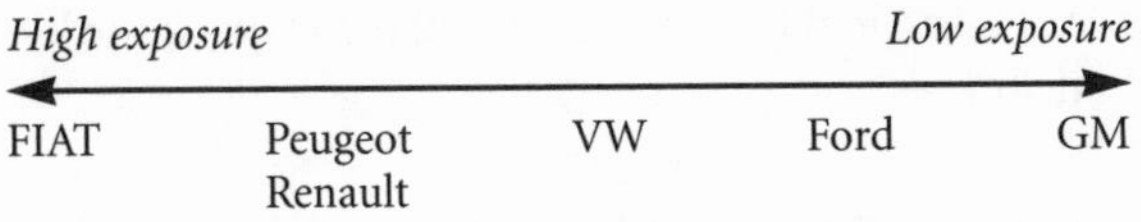

High exposure   Low exposure

FIAT   Peugeot   VW   Ford   GM
              Renault

Fig. 4.   Firm adjustment and industry liberalization

dependence of a firm on one single market and the more it was exposed to adjustment costs as market segmentation was ended.

These rankings cannot do justice to all the elements that determine the relative competitive position of a firm, elements that could change significantly over time and vary across model ranges. The discussion in chapter 3 provides a much richer picture. However, if the internal market meant anything, it meant that national market segmentation would be reduced, and so it seems reasonable to infer that those producers most reliant on that segmentation for their sales faced the most acute adjustment difficulties. In figure 4 the U.S. multinationals are shown to be the least exposed—they were easily the most regionally integrated producers. While the production of Volkswagen (VW) was concentrated in Germany, its sales mirrored more closely the pattern of the American multinationals rather than the pattern of the other three large producers—Peugeot, FIAT, and Renault, all of whom depended on their traditional national markets. Therefore I have located it between the two groups.

From this we may expect to observe a more liberal coalition of firms—the U.S. producers and VW—and a less liberal coalition—Renault, FIAT, and Peugeot. In the event, when the preferences of each automaker in each issue area were scrutinized, variation in this picture was discovered. Exposure to adjustment in each issue area depends on factors other than past market segmentation (for example, technology). However, the map presented above serves as a useful analytical starting point.

Summary

The discussion above has generated plausible, if merely illustrative, maps of the exposure of member states and the major auto-producing firms to adjustment. I argue that all parties wished to realize mutual gains from integration but that preferences over specific policy outcomes were likely to differ in predictable ways across states and firms, and that any effort at understanding these differences should begin with a knowledge of the distribution of adjustment costs. Agreement was easier for the member states when establishing the range of outcomes and more difficult for them, and for the firms involved, when addressing each issue area that related to the auto sector. What follows next is an analysis of the cooperation problem faced by states and firms, given the kinds of preferences discussed above.

Cooperation among States and Firms

The preferences examined above were translated into political outcomes at the level of the EU. These outcomes were a function of the success, or otherwise, of interfirm and interstate cooperation, mediated by the institutions and rules of the EU. In this section the limits on that cooperation are explored in the absence of institutions. The question to be investigated is the degree to which the member states or firms could accomplish their goals without an institutional arena of some kind. Where strategic dilemmas are discovered that could not be easily overcome in the absence of institutions, that is where I might expect to observe an important role for EU institutions, or, indeed, institutional innovation or adaptation of some kind.

Promises and Threats

If preferences were too dispersed, making it difficult for a coalition to emerge, promises (side-payments) and threats (imposed costs) might play an important part. Their existence and effectiveness depended on the issue area and institutional context. Consider the pattern of deal making that led up to the SEA. Britain and the Mediterranean members had to be induced to agree to a bargain close to the preferences of the Northern members. How they were persuaded suggests the ways in which bargains could be cemented by side-payments, or by threats.

Under a unanimity rule, which governed the process, the member with the minimalist position should have had the greatest influence. However, Portugal and Spain were in the process of joining the EU during bargaining over the SEA and were most susceptible to the influence of side-payments. (These countries are significant net beneficiaries of the Community budget.) In other words, they had little bargaining power. Britain, on the other hand, had begun the 1980s involved in an acrimonious and politically costly struggle over its contributions to the EU budget. The SEA could only move forward after the dispute had been settled (see Taylor 1989; and Moravcsik 1991). It was not with promises, therefore, but with a credible threat of exclusion that the other major players, mainly France and Germany, induced Britain to agree (Stephen 1994).

The foregoing suggests that, in a similar manner in specific issue areas, one way for different preferences over harmonization and integration to be adjusted (and to converge) might be for actors with preferences for a dramatic improvement over the status quo to make side-payments to, or threaten to impose costs on, actors whose preferences were to remain close to the status quo. Such side-payments would shift the distribution of welfare gains from integration toward those countries fearing greater political costs and so make them willing to agree to higher levels of integration. Threats make nonagreement less palatable and so also make a state's preferences shift toward those of the core coalition.

The institutions of the EU might play an important role in this area. For side-payments to work, promises must be credible and the complex set of payments between multiple actors must be managed. By granting the power to make side-payments to the institutions of the EU, the member states might be able to make a credible pre-commitment. (Of course, they might seek to renege on their contributions to the EU at a later date, but such action would call their membership in the organization into question and be politically costly.) They also had an institution that could help them overcome the tremendous practical difficulties of coordinating a network of side-payments across numerous issue areas over a long period of time. The effectiveness of threats can also be enhanced when bargaining in an institutionally rich environment. For example, the formal power to block action in an issue area in which the status quo is costly to some group of players could be used to extract concessions in some other area. In summary, normal political exchange (promises and threats) might not require an institutional context, but where it is complicated, spread across issue areas, and occurs over time, it could certainly be facilitated by the appropriate institutions.

It should be recognized, in passing, that the distributional consequences of integration were not only shaped by simple transfers. The character of regulation, or lack of it, adopted by the member states in any sector (as they were well aware) also had profound distributional consequences. The amount of integration that was acceptable was as much a function of the rules governing integration in any particular issue area as it was of a state's or firm's competitive position. From that it follows that rule changes, with distributional consequences, could be promised in lieu of side-payments as part of an effort to foster cooperation. As will be seen below, the institutions of the EU also had a role to play here, since they were in a good position to propose solutions to the problems of coordinating rules and regulations, given these distributional consequences.

Interstate Cooperation

Beyond the practical difficulties of managing political exchange, there were other elements in the strategic environment that intensified the collective action problem for states and firms. As noted above, completing the internal market was a "positive-sum" game, entered into in order to earn unrealized joint gains. As a result interstate cooperation over the SEA, with the objective of establishing a framework bargain over rule changes aimed at governing future policy outcomes, was politically possible.

However, the character of the game, or strategic dilemma, in each particular issue area might vary significantly, depending on variation in the distributional consequences and variation in the exposure of actors to exploitation. It should be possible to place each issue area on a continuum running between two limit conditions. One limit is a "coordination" game without distributional consequences, resolved easily by the exchange of information (see Stein 1990, 36). An example might be the allocation of radio bandwidth. The other limit is a "zero-sum" game, in which a gain by one party will require another to back down and endure a loss (see, among many others, Rapoport 1960, 130–39). For example, the division and allocation of a fixed quota on logging in old-growth forests has the characteristic of a zero-sum game.[7]

Those issue areas that fell under the purview of the internal market program fell between these two limiting cases. Some assumed the character of a coordination problem with acute distributional consequences. Other issue areas had the character of games of mutual aversion and possible exploitation. For example (as examined in depth in chapter 4), regulatory harmonization in auto emissions control could converge on a high or low level. However, even though all governments wanted harmonization, those who were home to producers of large, technologically sophisticated cars could obtain an advantage for their producers in the marketplace (relative to small-car producers) from harmonization at a high level. In other words, the common interest in harmonization had to be weighed against sharp divisions over the distributional costs. The crucial political struggle would be over how these costs were assigned, and the outcome might well favor actors who enjoyed an institutional advantage of some kind.

In other, slightly different kinds of strategic environments actors sought to realize mutual gains under conditions in which each was exposed to the possibility of exploitation by the other. For example, imagine countries A and B are members of a customs union. In order to make the playing field "level," they seek mutually agreed-on limits to the subsidies each national government may give its national champions. (Chapter 6 of this project addresses this issue in the case of the auto sector.) Each country is willing to give up its subsidies unilaterally, and so universal subsidies are the least preferred outcome for both. However, each much prefers that the other reciprocate, because in the event that they do not there is a danger that unsubsidized firms may be driven out of business or

A

	High	Low
High	1,1	4,2
Low	2,4	3,3

B

Fig. 5.   Coadjustment game

be the victim of "rent snatching."[8] Furthermore, each is tempted to exploit the other in the event that the other does reciprocate. This is the core of the problem; exploitation of one by the other (and vice versa) is a stable outcome.

A game-theoretic scheme examined by Martin (1992, 15–45) serves nicely to illustrate the character of this kind of game and yields very useful insights about possible levels of interstate cooperation in the absence of institutions. She calls this kind of problem a coadjustment problem (see Martin 1992, 21, fig. 2.4c). The payoffs and game matrix are depicted in figure 5. Imagine that there are two strategies available to each player. Each can choose to subsidize their firms at a high level (H) or a low level (L). The payoffs to each reveal that neither party has a dominant strategy (therefore, this is not a prisoner's dilemma), although there exist two pure strategy equilibria (H, L and L, H). In a simultaneous, single play of the game, which of these two equilibria will be chosen is indeterminate, although each outcome has significant distributional consequences. This is the essence of this kind of cooperation problem—there exists a stable outcome in which the distributional costs are all imposed on one player. However, under repeated play, in which an infinite set of strategies are available in the range between the two limit cases of H and L, there also exists an equilibrium strategy (the equivalent of a mixed strategy) under which the distributional consequences are eliminated, albeit at the price of a collectively suboptimal (Pareto-inferior) level of subsidization. Simply put, each player could subsidize at the same level, but at a level that would be collectively inefficient.[9]

Of course, the folk theorem tells us that under infinite iteration numerous perfect equilibria may exist and none is, a priori, to be preferred (see Rasmusen 1989, 92–94). But because payoffs are symmetrical when each subsidizes at the same level, this equilibrium can claim to be a "prominent" solution to the cooperation game and so might well be preferred by the actors involved.

What this tells us is that under these strategic conditions member states involved in a long-running subsidy game, who have a unilateral interest in mutual restraint, will still not be able to realize fully that interest because of the danger of exploitation and will still subsidize at a higher level than their collective preferences warrant. Martin's insights from this game can be easily translated into the terms of the subsidy game I have described: the greater the value to each of imposing costs on the other (in comparison to the value of cooperating to eliminate subsidies), the higher and more suboptimal the level of subsidy each will choose in equilibrium. It is unsurprising that countries should find mutual restraint difficult when opportunities exist to exploit the restraint of others, but this story highlights a crucial point: even when both actors have an interest in moving away from the status quo, distributional difficulties may make a mutual optimum elusive unless some mechanism—that is, an institution with the power to bind—can come into play.[10]

The interaction between the member states of the EU over internal market issues is well characterized by the strategic environments evaluated above. The analysis shows that it would be difficult for the member states to maximize the available mutual gains from cooperation under these kinds of conditions. The question is, therefore, what kind of institutions could resolve these kinds of dilemmas, and whether EU institutions were of that kind.

Cooperation among Firms

Just as the member states of the EU faced cooperation problems, so too did firms who, while competing in the economic marketplace, were perhaps in a position to cooperate to their mutual advantage in the political marketplace. Firms in different sectors may, of course, compete against each other in the political marketplace (Becker 1983). However, for the most part, policy spaces are discrete, and, especially in the context of the SEA and the internal market, firms either accepted policies devised by others or cooperated in order to shape them to their own ends (on policy spaces see Heclo 1972). One possible explanation for the kind of relationship that exists between firms in the same industry has been offered by Bowman (1989). His general point is that firms with differentiated products and divergent cost conditions (i.e., more or less efficient firms, doing more or less different things) find it difficult to cooperate. Differences in technological capabilities may also impede cooperation. But firms with homogeneous products under conditions of roughly equal costs find it easier to cooperate.

The argument behind this proposition is simple. The goal of interfirm cooperation might be anything, but assume it is some public good for the group in question, such as protection. Firms facing similar costs and producing undifferentiated products cannot easily obtain a private advantage from a political change that affects all the firms involved in that market. On the other hand, a firm with a cost advantage may feel that economic openness, which has the effect of driving competitors out of business, is valuable, even if the firm must give up normal profits in the short run. For this reason it might be tempted to break up any industry-wide cooperative political enterprise; under greater openness it would stand to inherit some of a less efficient firm's share of the market.[11]

As will be discussed below, the poor institutional capacity of EU institutions gave firms an opportunity to influence outcomes, but to do so they had to act in concert. Even if the elements identified above did serve to foster cooperation, some institution that would speak for firms with a single voice would be necessary. In short, as conditions favored firm cooperation, so they would give rise to appropriate interest group associations.[12]

If the forces at work shaping firm cooperation operate in the way that I have suggested, then it is possible to make a useful and plausible inference about the character of interest associations in the case of the auto industry. Assuming that mass-market auto producers faced the greatest adjustment costs following integration but were exposed to similar cost and technological constraints, then it would be they who had the interest and ability to cooperate in controlling the relevant transnational interest group association.[13]

These conditions that I claim are required to foster interfirm cooperation are at odds with the earlier discussion of the asymmetrical effects of integration, which are inevitably pronounced for firms in any particular sector. At the very moment when firms may wish to coordinate their responses to the political initiatives of the governments of the member states, they face being divided into winners and losers by the effects of greater economic openness, which works against such collective action. Furthermore, when governments make side-payments to lower the political costs of adjustment (payments to firms, or to other governments who pass them on to their firms), this also alters the conditions for subsequent transnational interfirm cooperation. While such payments might equalize the competitive position of firms (by sheltering inefficient ones) they would also be politically divisive. Firms without generous political patrons would resent—and seek to limit—payments to more fortunate competitors. In short, the conditions for firm cooperation would be, in part, a function of government action.

In conclusion, the central propositions on interfirm cooperation are as follows: where firms trade in homogeneous products, share similar cost structures, and so stand to gain or lose in roughly the same degree from changes in the status quo, they will find it easier to cooperate in pursuit of some political objective. But the availability of private goods (for example, subsidies) to be had from trading in the political market could prove divisive. Whatever levels of cooperation were accomplished would be reflected in the growth and character of the interest group associations to which the firms in question belonged.

The Institutions of the European Union

The discussion above showed how dilemmas exist that could limit the ability of governments and firms to cooperate, and how institutional arrangements might help overcome those limits. However, the many institutional arenas of the EU cannot be explained as some kind of inevitable response to functional needs. Their character is, essentially, an empirical question. The role they play is determined as much by a path-dependent and contingent historical process as by the strategic and farsighted choices of the principals, the member states. The purpose of the discussion that follows is to discover the range of possible roles that institutions of the EU might play, and to link this range of possibilities to the discussion above of government and firm preferences and cooperation problems. On occasion it may be that institutional adaptation and innovation are, in fact, associated with the need to surmount the dilemmas of joint decision making. However, it is also very likely that institutions exist and shape outcomes as exogenous features of the political landscape.

It is important not to speak of the institutions of the EU as if they were a single, undifferentiated mass. The EU is, in fact, a vast complex of separate (if overlapping) institutions, established and adapted at different times, serving different purposes, and therefore exhibiting different political properties. In the discussion that follows, institutional characteristics will be identified that may play an important role in some issue areas, or under some circumstances, but not elsewhere. By the same token, institutions of one kind that might foster integration in one issue area may coexist with other institutions that have very different effects on outcomes. The purpose is to determine the full range of possible institutional characteristics, knowing that the final picture will be heterogeneous and even contradictory, as are the institutions of the EU themselves.

As suggested above, some of the rules of the game and some of the powers of EU institutions were intentionally adapted at the time of the SEA. They were chosen with a view to the consequences they would have for outcomes: for example, the increased use of qualified majority voting was intended to limit the power of member states with minimalist preferences. Further, some of the dilemmas for the member states and for firms created by the need for coordinating their behavior may have led to other refinements of the institutional environment. But rather than beginning this project by trying to explain institutional innovations, this study begins by evaluating the role of EU institutions as independent variables in policy outcomes. Subsequent chapters go on to show how that role was played out in each particular case study. After carefully observing the effects of institutions, it may then be possible to analyze the political forces behind some of the institutional innovation and adaptation observed.

First, I investigate the way in which variation in the rules of the game might place a more or less severe premium on the ability of governments and firms to cooperate as they sought to control policy outcomes. In other words, the level of cohesion required to have a decisive effect may vary as rules varied. Second, I evaluate the conditions under which the institutions of the EU might be autonomous, and subject to some "private" institutional interest. Finally, I go on to investigate the rules under which the institutions of the EU operate, to discover if they are structured so as to favor some actors and some outcomes in a systematic way. The point is not to offer determinate statements or predictions about EU institutions, but to suggest the range of possible roles they might play in shaping outcomes.

The Rules of the Game

Even if the member states were able to cooperate sufficiently to articulate their collective preference, the question arises whether it simply reflected the ideal point of the median country (assuming single-peaked, symmetric indifference curves). That would depend on the rule governing the formation of coalitions. A unanimity requirement would yield a very different collective preference from a rule in which outcomes were decided by a simple majority. In the former case, that actor wishing for the smallest change over the status quo would be decisive, whereas in the latter case the number and character of alternative coalitions, and who enjoyed the power to propose them, would determine the ideal point for the group. Not only would the outcome be very different under unanimity, but it would be much harder to accomplish.

As noted, the SEA was an institution-building agreement characterized by peak bargaining among nation-states in which the supranational institutions themselves played a less important role.[14] Although it had to be agreed upon unanimously, the positive-sum character of the game, and the emphasis on the process of decision making rather than on specific outcomes, made such agreement possible—it was an incomplete contract promoting future interactions aimed at a cooperative "supergame" (see Snidal 1986). But when the time came to bargain over specific policies, the rules governing outcomes varied widely in the context of powerfully felt distributional divisions.

Bargains among the member states in issue areas relating to the internal market, as a result of the SEA, were subject to qualified majority rule, a less demanding form of group self-rule than unanimity.[15] But the role of the European Parliament (EP) was also expanded by these changes in a legislative process known as the cooperation procedure. Under certain circumstances the EP, in conjunction with the Commission, enjoyed the power of an agenda setter.

This meant that, where the EP and the Commission were in agreement on amendments to legislation (after the second reading), the member states would need to be unified in order to adopt an alternative proposal, or be willing to accept the continuation of the status quo. Change for the worse in the status quo, under these circumstances, would put tremendous pressure on the member states (see Tsebelis 1994a; Moser 1996; and Stephen 1995).

On the other hand, in order to accomplish a "level playing field" (i.e., an internal market in which political favors to privileged economic actors were restricted), other issues had to be addressed that were not technically internal market questions. For example, state aid to industry was governed by rules and procedures that pre-dated the SEA; to accomplish agreement on those rules, the member states acted unanimously. (In the event, much was delegated to the Commission—the implications of which are discussed below.) In other matters the role of rules was altogether reduced. In the area of external trade for the auto industry, EU policy toward Japan on imports was entirely informal and resulted in an informal agreement. Indeed, the agreement could not be formalized in the context of the EU's own rules on free circulation, or under the rules of the General Agreement on Tariffs and Trade (GATT). This may have been why a policy was successfully adopted in an issue area characterized by widely divergent preferences, and why the policy limited rather than fostered economic openness. (I return to this in one of the case studies.) Here, of course, the lack of rules was clearly endogenous to the political forces at work—rules existed, but they prescribed a liberal outcome and so were ignored.

In general, this variation in the rules of the game across issue areas would also have systematic effects on the level of cooperation among firms, as well as on the member states. For example, where the Commission was a powerful agent (as in the bargaining over external trade), the imperative to influence it would be very great, fostering cooperation. Where the agenda control of the Commission was shared with other actors, or supplanted by high levels of cohesion among the member states, the incentives for firms to seek transnational cooperation were reduced.

In summary, the formal rules under which policy was decided varied, and so for any given level of cohesion among governments and firms we might expect to observe variation in control over outcomes. In addition, the relative power of the Commission as an agent of the member states varied across issue areas, and so the incentive for firms to cooperate in seeking influence over it could also be expected to vary.

This discussion has taken the rules and institutions to be "neutral" and merely examined their mediating effect on actors as a function of the simple mechanics of policy-making. I now go on to investigate whether the institutions of the EU could have enjoyed some measure of autonomy, giving rise to "agency drift" in the way in which the staff of these institutions discharged their responsibilities.

The Composition of EU Institutions

Once the time came to complete the contract represented by the SEA, the three main EU institutions might be expected to play a more important role, beyond the question of the rules of the game. Of them all, the Commission may be the most important because of its role as an agenda setter, and as an institution with significant delegated powers. It is therefore important to estimate the probability with which it might pursue an agenda of bureaucratic expansion and/or political legitimacy. While the Commission responded to the political influence of firms and states acting in concert, it might also wish to shape policy outcomes in systematic ways congruent with its own institutional interests.

Different aspects of the Commission and its environment yield different incentives for agency drift. The Commission was specially charged with forwarding the purposes laid down in the Treaty of Rome (and subsequent amendments to that treaty, especially, of course, the SEA). This is the basis of its institutional identity and the source of its political legitimacy. This suggests that any institutional interest was likely to be more "pro-integrationist" than, for example, some or all of the member states. In addition, it answered (in the 1980s) to 12 principals, who were themselves divided over policy. Multiple principals allow, it can be argued, for greater autonomy in an agent (Pollack 1997). Furthermore, in keeping with the political logic of delegation (see the discussion in chapter 1), the Commission may enjoy a deliberate grant of autonomy in order that blame may be avoided (by national governments) for the consequences of its choices, and so that it can propose impartial "prominent" solutions to coordination problems with distributional consequences.

Against these factors must be set others, working in the opposite direction. As a relatively recently established transnational institution the Commission was likely to be especially solicitous of the interests and political preferences of the member states. To be ignored, or subsequently overruled in the Council of Ministers, would be costly and was to be avoided. Furthermore, as a result of its recent establishment and modest resources, it lacked the institutional capacity to remain autonomous of the various interests it had to regulate. Consistent with this view is the fact that in technical matters it relied on the information provided by outside interested parties.[16] Finally, mindful of the "democratic

deficit" commonly attributed to EU institutions and only remedied in part by
the innovations of the SEA, the Commission might have a strong preference for
consulting widely before drawing up proposals or making rulings. (This suggests why the EP may have a significant informal as well as formal role.)

How these cross-cutting pressures played themselves out is an empirical
question, but the formal argument is as follows: Because the Commission did
not pursue integration in a way that placed it "out on a limb," the policies it proposed, in a two-dimensional policy space, were always constrained by the Pareto
surface described by the preferences of the member states, and of those well-
organized and well-mobilized constituents with an interest in the issue areas being addressed. This surface, of course, was more or less spacious depending
upon the differences among the various actors. Within this constraint I expect
Commission efforts to be biased toward greater integration, and the effectiveness of those efforts to be a function of the rules of the game.

Of course the Commission is not the only EU institution, and its policy output may have been shaped by other institutional actors. For example, Goldstein
(1996) has shown how the composition of dispute settlement panels can lead to
a change in the character of settlements and, in turn, to a rational (moderating)
response by an agency that may come before the panel. In the case of the EU,
dispute settlement is delegated to an even more autonomous, transnational institution—the European Court of Justice (ECJ), which may also have an "integrationist" bias due to its "constitutional" responsibilities. However, it too, like
the Commission, has to tend to the preferences of the member states if its legitimacy is not to be eroded by noncompliance or other challenges to its authority
(Garrett and Weingast 1993). But if the member states cannot agree (in other
words, when the Pareto surface is very spacious, so much so that under any given
rule no bargained outcome is possible and the status quo is controlling), the
Court may take the opportunity to make rulings that advance integration (this
explains the significant departure represented by the *Cassis de Dijon* ruling, according to Alter and Meunier-Aitsahalia (1994). Furthermore, as discussed below, the logic of the law and the terms of the Treaty of Rome may give the Court's
rulings a pro-integrationist tendency (the logic of the EU legal order also played
a part in the administrative law under which antitrust policy was discharged by
the Commission—see chapter 6). In general, therefore, while the role of the
Court needs to be discovered in each case study, the same logic applies to it as
to the Commission. Divisions among the principals allow more-integrationist
rulings.

Finally, given that the EP shared agenda-setting powers with the Commission (more on this below), some estimate of the forces shaping its institutional

interest should be made as well. It is reasonable to assume that the officials, members (MEPs), and staff of the EP have a vested interest in forwarding and expanding the "European project" (see Eichener 1993, 53–57). They tend to be self-selected for that purpose, although following the domestic divisions in a variety of countries over Maastricht some anti-EU MEPs have joined the Parliament. Indeed, inasmuch as the EP is directly elected and not a true agent of the governments sitting in the Council of Ministers (rather, they share the same principals—national voters), this is one EU institution likely to be less constrained by the spread of preferences among the governments and mobilized interests of the EU. In short, it may make proposals outside the Pareto surface.

On the other hand, conventional constituency politics could be expected to play a role as well. Indeed, it seems reasonable that the more consequential the EP becomes, in part due to institutional changes in the SEA and Maastricht, the more it will reflect a plural struggle between interests and the less it will promote a European "project" detached from any specific coalition of political forces. Furthermore, questions of legitimacy are just as likely to weigh heavily in the minds of MEPs—it is an institution that has historically had little respect. This may make it inclined to act "responsibly" in order to foster its credibility.

In short, the Commission, the EP, and the ECJ are at the center of the action, albeit with limited autonomy and limited institutional capacity. They realize their preferences within the constraints imposed on them by other political actors, such as states and firms. But where such actors cannot cohere, an institutional interest in favor of integration stands a greater chance of being realized. In other words, the institutions of the EU may operate as independent variables on policy outcomes under certain conditions. The first, acting as a general constraint, is the spread of preferences among other powerful actors (as discussed above). The other is the character of the rules of the game as they affect each institutional player.[17]

Rules and Institutions

Ultimately the member states of the Community are the principals, and the institutions of the Community are their agents. The institutions were adopted with a view to realizing the maximum mutual gains from the EU for the governments of the member states at the lowest possible political cost. However, once Community institutions were in place, or innovation in existing institutions complete, the rules to which the member states had committed themselves also conferred specialized roles on these institutions, which gave them a more or less formal source of power. What needs to be evaluated, therefore, is the way in which these rules operate from the point of view of EU institutions, and what systematic consequences (if any) they may have for policy outcomes. I argue that under certain conditions EU institutions may have an institutional capacity to limit the set of possible outcomes, weighting them toward maximalist (i.e., most pro-integration) positions and reducing the opportunities for minimalist positions to triumph.

This could occur in a number of different ways. For example, the control over the agenda enjoyed by the Commission and the Parliament, in combination with qualified majority voting, might circumscribe the ability of even a combination of states to take the initiative. Also, the control enjoyed by the Commission staff in the functional committees of the Commission, which, in a process known as comitology, reviews the technical details of legislation, might limit the influence of the member states. Finally, the manner in which the ECJ encourages private legal suits that limit national authority and promote the doctrine of direct effect, while refusing to hear suits that argue for limiting the supremacy of EU law, has pro-integrationist consequences.

The power of the Commission and the Parliament as "conditional agenda setters" has been underestimated (what follows relies on Tsebelis 1994a, 1996; and Moser 1996). The fundamental consequence of the cooperation procedure was that if the Commission and Parliament shared a position (for example, a position on auto emissions), they could present to the Council of Ministers (after the second reading) a winning proposal that some qualified majority (QM) of the states preferred over the status quo. Given that both the Commission and the EP have an institutional interest in more integration rather than less, it is reasonable that their proposals will be aimed at a QM of the member states whose preferences are closest to the maximum. Of course, in order to pick off the ideal coalition the Commission must have good information about member state preferences.[18]

It is for this reason that the Council of Ministers, which in theory might contain a variety of coalitions among the member states, may be constrained on occasion to accept either maximalist positions or the status quo. The power of EU institutions as agenda setters imposes a severe cooperation problem on the member states. To amend a proposal by the Commission (after the second reading) requires unanimity, and there may be no agreement on maintaining the status quo, let alone on some less integrationist alternative.

There remains another avenue for the member states to shape Commission proposals—through the process known as "comitology."[19] There are over 1,000 committees of experts, made up of delegates from the member states and representatives of industry, with the general role of supplying the skills necessary to write, monitor, and help implement regulation in highly technical areas. However, some have strictly advisory powers, and others that do have legislative tasks delegated to them are structured so that the Commission representatives (who chair them) may pick "maximalist" recommendations from the set under discussion. In order to prevent this control by Commission representatives, national delegates and industry representatives have to form coalitions, know the powers of their particular committee (frequently not the case), and settle on alternative proposals. The burden is on the representatives of the member states, and industry experts, to accomplish high levels of cooperation over very technical matters if they are to control the formation of Commission proposals. In short, "comitology" may act as a mechanism that structures external influences by privileging maximalist proposals.

On the other hand, of course, Commission capacity is slim (as noted above). This is clearly recognized by the "model directive" on technical harmonization (part of the SEA proposals), which delegated standard-setting to private bodies (OJ 1985, C 136/1). In other words, Commission experts may be constrained to entertain a set of proposals devised for them by others. The question of who is setting the agenda under such circumstances is far from clear. Once again, a general expectation is that Commission autonomy depends upon divisions among other actors. The set of proposals from which Commission representatives may choose will be large where divisions are pronounced.

In the case of the ECJ, where the process is, at least on the surface, legal rather than purely political, judicial appeals over the implementation and monitoring of laws are entirely beyond the control of the Council of Ministers.[20] At bottom, the manner in which the doctrine of direct effect operates empowers private individuals and groups with pro-integration interests. Those seeking to declare any act of the Council or Commission ultra vires are denied standing, while those seeking to force member states to conform to Community law and practice, as interpreted by Community institutions, are encouraged to appeal to the Court (see Burley and Mattli 1993, 60–62). The member states themselves, when appealing to the Court, are constrained to rely on the ratchet of precedent; the ECJ not only never reverses itself, it is never asked to do so. In short, the legal structure that monitors and enforces compliance with the rules of the Community may tend to make "maximalist" rulings.[21]

In summary, the rules by which states and other interests must interact with the institutions of the Community might favor pro-integration interests and coalitions. It might also be the case that the institutions themselves shaped the agenda and therefore outcomes. Such institutions, for reasons of corporate identity and purpose, would, in that event, seek or favor pro-integration outcomes. Losers opposed to the position of EU institutions might have had few legal remedies, while other institutional avenues required high levels of inter-firm and interstate cohesion. Yet the constraint imposed by legitimacy and the formal authority of the principals never disappears. How closely drawn that constraint was, and the conditions under which it allowed for institutional autonomy, must be discovered by the research reported below.

Conclusions

The discussion in this chapter has consisted of a series of arguments about the preferences of states and firms, their ability to cooperate, and the role that could be played by the institutions of the EU. What follows is a general picture of the ways in which the elements of this framework can be linked together.

The distribution of the political costs of adjustment among states and firms sets the conditions governing their strategic interaction, and the degree to which EU institutions can have an independent effect on outcomes. This distribution is a function of their exposure to adjustment costs. In the case of governments, the function describes the way in which political leaders weigh the preferences of voters as against the influence of sheltered interests. In the case of firms the distribution of costs is determined by the competitive position of each firm.

In an issue where the interests among firms and governments are closely shared—in other words, where the political costs and benefits are closely shared—I expect strategic dilemmas and formal institutions to be of less consequence. Where differences among crucial actors are significant, there exists a greater possibility that cooperation among actors will be harder to accomplish, and that institutions will play an important role. This is a probabilistic claim. The interaction of interests and institutions—so often separately investigated, so hard to capture simultaneously—is subject to numerous contingencies. The way various constraints shape outcomes in any particular case requires careful empirical scrutiny. That is what I go on to address in the case studies that follow.

CHAPTER 3

The Political Economy of the European Automobile Industry

Introduction

In this chapter I describe the postwar performance of the European automobile industry, analyze its market structure and competitiveness, and map the public and private institutional environment on the eve of the Single European Act. The purpose is to supply the empirical material necessary for applying the analytical framework developed in the previous chapter. For that reason, emphasis will be laid on those elements fostering divisions or cohesion among governments and firms, and those national institutions that mediated firm interests before the SEA came into force. The material provides a crucial starting point for the case studies in European Union policy-making that follow.

First I account for the divergent experiences of each major producing country in Europe since the Second World War.[1] I describe the history of state support for national champions, a pattern of government intervention commonly observed in the European political economies. This is followed by a comparative survey of the structure of the auto industry. I begin by accounting for those general structures of the auto sector that fostered or inhibited cooperation among firms and governments over the move to economic integration. I go on to estimate the preferences of governments and firms over a set of specific issue areas based on the following elements: the balance of trade in autos for each producing nation, the degree of specialization in auto production, the patterns of market segmentation, the variation in factor costs across Europe, and the extent of nonprice competition. In the case studies to come, these preferences will be refined and extended.

I then examine the role of private industry associations and the character of state-firm relations within the producing nations. I show how these connec-

53

tions influenced the role played by the EU in the integration of the sector, and I account for the early stages of transnational association building among European automakers. The variety of institutions at the level of the member state, in combination with the institutional environment at the level of the EU, could and did have a systematic effect on the way firm interests were articulated and the relationship firms enjoyed with their respective national governments.

A Short History of the European Automobile Industry

The extraordinary growth of the European auto industry between 1950 and 1973, when the first oil shock occurred, is a clear indicator of the general economic boom enjoyed by Western Europe during this period. Output in the four major producing nations of Europe rose from 1.75 million units annually to 11.67, an increase of more than 650 percent. This performance was a function of highly favorable economic conditions, and while some producers may already have begun to show signs of competitive weakness by the late 1960s, it is clear from figure 6 that all boats were lifted by the rising economic tide.

The industry then began to experience difficulties between 1973 and 1984. The first oil shock, followed by inflation and a sharp rise in raw materials costs, and much lower rates of economic growth, brought on an extended period of retrenchment and industry concentration. The oil shock caused the first Europe-wide downturn for the industry in the postwar period. A recovery in 1976 was followed by the second oil shock in 1979 and a recession in 1982. It is important not to underestimate the effects of such fluctuations in production. The difference between 500,000 units more or less might be the difference between having the money to invest in the next product cycle and bankruptcy.[2]

What is clear from figure 6 is that the four major producing countries, setting Spain aside for the moment, have had divergent experiences since the early seventies. These are the result of the interaction of a variety of factors. Different underlying rates of economic growth in combination with distinctive patterns of industry management practices resulted in, among other things, more or less satisfactory labor relations and different levels of firm concentration. These differences, added to variation in macroeconomic management and industry-government relations, led to increasing divergences in firm competitiveness across the member states of the EU. What follows will examine these factors as part of a general account of the experiences of each country. This account relies, in part, on Chanaron and de Banville 1991; Hart 1992; Maxcy 1981; and Quinn 1988.

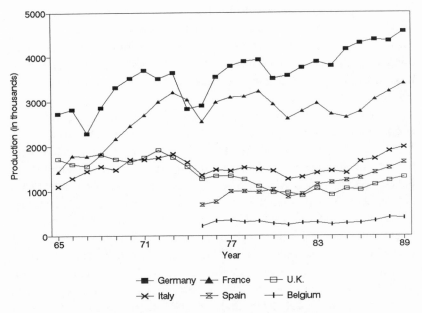

Fig. 6.   Automobile output (Data from MVMA 1988, 1992)

The British Auto Industry

In many ways the most remarkable story is that of the British auto industry's decline (and recent revival). Even by the time of the first oil shock it was clearly the most troubled of the four major producing countries. The fragmentation of the domestic industry, poor management and labor practices, and the harmful government practice of using the tax on auto sales and the control of consumer credit as macroeconomic levers (during the height of the so-called stop-go economic cycles) placed the industry, which depended largely on its domestic market, in a weak position at the very moment that Britain entered the EU and tariffs were eliminated. As figure 6 shows, British production went into a steady decline after the oil shock, and imports captured an ever increasing share of the national market. This decline was only arrested by the end of the 1980s, under very different political and economic circumstances.

This poor performance occurred in the context of an avowedly liberal, or "hands-off," approach to government policy. But while the British government never set out to engage in systematic management of the sector (nor did it have the institutional capacity to do so), a series of increasingly unsuccessful exceptions to this policy were forced on it, beginning as early as 1960 (when it subsidized the Rootes group to invest in a plant in Linwood, Scotland, to be a downstream consumer of the government-established Ravenscraig steelworks; see Wilks 1984, 75–78). In spite of the rationalization of British domestic producers, culminating in the unwieldy and inefficient firm of British Leyland (BL), later to be known as Rover, and the expenditure of vast sums of public money, performance continued to sag.[3]

Foreign-owned firms did not perform much better. In keeping with a liberal approach, multinational producers (that is, U.S. multinationals until the 1980s) were traditionally welcome in the United Kingdom and indeed were treated with scrupulous evenhandedness by the postwar British authorities.[4] But as productivity in the Ford and Vauxhall (GM) plants declined in the 1980s, in conjunction with the dramatic overvaluation of the British pound in the early 1980s, these producers increasingly moved production to other locations, chiefly in Spain and Germany. This, in combination with the steady decline of BL, had serious consequences for the U.K. balance of trade in automotive products, as can be seen in figure 7, and for the vitality of the components sector, which represents roughly as much manufacturing value added as generated by an assembler. For example, by the mid-1980s GM was running approximately a $1 billion deficit in its intrafirm trade between Britain and the rest of Europe (House of Commons 1987, 82). As a result GM became subject to political pressure; earlier warnings by the Department of Trade and Industry culminated in public criticism by the minister, Sir Leon Brittan (*Financial Times*, 4 July 1986).

The American multinationals were not the only producers coming under political pressure. By 1977 the Japanese share of the British market was roughly 10 percent, and informal talks seeking "a gentleman's agreement" on voluntary restraint had the effect of limiting future increases in Japanese sales in the United Kingdom (*Financial Times*, 11 February 1977). This restraint never became a legal agreement—which would, of course, have been contrary to the General Agreement on Tariffs and Trade (GATT)—but remained an informal one between the Society of Motor Manufacturers and Traders (SMMT), the British industry association, and the Japanese Automobile Manufacturers Association (JAMA).[5]

In summary, the British auto industry was in a state of competitive decline until the mid-1980s. The remains of British Leyland, the Rover Group, was producing only a few hundred thousand units a year, while trying to compete in mass-market segments.[6] Licensing agreements between Rover and Honda, and the transfer of technology, did seem to promise some long-term improvement in productivity and quality, if they also suggested that Rover would ultimately be absorbed by its Japanese partner (in the event, BMW, the German specialist producer, bought Rover). The U.S. multinational producers had shifted a sig-

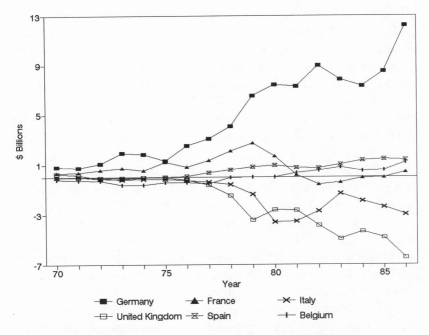

Fig. 7.   Balance of trade (Data from COMTAP; OECD 1987)

nificant amount of production away from the United Kingdom and spread it throughout Europe. Greater openness could result in further decline, and the past history of direct government involvement had been disastrous, both of which seemed to limit policy options.

In the event, the strategy chosen for the rehabilitation of the sector was to rely on British openness toward foreign direct investment (FDI) and the desire of Japanese auto producers to make investments within the EU in an effort to avoid tariff and nontariff barriers. From the importance of Japanese investment it may be inferred that the British government had a strong preference for completion of the internal market in autos, and for the persistence of a liberal investment regime. On the other hand its preferences over external trade were likely to be more protectionist since such barriers foster investment diversion.[7] What it also reveals is that no government of a major EU economy was willing to consider the exit option as a viable response to failure in this sector.

The German Auto Industry

The German government was involved in less formal public control over the sector than even the British government, especially if the time spent turning over Volkswagen (VW) to the private sector is set aside.[8] This is not to say that public policy did not take the importance of this sector very seriously, and Reich makes a strong case for his claim that there exists a "core" to the German political economy (to which, for example, Daimler-Benz and VW belong) and a "periphery" (to which the two U.S. multinationals, Fordwerke and Opel (GM), are consigned). As evidence he notes that VW's profit, taxes, and capital costs in the 1950s were obscured by government budgets, and that as a consequence Ford and GM were forced to avoid trading in the low-cost segment of the market (Reich 1990, 139).

The consolidation of the sector in the 1960s confirmed a pattern in which ownership was retained in "national" hands. The smaller firms of NSU and Auto-Union were taken over by VW, while the firm of Borgward disappeared completely and BMW went through a change of ownership and recapitalization. In the case of BMW, intervention by the state government of Bavaria prevented its purchase by the British General Electric Corporation. The subsequent purchase of Rover by BMW in 1994, and the "hands-off" policy of the U.K. government at that time, presents a contrast.

More recently, the superior performance of this sector, including the U.S. multinationals, has undoubtedly permitted local and national authorities to pursue a more strictly "liberal" policy in word and deed. What is more, the crucial supervisory roles played by the *Hausbank* for each manufacturer in many ways take the place of the kind of coordinating role attempted by the state in Britain and, more effectively, in France. For example, the Deutsche Bank played a vital role in the crisis at VW in the early seventies, when the firm was forced to make the transition from "Fordism" and the Beetle to the more flexible product range of the Golf/Rabbit (Streeck 1989, 120).

As can be seen from figure 6, Germany led Europe in passenger car production. What is more, due in part to the fact that the domestic market in Germany was the most fragmented and competitive in Europe, producers were willing and able to seek extra sales through exports. The result, shown in figure 7, is that Germany, alone of the major producing countries of Europe, enjoyed a large trade surplus with its partners in the EU. It also enjoyed a surplus with the rest of the world, especially the United States. The exception was Japan, although the specialist producers had met with some success in that market by the late 1980s and were relatively optimistic for the future.[9]

The Japanese slowly built up a 15 percent share of the German market, which is the largest share they have in any of the domestic markets of the major producing countries (in the smaller countries it runs as high as 30 percent). Yet many commentators claim that even the Germans have some kind of tacit agreement with Japanese producers that limits their sales (see Wilks 1989, 172;

and Smith and Venables 1990, 126). As discussed in chapter 5 in greater detail, Europe-wide monitoring of Japanese auto sales may have encouraged a "de facto" limit on Japanese sales in Germany.

In summary, on the eve of the SEA, Germany and the German auto industry were in a position to gain the most from the completion of the internal market. Germany, therefore, had a strong preference for the completion of the internal market and the adoption at the level of the EU of its own, mostly liberal political management of the sector. However, the interests of its producers were likely to be differentiated in significant ways. The specialist producers—Daimler-Benz and BMW, with strong links to the Verband Der Automobilindustrie (VDA), the industry association, and through it to the government—felt relatively invulnerable and in a position to have their political preference for openness realized. However, the mass producers faced greater competitive challenges, not least from the Japanese.[10]

The French Auto Industry

In France the role of the government in the postwar development of the sector is more prominent than in any other country in Europe (see Hart 1992, 112–21). With the confiscation of Louis Renault's company at the end of the war (Renault was accused of collaboration with the Germans), the French government itself became a major auto producer. Renault was to remain at the core of French postwar policy and planning. It was seen as a central element in French postwar economic recovery and a "porteur du progrès social." (For a description of Renault's place in the French political economy see Tacet and Zenoni 1986.) There were three other major French producers—Peugeot, Simca, and Citroën. When Citroën began to stumble soon after the first oil shock, it was the French state that orchestrated the sale of its passenger car operations to Peugeot and the truck division to Renault.

It is the French government's treatment of the U.S. producers that shows how far it would go in order to protect its national champions. Ford had its plant in France stripped by the Germans during the war but was constantly obstructed during postwar reconstruction in its efforts to reestablish what had been a significant prewar presence. It ended up selling its factory to Simca in 1954. Subsequently Ford applied to the French government to make a new investment at Poissy in 1964, and soon afterward GM applied to build a plant in Lorraine. Their applications were denied.

Chrysler subsequently succeeded in buying Simca on the open market, but it was unable to turn a profit, either in France or with its other investment in Britain, and it finally sold all of its European operations to Peugeot. As a result

FDI in this sector was completely excluded, and by the end of the 1970s the auto industry in France had become concentrated into two national producers, Renault and Peugeot.

This strategy did not, however, lead to an internationally competitive industry. Despite an "understanding" with the Japanese limiting them to 3 percent of the market, and a suspicion that even their EU partners in Germany had been warned to show some "restraint," both companies, especially Renault, were financially weak.[11] As can be seen from figure 6, French production recovered well from the effects of the first oil shock, but the second oil shock and the sluggish markets of the early 1980s created a crisis of overcapacity and profitability. Despite its tradition as the "private" alternative to Renault, Peugeot reluctantly accepted loans totaling $300 million in 1983–84, while Renault, required by a socialist government to hire workers during the deepest recession of the postwar era, lost over $2 billion in 1984 (Wilks 1989, 177–78). As is examined below, this subsidy was to be the focus of protracted negotiations in the late 1980s when the EU began to establish a regime for state aid.

Part of this enormous loss at Renault was the result of a disastrous attempt to pursue a global strategy by buying the ailing American Motors Corporation (AMC). This highlights a serious difficulty that faced the French auto industry: on the eve of the SEA the French producers were still overdependent on the French market. This overdependence placed them at a relative disadvantage in an integrated market, at a moment when they needed to reduce total costs by 5 percent and increase labor productivity by 15 percent in order to stay competitive (CEC 1988d, 22–23).

For French producers the important question was whether the French government would be willing to shoulder the political and economic burden of limiting the costs of adjustment. The preference of the French government, in an effort to avoid any further costly financial commitments, was probably for the EU as a whole to shoulder the burden of lowering adjustment costs in this sector. It would wish for side-payments from the EU (i.e., other members) in place of the French taxpayer support of the past, and also for other policies to protect the sector, such as relative closure in external trade.

The Italian Auto Industry

The postwar story of the Italian auto industry is close to that of France. While Alfa-Romeo was a state-owned automaker, controlled by the state holding company Istituto per la Ricostruzione Industriale (IRI) from 1933, the autarky of the Mussolini years benefited FIAT most of all, due to its dominant position in the Italian market. Being the only mass producer in a market characterized by an unusually small average vehicle size, FIAT was able to make the most of economies of scale, while remaining insulated from competition from other European producers, whose model ranges tended to feature heavier models with larger engines.[12] Ford, the foreign producer most interested in investing in Italy, had been excluded by the Fascist regime of Mussolini and never found a way to return.

As a result, by the early seventies, FIAT was Europe's leading mass-market passenger vehicle producer. But, as in the United Kingdom, a significant rise in labor militancy, due in part to the fragmentation of the labor movement, had a very disruptive effect on the quality of output throughout the rest of the decade (see Golden 1988). FIAT began to lose market share in Italy without being able to compensate for it with gains in other European markets. After a 1980 showdown over layoffs, FIAT did succeed in regaining control of the shop floor in its large plants in Turin. As a result of the introduction of some successful new models, and an expensive commitment to automation and robots (partly as a consequence of its experiences with militant labor), FIAT accomplished a turnaround in the company's fortunes, increasing quality and overall productivity in the early 1980s.

However, the true state of FIAT's bottom line is obscure, and this obscurity is nowhere more evident, and the relationship between FIAT and the Italian state more important, than in the episode of Alfa-Romeo's privatization.[13] FIAT had acquired the ailing specialist producer Lancia in the sixties in order to keep out of the Italian market any foreign competition, Ford in particular. In 1986 the board of the IRI made a surprise decision to sell off Alfa-Romeo, and Ford made a good cash offer for the firm. FIAT was faced with another foreign threat. Alfa-Romeo was recapitalized with state funds in the late 1970s and had a large new plant outside Naples, established as part of the Italian government's continuing efforts to develop the Mezzogiorno. In theory the firm owed the Italian government a lot of money (partly as a result of this investment). After a series of murky maneuvers, FIAT defeated the Ford bid by agreeing to the same price and so acquired the firm. In fact, not only was the Italian government not paid by FIAT, but Alfa-Romeo's debt vanished (in a compromise with the EU over state aids, to be discussed in chapter 6, FIAT agreed to begin payments in 1995).

FIAT was also assisted in other ways. The cost of the layoffs that sparked the strike in 1980 was eventually shared with the "casa integrazione," a public system for managing layoffs in which workers do a short workweek and the government makes up the difference in their pay. Also, as Italy's premier industrial enterprise, FIAT shares in all kinds of public projects, recently being made one of the principal contractors on the Italian high-speed train project. Given the porous character of Italian state institutions, it is no surprise that foreign investment, public spending, and even the specifications for government contracts should be subject to significant informal control by FIAT.

Overall, since the first oil shock FIAT has exhibited an ability to renew itself and hold its own. As can be seen from figure 6, Italy in the mid-1980s was the third-largest producing country in Europe, and FIAT was the second-largest producing firm. The problem was the same as for the French producers, only it was even more pronounced. FIAT depended on the Italian market for its sales. A relatively weak export performance in EU and other countries resulted in a significant trade deficit in auto products for Italy (see figure 7)—in spite of the fact that the Japanese producers were limited technically to only 3,000 imported units every year (some 40,000 cars were registered for one day in the EFTA countries of Switzerland and Austria and then shipped to Italy and sold legally as used cars).[14]

In summary, the prospect of completing the European market after 1985 increased the threat to the Italian balance of trade. What is more, it would have been politically difficult for the Italian government to commit itself to any EU regulation of the sector that might upset the cozy relationship that bound together the state, the political parties, and such powerful domestic actors as FIAT. (The political explosion at the beginning of the 1990s could not be foreseen.) Just as southern Italy benefited from EU structural funds, so it might be expected that the Italian government's preference would be for FIAT to receive assistance and protection from the EU, in place of that which it had received from the Italian government.

The Spanish Auto Industry

Short mention will be made of the Spanish experience. As figure 6 shows, Spain was a success story by comparison, for example, with Britain. It passed the United Kingdom in auto production in the early 1980s. Of course, as a market for cars it was still much smaller than the other four major producing countries, but its success, as noted above, was due to its locational advantages for multinational production. The only significant domestic producer, SEAT, was sold to VW in 1986 after years of losses paid for by the Spanish government and also, in part, by FIAT, which had a controlling share in SEAT until 1980. All other passenger car production was conducted by foreign producers, principally the U.S. multinationals, Peugeot, and Renault.

The reasons for its locational advantage lie in the very high external trade barriers maintained by both Spain and Portugal before their entry into the EU in combination with low wages and location subsidies. These factors made Spain an attractive export platform. It was the first country to benefit from a development that was likely to become more pronounced as companies adjusted to higher levels of competition: that is, the shift of production to the low-wage European periphery, a shift lubricated by the EU's structural funds for regional assistance.[15] In summary, the Spanish government had a strong interest in the completion of the internal market, because this would increase export opportunities, and also an interest in the maintenance by the EU of a liberal foreign investment regime (even if the source of its FDI was mainly intra-EU).

Small Member States

With the exception of Belgium, the small member states were not home to any significant production activities. As a result the treatment of this sector by the national governments of these states reflected a wider set of purposes than those observed among the governments of the producing nations, who shared a common interest in fostering this economically important activity.[16] In the small states various tax and environmental regimes reflected other priorities, imposed on the sector without regard for producer interests. For example, in Denmark autos were subject to an extraordinary 100 percent sales tax, while Holland was disposed to impose very high emissions control standards, as will be discussed in much greater detail below. While small states, therefore, had a preference for free trade, preferences for widely varying regulations in other areas would make harmonization much more difficult to achieve.

Conclusions

In keeping with the argument in chapter 2, the consequences of increased integration were likely to be unequally distributed among firms and governments. Some firms stood to make significant gains—among the mass-market producers the U.S. multinationals and VW seemed well-situated—while others, in particular French and Italian producers, faced costly adjustment. This was sure to impose political costs on their governments. These general remarks must now be supplemented by a more precise, comparative evaluation of the characteristics of the industry.

Factor Prices, Specialization, and Segmentation

This section accounts for the strengths and weaknesses of the member states and firms in this sector by more refined comparisons of costs and performance and describes the market structures in which they operated. I identify forces that favored or hindered interstate and interfirm cooperation, and I specify the preferences of firms and states for policy in the various issue areas addressed in the case studies to come.

Market Growth and Factor Prices

One general factor worked against interfirm cooperation in the late eighties. As can be seen from figure 6, after 1985 the European car industry went into an unexpected boom, breaking out of the doldrums it had been in since 1978. Five-country production of 10.46 million units in 1985 had increased to 12.88 million units by 1989, an increase of over 20 percent. French production alone increased by 777,000 units between 1985 and 1989. Under these circumstances each firm might see a chance to increase output, and perhaps market share, by relying on its own efforts, rather than protecting its market position through cooperation of various kinds with its competitors. However, this disincentive to cooperate ended when the European market peaked in 1989 and turned down in 1990. (The exception was Germany, because of the effects of unification.)

Labor

These buoyant conditions must be set against changes in factor prices. It was argued in chapter 2 that firms facing similar factor costs could cooperate more easily. Where factor costs varied across firms, a firm might find greater advantage from private strategies in the economic marketplace than from pursuing cooperative strategies in the political marketplace. Since the Stolper-Samuelson model of international trade suggests that increased international exchange results in factor price equalization, and since Europe had experienced a large increase in exchange of all kinds since the war, it could be expected that factor prices converged, and that the strategic environment faced by the major producers became, in general, more favorable to cooperation.

The extent to which this equalization has occurred in Europe as far as labor costs are concerned is still something of an unresolved question. Erickson and Kuruvilla (1993, table 4) have attempted to measure total labor costs after correcting for cross-national differences in compensation that are due to variation in the level of productivity. They find that, even after allowing for differences in productivity levels, total unit labor costs among all the member states between 1980 and 1986 did not converge as might have been expected. This finding is supported by Flanagen (1993). However, among the four major producing countries the standard deviation in unit labor costs in manufacturing did decline between 1980 and 1986 (from 20.80 to 11.92 in current U.S.$). In other words, among these four there was convergence in the factor price of labor, although Spain, as noted above, enjoyed a significant advantage in this respect until the early 1990s. There is also other evidence that labor costs in manufacturing (taking into consideration labor productivity) converged in Europe by the late eighties (see *Financial Times*, 17 December 1991, 2).

In the auto industry alone the picture is a little more mixed; the wage costs of autoworkers among the three largest producing countries (excluding Germany) have converged (VDA [Verband Der Automobilindustrie] 1991, 39–40). This convergence is confirmed by Swedish data, in which the standard deviation in unit labor costs (in kronor, uncorrected for productivity) among these three large producing countries and Belgium shrank between 1980 and 1985 (SAF 1992). Inclusion of German figures increases the standard deviation over the period. In the past this difference between Germany and its competitors was counteracted by the well-known labor productivity of German workers. In fact, labor productivity grew more slowly in the German auto industry in the 1980s than in competing producing nations.

Capital

A good way to measure the degree to which market rates for capital in the EU were converging, a method employed by Frankel, Phillips, and Chinn (1992, 21), is by estimating covered interest rate differentials (between each currency and the deutsche mark [DM]). They find that the trend for all the EU members for the period between September 1982 and April 1988 converges on the DM rate, with the exception of Belgium and Ireland. However, this convergence in rates is less a function of factor price equalization, they argue, than of increasing confidence (misplaced, as it turned out) in the European Monetary System (EMS) in the late 1980s. The removal of capital controls in France and Italy also played a part in this convergence. Indeed, European Monetary Union (EMU) was perceived by the major European auto producers as a vital accompanying step to completing the internal market, as it would give them easy access to a Europewide capital market; they saw themselves at a significant comparative disadvantage, in world terms, in the cost of capital, against Japanese producers who were able to obtain very-low-cost capital during the 1980s because of the bubble in Japanese equity markets.[17] To the extent that the cost of capital converged across the member states, so would the prospect for interfirm cooperation be enhanced.

However, the market rate for capital, as far as the auto producers were concerned, was dominated until the mid-1980s by the subsidies provided by various national governments. As noted above, the French, British, and Italian governments all provided assistance at below-market rates (or even 0 percent) to their national producers. This clearly worked to the disadvantage of the other producers—VW and the American multinationals—who traded in private capital markets. But by the mid-1980s the EU had begun to place limits on state aid (to be examined in much greater detail below). These limits reflected, in part, the unwillingness of various governments to continue to give subsidies and favorable loans to national champions that continued to perform badly. The desire of European governments in the 1970s to protect employment gave way, in the 1980s, to fiscal restraint as part of the battle against inflation. (These preferences may have varied due to partisan differences across governments; see Verdier 1995.)

On the one hand, a level playing field once subsidies were ended might foster cooperation. By contrast, the possibility of continued subsidies would inevitably prove divisive. Firm preferences over this were, no doubt, a function of what they had received in the past. Past receipts have been conveniently estimated for the period 1977–87 by the Commission of the European Communities (CEC 1990a, 57) and are presented in table 4. As the discussion above suggests, Renault and FIAT enjoyed the most subsidies. Conspicuous is the sensational amount of money given to Alfa-Romeo by the Italian government (amounting to roughly ECU 1,600 per car produced over the 10-year period). If this sum is included in FIAT's total, then it was easily the most heavily subsidized firm. At the other end of the spectrum were the U.S. multinationals and VW (although it is interesting to note the degree to which all enjoyed assistance of one kind or another). Taken as a whole, table 4 gives a good picture of what firms might expect for the future, based on their experiences in the past, unless increased restraints on subsidies had a significant effect.

TABLE 4.   Total Estimated State Aids, 1977–87

Producer	Aid Levels (millions of ECU)	Rank
FIAT	3,212	3
Alfa-Romeo	3,487.2	2
PSA	1,138	5
Renault	4,494	1
VW	1,563	4
Ford	654.8	7
GM	1,102.5	6

Source: CEC 1990a, 57.

Government Preferences and Factor Prices

The convergence of factor prices could have shaped the preferences of the member states in a similar manner. Preferences over openness, internal or external, are partly determined by the degree to which any individual country enjoys some price advantage. The case of the United Kingdom is interesting in this respect. Labor market reforms and the political defeat of the unions were part of a strategy to reduce labor's total share of national income. To the extent that the success of this strategy lowered the cost of labor in the United Kingdom, it would have the effect of diverting FDI to the United Kingdom at the expense of its partners in the EU, an inherently divisive strategy from the point of view of other European governments.[18] On the other hand, to the extent that factor prices generally converged within the EU, so the advantages to governments of integration were likely to be equally shared, thus fostering cooperation.

In summary, it is reasonable to say that the price differentials across the member states for capital and labor had narrowed by the late 1980s. I argue that this narrowing favored greater cooperation between the mass-market auto producers (all other things being equal) and the member states. In the specific issue area of state aid the differential political access of firms could have led to divisions. The mixed motives of the member states in this issue area were examined in chapter 2. The discussions that follow here will address other general elements that permitted or hindered cooperation and will also identify specific elements operating within particular issue areas that led to variation in cooperation over different policy outcomes.

Performance and Specialization

Notwithstanding the fact that factor costs may have converged, decisive differences in performance could have persisted among producers and national industries as a whole. These would also have shaped the strategic environment. I begin with an analysis of the relative performance of the major producing countries, which will yield their preferences over integration in general and over external trade.

Intra-European trade in manufacturing as a proportion of GNP—that is, trade between the member states of the EU as opposed to trade between member states and the rest of the world—has steadily increased throughout the postwar period (see Frieden 1994, table 2). In like manner, from a state of the world in which the national markets were almost completely shut off from one another, intra-European trade in autos has also increased dramatically. The tariffs on cars traded between the member states of the EU (in conjunction with tariffs on a wide range of other manufactured goods) were finally eliminated on 1 July 1968. This mutual exposure was bound to have an impact on import penetration and industry concentration (a move to fewer and larger firms), the former leading to the latter.

The different consequences of integration on the balance of trade for each of the producing countries were depicted above in figure 7.[19] While France and Germany were able to make progress in the 1970s in improving their balance of trade, both Italy and Britain immediately began to experience chronic deficits in this category. By the mid-1980s this development had become even more pronounced—Britain's deficit exceeded $6.5 billion, while Germany's surplus approached $13 billion. France struggled to maintain a rough balance in its trade, while Spain and Belgium enjoyed a slight surplus. (As a share of its overall trade balance, of course, this surplus was important for Belgium.)

It has been observed that intra-industry trade is characteristic of exchange between the advanced market economies in the postwar world, a pattern supposed to be especially pronounced in the case of trade within the EU (see Grubel and Lloyd 1975; and Krugman 1989). However, only the French experience, of a balanced increase in exports and imports in this industry, is really consistent with this claim. In fact, as depicted in figure 8, the degree of intra-industry trade in this category for four of the six producing countries declined in the 15-year period following the elimination of the last tariff barrier to intra-European trade.[20] This decline suggests that greater openness within the EU had the effect of fostering specialization in the member states of the Community, even though most of the producing nations shared roughly similar factor endowments. In effect, intra-industry trade increased at first, following the removal of tariffs, before giving way to inter-industry specialization. Such specialization indicates that auto production was being displaced from some countries (Britain and Italy) and concentrated in others (Spain and Germany).

The preferences of the member states for further economic integration, therefore, would be shaped by the degree to which they imagined it would foster even greater specialization and increased concentration of production in a few countries, with inevitable consequences for the balance of trade in this sector for those other member states that did not enjoy this increased specialization. (These comparative data simply confirm the conclusions drawn from the discussion above of each national industry.)

There is an interesting aspect to this: it is likely that the fate of firms, as the regional market became integrated, became increasingly detached from the fate of the industry in any particular member state. This is sharply revealed by a comparison of figures 7 and 11 (see below). While the elimination of tariffs led

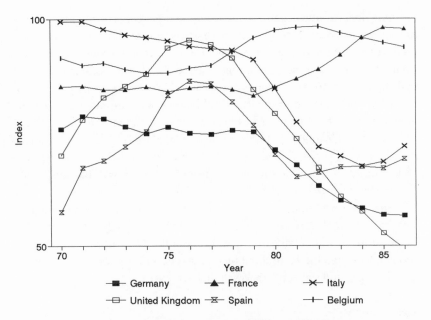

Fig. 8. Intra-industry trade (COMTAP; OECD 1987)

to a division of the producing states into winners and losers, the major auto producers, with the exception of the hapless British Leyland/Rover, continued to
share the market roughly equally (the character of the producers' oligopoly is
discussed below).

The problem of imputing preferences over integration to the member
states based on past economic performance (as noted in chapter 2) is that it
is difficult to take into consideration the range of responses open to governments. For example, what of the choices before the British government, given
the poor performance of the auto industry in the past? It might be willing to
allow the industry to disappear, and so release factors for use in more competitive sectors, but this was never considered. They might seek to restore
competitiveness with a variety of government policies. They might, however,
be politically constrained from making an exit but unable to make alternative,
necessary adjustments (this may be more illustrative of the Italian case). Atti-
tudes over openness would vary accordingly. However, I will begin by taking
past performance as a starting point. The degree to which past performance
is not a good measure of the preferences of any particular member state will
serve as a useful guide to other, possibly contingent political forces shaping
outcomes.

One final comment must be made on the preferences of the EU member states toward Japanese imports. Because of significant differences in relative productivity between EU and Japanese producers, radical economic openness would result in a significant worsening of the already unfavorable balance of trade between them (this difference is discussed in detail below). By the end of the 1980s, notwithstanding the VERs (voluntary export restraints) imposed by some countries, the EU had a $6 billion trade deficit in automotive products with Japan (CCFA 1991, 4). It is therefore reasonable to suppose that the member states, while perhaps divided over the degree of internal openness because of their different experiences following the eradication of trade barriers, would be united in their reservations over external openness.

Another way of obtaining information about preferences over integration is to estimate the differences between firm performance and national markets. These estimates will provide information about the different competitive situation of firms, and therefore about their preferences over integration. They will also yield firm and state preferences in each issue area.

Segmentation

While specialization is the concentration of production in certain areas, market segmentation is used to describe the concentration of sales by particular producers within one national market. Market segmentation also describes the way in which different markets are characterized by different product mixes. By analyzing segmentation I obtain a measure of the relative exposure of firms to adjustment costs, and I discover some of the particular elements influencing firm and state preferences in specific issue areas.

The persistent segmentation of European markets, notwithstanding 15 years of intra-European free trade, may have been the result of product differentiation, economies of scale, and consumer preferences. However, these elements are not the whole story. Segmentation was also a product of different national regulation of the sector: for example, taxation, state aid, and environmental and safety regulation, to name just the most important. An analysis of this segmentation will help to establish firm and state preferences in two important issue areas: external trade and environmental regulation.

The effective segmentation of the European market is clearly indicated by figure 9. Were the markets of the major countries of Europe fully integrated, in the way the U.S. market is integrated, the European market shares of each of the major mass producers ought to be roughly similar to their shares of each national market, although due to transportation costs, firm strategies, and varia-

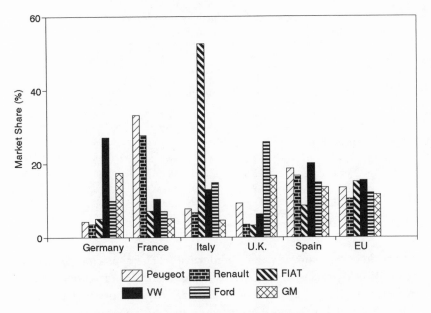

Fig. 9. Firm share national markets (CCFA 1990)

tions in consumer preferences national market shares would never be exactly the same. Yet the experience of each firm in each national market was very different from its experience in the EU market as a whole, even though the six major producers were roughly comparable in size.[21]

Figure 9 reveals the greatest regional imbalance (that is, national concentration) in sales for FIAT. At the other extreme the U.S. multinationals had the most evenly distributed sales. It is not surprising that the least "national" producers have the least segmented pattern of sales. The French producers have an imbalance close to that of FIAT, and the structure of VW's sales is closer to that of the U.S. multinationals. These patterns yield a very clear picture of the potential adjustment costs faced by each firm, as argued in chapter 2.

This exposure to adjustment difficulties can be measured in other ways. For example, de Banville and Chanaron (1991, 35–38) estimate the relative productivity of each firm as a function of the number of vehicles produced each year by each employee. Table 5 reports both their findings and calculations designed to address one of the serious drawbacks to this kind of estimate.[22] Less productive firms, under radical integration, will be forced to restructure and may even be put out of business. In column c, table 5, it is clear that the U.S. multinationals and VW enjoyed a slight advantage in productivity, while the

TABLE 5.   Labor Force Productivity (vehicles per man-year)

	(a)	(b)	(c)
Producer	Index of Productivity	Index of Integration	$a_i(b_i/\bar{b})$
FIAT	14.1	51.1	25.0
PSA	17	25.7	15.1
Renault	21.6	19.2	14.4
VW	9.8	49.3	16.7
Ford	15.5	38	20.4
GM	9.8	50	16.5
Toyota	57.6	19.6	39.2

Source: Banville and Chanaron 1991, 30, 37.

French producers rank lowest in productivity. (The apparently anomalous figure for FIAT reflects, in part, the distinctive character of its product line of smaller, low-value autos; fewer man-years are required per unit produced, although the total value added per man-year may be no greater.)

The differences in productivity among the EU mass-market producers tell us a certain amount about their preferences for internal economic integration. The U.S. multinationals seem to have the most to gain. On the other hand, the dramatic difference between Toyota and all of the EU producers reveals the danger to the Europeans of radical external openness. This disparity is confirmed by Womack, Jones, and Roos (1990, 85).

The foregoing discussion has measured market segmentation by differentiating among firms on the basis of their relative competitiveness, using the geographic concentration of their sales as a guide. It has also suggested other ways to measure differences in interfirm competitiveness. In order to establish the preferences of the auto firms and the member states in other issue areas, it is helpful to distinguish between them on the basis of the product range in which each specialized. In figure 10 the output of four producing nations is compared, revealing the differences in the characteristics of the fleets sold in each market, as measured by engine size. Firm output was not generally coterminous with patterns of national production. However, this was much more nearly true for those firms dependent on their national markets (FIAT, Peugeot, and Renault) than for those that were more perfectly regionally integrated (Ford and GM).

The patterns observed for each country reveal significant specialization, with Italy concentrating in cars with smaller engines, Britain in cars with mid-

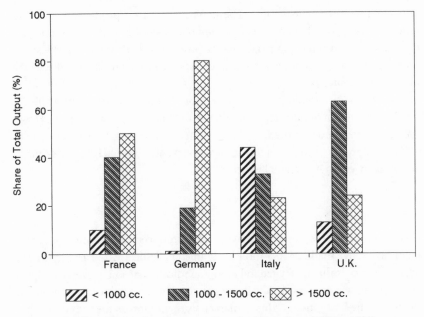

Fig. 10. National output by engine size (Data from MVMA 1991)

sized engines, and Germany in large, powerful cars. The significant concentration of large-car production in Germany reflects the role of the German specialist producers who, unlike VW, based all of their production in Germany until the early 1990s. These different patterns reflected not only national preferences, but also regulatory/tax differences: Italy taxed large-displacement engines at higher rates; in Britain tax laws favored the "company car" for many years, which inflated the market share of mid-sized cars; and in Germany the lack of a speed limit on the autobahn fostered the production of fast, sturdy autos.

These differences in fleet characteristics would be reflected in different preferences, across firms and states, with regard to any EU regulation that had a differential impact on autos of different sizes. Environmental regulation, of course, was exactly of that kind; the costs of such regulation were greatest for small vehicles, when expressed as a share of the total value of the vehicle. Those firms that specialized in small cars, and the states in which their production facilities were concentrated, were likely to have very different preferences over the appropriate level of regulation by comparison with firms specializing in larger autos, or with the states in which little or no small-car production occurred. In other words, Italy, France, and to a lesser extent the United Kingdom might be opposed to the preferences of Germany and the small, nonproducing member states in environmental matters. The mass-market auto producers would be much less likely to welcome such regulation than specialist, niche producers. (In the event, even among the mass-market producers divisions arose, divisions provoked by variation in technological capacity across firms. This is discussed in the next chapter.)

In summary, differences in firm exposure to adjustment difficulties following the completion of the internal market would limit cooperative efforts. However, firms were much more likely to be united over external trade issues. Differences in product mixes and technological capacity were likely to divide firms and states over environmental issues.

Prices

Given that the preferences of the mass-market producers and the member states identified above made cooperation likely in some issue areas, if not in others, what evidence is there, of a general kind, to indicate that some level of cooperation (possibly tacit) was already being practiced by the producers on the eve of the SEA? The best guide to this is market segmentation as measured by price differentials for the same product; where prices varied significantly across national markets, and the variations cannot be attributed simply to barriers to trade or regulatory differences, the cause must lie in firm strategies (of course one factor influencing prices in the U.K. market is that the British insisted on driving on the left). In a purely competitive industry such variations would be largely traded away. However, where significant market power existed such variations might persist if the different geographic concentration of sales (as observed above) were the consequence of a tacit agreement between firms in which each home market was sheltered from intense price competition.

Notwithstanding the differences in product ranges that persisted, many other aspects of automakers' products had become more standardized. Furthermore, the number of products offered had increased, limiting the degree of monopolistic competition, or niche specialization (see Helpman and Krugman 1985). Also, the quality revolution in manufacturing techniques had been increasingly diffused throughout the global auto industry, albeit with different levels of success, making differences in reliability and finish between autos less pronounced. Compared with the late 1970s, therefore, many important characteristics of the principal products of the major producers in Europe had converged, and the number of uncontested niches had diminished.

If it is true that the products of the mass-market producers had converged in terms of quality and design and that they faced an increasingly similar cost structure, then price competition should have become more intense. On the other hand, such developments also increased the incentives to practice tacit collusion, for reasons suggested above.[23] In fact it appears that not only were national markets segmented in terms of the kind of autos sold, but also in terms of the prices charged for the same autos across different countries. In other words, price competition had not become more intense, and tacit collusion was already being practiced on the eve of the SEA.

In 1992 a study by Directorate General (DG) IV (one of the divisions of the Commission) suggested that price dispersion ranged as high as 45 percent for any one particular model across the various European markets. More information on this matter is difficult to obtain. Producers have a strong disincentive to generate and reveal data on prices that are costly and time-consuming to assemble, and which will only be used to make difficulties for them. The result is that with the exception of the Brittan report, as it was called, and a report by the Monopolies and Mergers Commission in the United Kingdom earlier in 1992 that focused on U.K. prices, no one really knows the true pricing strategies of the producers.

While it is therefore difficult to fully substantiate the claim that the auto producers acted as a "rent-seeking" oligopoly, the fact that over 70 percent of the entire market for autos (including specialist products), with 320 million consumers, was controlled by six producers is at least a prima facie reason for thinking that oligopolistic pricing practices of some kind may have occurred. The mass-market producers all enjoyed market shares of roughly between 10 and 15 percent throughout the late 1970s and the 1980s, as shown in figure 11. The pattern for this period was that each firm in turn enjoyed relative success, usually on the basis of a particularly successful model, only to be subsequently eclipsed by some other competitor. No firms were eliminated, and none achieved commanding leads. This kind of balance is suggestive of a "comfortable" competitive environment. The long product cycle and huge sunk costs of the auto sector created even more of an incentive for the major producers to live and let live.[24]

Summary

The various elements examined above have various effects on interstate and interfirm cooperation. The growth of the market in the late 1980s may have limited firm interest in cooperation. Over the 1980s as a whole, factor prices converged, roughly speaking—one element that may have fostered cooperation among firms, and also among some states. Some states were losers after tariffs were eliminated, some winners, a result that implies potential divisions over

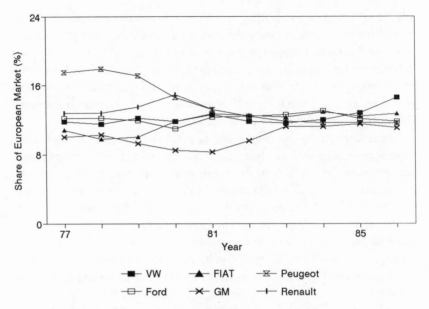

Fig. 11.   Firm market shares (CEC 1990a, 54)

more internal economic integration, although preferences over external openness were much more similar. Firms, too, faced different adjustment costs but
enjoyed roughly comparable market conditions (of course divisions over state
aids may have persisted). Furthermore, they had less divergent experiences following the elimination of tariffs, by comparison with the member states, which
also suggests a cooperative environment. Above all, their performance as a
whole was weak by comparison with third-country producers—that is, the
Japanese—and so their preferences were likely to be very similar on the issue of
external trade. Interfirm differences over policy were likely to be greatest over
environmental regulation. Finally, in pricing and sales, some evidence exists that
the EU market for autos was already subject to oligopolistic and possibly collusive behavior on the eve of the SEA. Taking all the factors enumerated above
together, I argue that the sector enjoyed increasing, but not comprehensive,
opportunities for interfirm cooperation. The situation for the member states
was more mixed.

Private, National, and European Union Institutions

The patterns of private, national, and EU institutions described below suggest
the ways in which the preferences imputed to states and firms above were ag-

gregated in the period leading up to the SEA. While the spread of preferences is one factor determining the ability of actors to cooperate, the institutional environment also played a crucial role. What follows shows the consequences for interest cohesion of mediating institutions on the eve of the SEA. Of course, the changes in EU institutions made by the SEA, and the changes in other interest-institution relationships as a result of the pressures created by the internal market project, mean that this picture was sure to evolve over time. What follows is a map of the starting point.

National Governments and Their Firms

It is no surprise that while the auto sector as a whole—that is, the assemblers, component producers, etc.—very often shared the same interests when it came to government policy, such shared interests need not always be the case. By way of illustration, the Retail Motor Industry Federation (RMIF) in Britain lobbied energetically and successfully during the 1992 budget negotiations in Whitehall for further reductions in the tax relief available for company cars.[25] This reduction would have the effect of returning car sales to the retailers, rather than maintaining the direct relationship that existed between producers and fleet buyers. Obviously the producers would oppose this change, but the retailers were able to make their opposition felt because they had their own interest group association. In other words, how the industry had its interests articulated had consequences for policy outcomes.

The industry associations in each of the producing nations differed in significant ways. One of the most important was the way in which mass-market producers did, or did not, have to share the stage with other elements of the industry. This factor influenced the degree to which these producers were able to make their influence felt on their respective national governments. Of course the U.S. multinationals did not have a home base in this sense, which would strongly determine their attitude toward interest group arrangements at the level of the EU, arrangements that could include other, like-minded automakers.

In France the Comité des Constructeurs Français d'Automobile (CCFA) has only two members, Peugeot and Renault. The components sector is represented by FIEV (Fédération des Industries d'Équipements pour Véhicules). In Italy ANFIA (Associazione Nazionale Fra l'Industrie Automobilistiche) represents both the principal manufacturer FIAT and the component makers. There exist numerous important overlapping organizations for the network of small and medium firms that go to make up the "metal-bashing" sector in Italy, but for technical questions and issues involving international relationships in the auto sector ANFIA has primacy. In Britain both the producers and component makers, importers and distributors, are represented by one organization, the SMMT (Society of Motor Manufacturers and Traders). Retailers also have their own organization, RMIF, as noted above. In Germany the industry association, the VDA (Verband Der Automobilindustrie), also embraces all areas of the industry.

In general the SMMT and the VDA shared a common characteristic. Both represented numerous interests, and this meant that the major producers had to share the stage with, and have their preferences moderated by, other actors. Consider the British case. The decline of the sector during the 1970s, and the acute effect this decline had on the British balance of trade, was noted above. The response by the British government was to solicit inward investment by Japanese auto producers; Nissan and Toyota both built assembly plants and engine plants in Britain. Whatever the long-term gains from this strategy, it immediately called into question the very existence of Rover as an independent entity (Honda, as part of its strategy for gaining a foothold in Europe, bought 20 percent of Rover) as well as posing a severe threat to the traditional market leader, Ford.[26] Nissan and Toyota are, of course, members of the SMMT. Ford may feel "betrayed" by the British government, but its own industry association, perhaps prodded by component producers and toolmakers who saw their opportunities increased by the arrival of the Japanese, welcomed this development.[27]

In truth, neither Ford nor GM felt as though they had a national government prepared to take their part in the way, for example, the French government took the part of the French producers. In Britain this may have been the result of the way interests were organized. Yet it is also true that ownership "mattered" in some way, and that "national" producers received special treatment. Ford briefly considered buying Rover, and part of the reason might have been a desire to thereby acquire a "parent" in the form of the British government (Wilks 1989, 175). Yet while the U.S. multinationals were never "British" or "German" in the way Rover or Daimler-Benz were, they were certainly good citizens of Europe. Intrafirm trade between Europe and North America was very modest and, if anything, ran in Europe's favor. Nearly all products were fully engineered in Europe for the European market. It is no surprise, therefore, that eventually Ford and GM would be strong supporters of an effective transnational, Europewide industry association.

In Germany the VDA reflected in particular the preferences of specialist producers, truck makers, and component makers such as Robert Bosch GmbH. These were some of the most internationally competitive and successful manufacturing firms in Europe. While Reich places VW in the core of the German political economy, it is perhaps more accurate to say that both VW and the two U.S. multinationals were slightly outside this charmed circle. Streeck even notes the geographical division between the specialists in the south of the country and the mass producers in the north (1989, 119). Also worth noting is that the National Socialists began the project of a people's car by trying to persuade the Reichsverband der Deutschen Automobilindustrie (the forerunner of the VDA) to undertake the project. Not surprisingly, they obstructed the enterprise, and the government undertook the project itself (Reich 1990, 152–53). The story of its origins illustrates the way in which VW was set apart from the rest of the German auto industry from the start.

Since the war, VW has had a unique legal status, with 10 seats on the board reserved for representatives of IG Metall (the autoworkers' union) and 20 percent of its stock held by the state of Lower Saxony. Its special legal status and its close relationship to organized labor have encouraged VW to rely on its own direct contacts with the German government and the authorities in Brussels, in order to avoid the fragmented interests within the VDA (interview with Dr. von Mobelen, Volkswagen AG, 17 June 1992). By contrast, the VDA had a less clearly positive relationship with its European counterparts, partly as a result of divisions over environmental issues but also because the interests of the VDA's highly competitive, specialist membership were better served by the liberal line pursued by the German government (rather than by a European Commission suspected of ambitions for a Europe-wide "industrial policy"). Therefore it is unsurprising that VW was to part company (to a degree) with the VDA and become another early supporter of transnational organization.

In France the situation was much less complicated. While the CCFA represented only producers, both Peugeot and Renault also dealt directly with the French government, which had in the past faithfully tended to their interests. On the other hand, the French government's preferences underwent a transformation after 1981. Until the early 1980s, in conjunction with the staff at the CCFA and the producers themselves, the French government technically was responsible for setting the prices of automobiles. By the late 1980s the relationship between the French state and the auto industry had changed completely. This is best illustrated by the changes in the legal status of Renault. After protracted bargaining with the Commission, to be discussed below, it gave up control of Renault. The legal status of Renault was altered, and its status as a "régie nationale" was ended. This then permitted Renault to form a strategic alliance with Volvo (which effort eventually failed, to be followed much later by an alliance with Nissan).

The realization had finally taken hold within the ranks of French government officials that completion of the internal market and openness to world markets were the only viable strategies for maintaining the competitiveness of French industry (Commissariat Général du Plan 1992, 8). While it cannot be doubted that the well-being of the auto sector remained a high priority for the French government, it also had to be weighed against France's deep commitment to the European (and by implication German) connection. Thus the French producers, while in constant dialogue with their government, may also have had an interest in organizing their efforts at the level of the EU in order to seek direct representation in Brussels.

In Italy, as noted, FIAT had powerful connections with the Italian government. Yet that government also had an overriding interest in integration as a whole. In particular the prospect of monetary union governed Italy's preferences in the 1980s, because the connection was seen to be the long-term solution to the problem of inflation. The international commitment to fiscal discipline, required by EMU, was used by the Italian state to pry loose some of those domestic interests whose claims sustained its budget difficulties (see Frieden 1994).

In general, therefore, the domestic strategic environment faced by mass-market auto producers varied across countries, but it had changed for all of them in ways that would encourage the formation of a transnational interest group. Although their national governments played a crucial role in bargaining over EU policy in the Council of Ministers and could be expected to tend to the needs of powerful constituents, this attention would inevitably be moderated by the overarching imperative of the "European project." But the response of each firm would be shaped by the specific character of domestic interest group aggregation. Because there were a variety of institutional and structural forces at work on the firms in question, they were inevitably inclined to pursue a variety of political strategies toward EU policy-making. Many of them were sure to pursue the creation of an effective transnational interest group association, but individual strategies, directed at national governments or at the Commission and other EU institutions, would also be chosen.

The formal reorganization of a transnational interest group, the Association des Constructeurs Européens d'Automobile (ACEA), at the level of the EU in 1991 was the culmination of a long process. The proximate causes will be examined in much greater detail in the case studies. The purpose here is to provide the relevant background, inasmuch as it shaped subsequent institutional innovation. It was not the first transnational auto producers' association. In fact, there had been two: the Comité de Liaison des Constructeurs d'Automobile

(CLCA) and the Comité de Constructeurs d'automobile du Marché Commun (CCMC). The former was a liaison committee that represented the views of the industry associations of each member state. The latter represented European producers directly but did not include the U.S. multinationals. Of the two, it was the CCMC that played the leading role in representing the interests of the assemblers. However, some members (in particular the mass producers) felt that the division between the two groups when representing the interests of the sector diffused its views. Notable was the exclusion of the U.S. multinationals from membership in the CCMC. It is fair to say that on the eve of the SEA the mass-market European producers had their interests at the level of the EU represented in ways that limited their opportunity to cooperate effectively.

Grant, Paterson, and Martinelli (1988, 72–73) note how most studies of business political activity focus on business interest associations. By contrast, I wish, as they do, to retain the firm as the focus of my attention. This is inevitable given the kinds of firms I examine. The automakers were vast enterprises. As noted above, over 70 percent of the market was concentrated in the hands of the six mass-market producers. It is natural, therefore, that while each firm was involved in domestic interest group associations, and also had an incentive to operate as a member of a transnational interest group, it will also be apparent, in the case studies to come, that large firms retained direct links with their own national governments and sought direct links with the institutions of the EU, whenever the strategic environment allowed and such links appeared to be useful. One objective of this research project is a systematic explanation for when and why a firm varied its strategy between cooperation with others and direct action on its own.

In summary, there were forces that served to detach firms from their former relationships with their "home" governments. Yet their representation at the level of the EU was deficient in certain institutional respects. The case studies to come explain the broken path by which the institutions adopted by the industry for its self-government were adapted in response to cooperative efforts in pursuit of collective political goals.

Early European Union Regulation

EU regulation before the 1980s had few important consequences for the industry, except, of course, the elimination of internal tariff barriers. The SEA was, by any measure, a departure from previous practices, and it meant more to the auto industry than to many other sectors. What follows is designed to set the stage for EU policy-making in the late 1980s, if only to indicate how little had been done before that. Interest group activity generally, and the auto sector was no exception, only increased following the passage of the SEA (Camerra-Rowe 1993).

Technically, the EU had been involved in policy-making toward this sector for a long time, but the sensitivity of the member states toward any Community developments that might threaten their "national champions" severely limited progress in the elimination of barriers to free trade. The best example of this is the question of type approvals (product standards for automobiles). A Commission "framework" directive in 1970 laid the basis for the harmonization of type approval across the member states (Directive 70/156/EEC). This meant that a car approved for sale in one market would be automatically approved in all the markets of the member states. Forty-eight specific type approvals were agreed upon but not implemented, because three remained blocked by France. The reason was that without the power to withhold type approval no legal control over imports—that is, Japanese cars—was possible. Article 85 of the Rome treaty explicitly allows for free circulation of goods in all member states after they have paid the duty to enter any one of the markets of the member states.

The institutions of the EU had also begun to examine the trading relationship between Europe and Japan some time before the passage of the SEA. Beginning in the early 1980s the European Parliament issued several reports on the auto sector, and it often focused on trade with Japan (Committee on Economic and Monetary Affairs and Industrial Policy 1-137/80; 1-1505/83; 2-171/86; Committee on External Economic Relations 1-997/82). In the first of these reports the motion for a resolution noted "the disturbing loss of markets . . . as a result of the trade offensive by aggressive non-Community industries." The Commission's role started as a result of the efforts of Commissioner Davignon to "monitor" several categories of manufactured goods. It was this effort that led the Japanese Ministry for International Trade and Industry (MITI) to set public targets for the European market share of Japanese producers. However, while these targets signaled some level of self-restraint, the main barriers to Japanese imports were the national restrictions described above.

In conclusion, although the EU had succeeded in eliminating intra-Community tariff barriers, the further integration of the sector had been halted—publicly by France, although it is likely that this opposition was tacitly approved by more than one of the other member states. It was only after signing the SEA that they faced up to the challenge of fully integrating this sector, including the related and crucial question of external openness (to Japanese producers). These connections are part of the paradox in the role played by the SEA. Some of the policy-making episodes in the auto sector I am going to examine did not fall under the heading of the internal market. The crucial factor is the interdependence of issues, which resulted in an institutional change in one area carrying forward integration across the full range of issues to be addressed. Type approvals were an internal market issue. They could now be pushed through with a qualified majority. However, questions of external trade were also thrust onto the agenda as a result.

Conclusions

In this chapter little mention has been made of a wide variety of other potentially significant actors, such as organized labor, local and regional governments, consumers, and the component parts industry, to name just a few. In the case studies to follow, such actors will play a part on occasion; however, it is the purpose of this project to focus on the role of the major firms in the sector and on the governments of the member states of the Community. I do so for two reasons, one empirical and one methodological. First, the history of the individual member states during the postwar period suggests that, notwithstanding the claims of other groups and interests, these firms have held, and continue to hold, a privileged place in European political economies. What is more, this special place at the political table was likely to be reproduced at the level of the institutions of the EU. Second, to make any analysis tractable and generalizable it is preferable to reduce the number of actors and limit its purview. The empirical claim tends to make acceptable this methodological choice.

In summary, the promise of the 1992 project made uncertain long-established patterns of interaction between firms and governments. The regionalization of the market and the movement of firms away from a purely national orientation promised a highly fluid, and novel, pattern of political bargaining over the policies of the EU. How firms and states approached these bargains was shaped by the strategic environment they faced—that is to say, the manner in which the economic structures and the institutional arenas discussed above encouraged or inhibited cooperation. As these forces and institutions were subject to change, so the level of cohesion between firms and states would also change, in a manner largely congruent with the preferences evaluated in this chapter.

CHAPTER 4

The Politics of Automobile
Emissions Control

Introduction

The first set of common European standards in the issue area of automobile emissions, finally enacted in December 1987 (Directive 88/76/EEC), was strongly contested. The outcome was seen by many to have favored the interests of the auto producers: standards were harmonized, but at a low level. This was very soon followed by a second round of regulation on small automobiles, which was much more favorable to those wanting high environmental standards and imposed considerable costs on producer interests. What explains this change in outcome over such a short period of time?

This episode has been the subject of much analysis, which has tended to focus on particular institutions or actors in the policy-making process, for example the European Parliament (Tsebelis 1994a) or small member states (Kim 1992). The strength of the analytical approach adopted here is that it shows the way interests and institutions interacted. The analysis gives the analytical scheme presented in chapter 2 comprehensive empirical support; the cohesion, or lack of it, among states and firms over linked issues was crucial. This episode also shows how some of the institutional changes of the SEA may have unintended consequences, which the member states did not foresee.

The explanation is a simple one: two sets of preferences were bound together in the issue area of environmental regulation, preferences over the level of emissions control and over the degree of market harmonization (centralized, uniform regulation). Firm and government preferences over emissions control were divided, while preferences over harmonization converged. This condition led to a shift in policy outcomes over time, following institutional change.

The institutional environment of the early 1980s permitted a coalition of member states, acting in concert with the interests of several producers, to introduce emissions control regulation at a low level, which increased the level of harmonization by fostering a Europe-wide standard. However, following the SEA, harmonization was disrupted by the unilateral policies of a subset of the member states, for which there was no longer any legal sanction easily available. Harmonization could only be restored by introducing emissions control regulation at a high level. This new institutional environment, in combination with the structure of interest, gave agenda-setting power to the European Parliament (EP). This shift in power, in turn, changed the outcome.

Of course, it will be apparent that other conjunctural forces were at work. For example, a crucial turn in policy proposed by the Commission came on the eve of European Parliament elections, in which the environment was a salient issue. However, ad hoc explanations for decisive elements of the story are avoided. The outcome depended on the spread of firm and government preferences, on their ability to cooperate given those preferences, and on the way in which that cooperation was mediated by institutions.

The chapter begins with an analysis of firm and government preferences for harmonization and for high environmental standards. Next I present a short history of EU regulation in this area up until the early 1980s, including a discussion of the legal basis for EU regulation, and its consequences for the policies adopted by individual member states. The first agreement, in 1985, is then examined and the role of firms, governments, and the institutional environment identified. Then follows an account of the institutional and legal changes brought about by the SEA, and their consequences. Finally, I explain the subsequent bargain and show the way firm and member state preferences, in combination with a new institutional environment, resulted in a significant change in outcomes.

The Preferences of Governments and Firms

The tension that existed between harmonization and high environmental standards is at the heart of the explanation that follows. The structure of firm and member state interests was different for each of these issue areas. In environmental issues there was a wide variation in preferences across firms and across governments (and high preference intensity). In issues relating to harmonization, preferences more nearly converged.

Firms and Technology

The preferences of firms and governments over emissions control were discussed in chapter 3, and a review of that discussion follows shortly. However, while the character of the product range in which firms specialized was a cru-cial determinant of interest, it was also shaped by differences in technological capabilities. Emissions control systems are an expensive addition to an auto-mobile, and the smaller the automobile, the greater the added cost of the sys-tem, when expressed as a percentage of the whole cost of the car. There were two technologies considered to be solutions to the emissions problem, which dif-fered in important respects. Catalytic converters (CATs) represented a technol-ogy already in use in North America. They could be used to reach even strin-gent requirements, but they were expensive. In addition, they required unleaded gasoline and electronic engine controls and made cars less fuel efficient. A dif-ferent solution, "lean-burn" technology, was still in the developmental stage and was unlikely to be able to meet very strict requirements. However, it would be cheaper and would increase fuel efficiency. It was seen as especially valuable for smaller cars.

The technical arguments for and against these different approaches are complicated; suffice it to say that the choice would be made for political reasons. The important point is that those two firms that were especially committed to lean-burn technology, Ford and Peugeot, preferred moderate standards and a long lead time for their introduction. A generous lead time would give what was an embryonic technology time to be fully realized. Of course Ford, which used CATs in its North American operations, was less dependent on this technical outcome than Peugeot.

Preferences over the Level of Regulation

The discussion of firm and state preferences that follows will take as its starting point an examination of national output by segment (chapter 3, figure 10). Al-though, as noted, firm output was not coterminous with patterns of national production, the data readily suggest the positions of various producers and their respective national governments. These are depicted in figures 12 and 13, pref-erences over regulation being set against preferences for harmonization, to be discussed shortly.

Those firms most dependent on their national markets—FIAT, Peugeot, and Renault—also specialized in smaller cars. It was no surprise, therefore, that France, Italy, and Spain (and the producers Peugeot and FIAT) were all opposed to high requirements. Italian production was made up of the highest percent-age of small autos, and roughly half of French production was concentrated on small and medium-sized vehicles. The production of smaller autos was con-centrated in Spain due to its low labor costs (see chapter 3). Medium and small vehicles were the most intensively traded category, in which all producers went

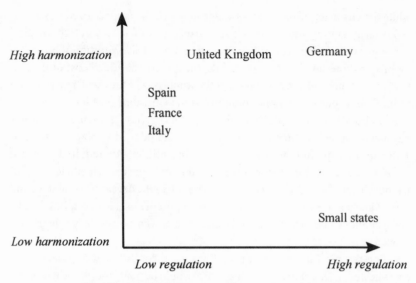

Fig. 12.   Governments: harmonization and regulation

head-to-head, and in which margins were smallest. It was here, therefore, that the producers were most sensitive to the impact of regulation. Without any countervailing pressures from ecological groups, the governments of France, Italy, and Spain, in keeping with long-established patterns of privileged treatment, were willing to represent faithfully the views of their producers. The only anomalous element was the French producer Renault, which, while opposed to high levels of regulation, was also looking toward an alliance with Volvo—which would tend to give it a stronger interest in harmonization and a weaker interest in low levels of regulation, given that its putative partner already met the highest levels.

The British government played an interesting role. While the fleet of cars produced by firms based in Britain had a profile similar to that of France's, if with a slightly greater emphasis on mid-sized autos, the most important producers were the U.S. multinationals, who had to meet the higher U.S. standards in their home markets. It might be assumed, therefore, that the technical hurdle of CATs meant less to them. Yet, as noted in chapter 3, their European subsidiaries were quite separate entities, with very different product ranges; it was much easier for the U.S. parent to meet U.S. standards in the United States than for its subsidiary to do so in the European market. Instead of CATs, Ford of Europe had worked hard on lean burn as a solution to emissions problems. What is more, Ford had an agreement with the British government: the lean-burn

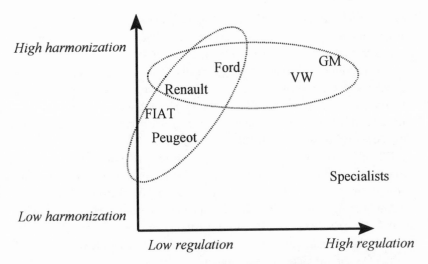

Fig. 13.   Firms: harmonization and regulation

engines would be engineered in the United Kingdom, and the British government would go to bat for the firm in Brussels (Wilks 1989, 181; EP [European Parliament] 1985, 17). Therefore both the British government and Ford were opposed to high standards for medium and small autos, unless the lead time was very permissive, because this would make lean burn an impractical technical solution.

As might be expected, the German specialist producers, because they made large cars and sold many in the United States, were comfortable with the prospect of CATs. The imposition of high standards on a Europe-wide basis would play directly to their competitive advantage. The main German mass producer, VW, was also, at first, content with the prospect of CATs. The German government, as part of its negotiating position, proposed to introduce fiscal incentives to encourage people to buy cars that exceeded the minimum emissions requirements. This use of incentives would have moderated price resistance among consumers. Furthermore, this tax relief was to be extended to diesel engines, to which VW had a large and successful commitment.

In the long run, on the other hand, diesels would be problematic from the point of view of the environment, for while they are economical they are also sooty, and only second- or third-generation lean-burn technology could be used for them if high emissions requirements were to be imposed. Also, VW's preferences for high emission standards must have been somewhat moderated after the acquisition of small-car producer SEAT (in Spain) in 1986.[1] Therefore the issue of the lead times set for placing CATs on all smaller cars would be very important for a company that was, at the same time, engaged in a massive amount of investment worldwide in the late 1980s and early 1990s.[2]

The relationship of the German government to its producers has been indicated in a general way in chapter 3. Sensitive to the demands of well-organized environmentalists, Germany had a strong interest in high environmental standards. It had led the Commission to make its earlier, very modest proposals for a directive on emissions control and lead in gasoline (Com 84, 266 final; Com 84, 532 final; and Com 84, 564 final). The VDA supported the German government. It reflected the interests of the specialist German auto producers, who were content to supply cars with expensive CATs, and Bosch, which had an overwhelming competitive advantage in Europe in the necessary electronic engine controls (Streeck 1989, 141–42). In this context, any reservations VW might have had about higher emissions controls would have been somewhat neglected by the VDA and the German government.

The smaller EU member states, of course, did not produce automobiles. This left them free to accede to the political pressures of the environmentalists, which in the Dutch and Danish cases were well developed. The acute air pollution in Athens also made the Greek government intransigent. The smaller states, therefore, were generally in favor of high requirements.

In summary (see figures 12 and 13), France, Italy, Spain, and the French and Italian producers were opposed to high levels of regulation. So too were the United Kingdom and Ford, in order to keep lean-burn technology viable. GM and VW were less seriously challenged by high standards, and specialist producers, particularly German companies such as BMW and Daimler-Benz, positively welcomed them. The German government and small member states were most in favor of higher standards.

Preferences over Regulatory Harmonization

The threat to harmonization, as many saw it, was that the introduction of environmental standards piecemeal, which created different standards in different national markets, would have two adverse consequences: such standards could act as barriers to trade because national standards might privilege national producers, and a proliferation of technical regulations would drive up the unit cost of autos by limiting the economies of scale available to firms. In this sense, while the distributional consequences of emissions control regulation made it an issue area toward the purely conflictual end of the spectrum of cooperation problems, harmonization that increased economies of scale for everyone was more nearly a variable-sum game.

It would be reasonable to expect that the mass-market producers had interests over harmonization that varied, depending on the degree to which their sales were segmented by market (see chapter 3, figure 9). In fact, four out of the six—the American producers, of course, VW, and Renault—preferred high harmonization. Increased harmonization would give them the opportunity to sell in all markets, while a range of different standards might put them, but not some other producer ready to meet those standards, at a competitive disadvantage. As will be seen, their respective governments reflected these preferences; in particular, the French government valued harmonization highly and sought both low standards and EU actions designed to centralize them. Only Peugeot and FIAT would accept lower harmonization, if that could mean lower standards in their national markets (interview with Tristan D'Albis, Peugeot, 26 June 1992).

The British government was also concerned about the autonomy of each country to introduce unilaterally, or encourage, its own standards. For example, given the German competitive advantage in CATs and diesels, the United Kingdom believed that any incentives promoting their sale had the potential to operate as a structural impediment, or de facto protection (interview with Thoss Shearer, Department of Trade and Industry, 27 May 1992). Ford and GM, as the most regionally integrated producers, also had an interest in harmonization. In other words, while high standards were objectionable, the appearance of different standards and fiscal incentives within the EU, and in the European Free Trade Association (EFTA), was also a very undesirable outcome.[3]

While Germany had a strong preference for high environmental standards, it was also inclined to put a high value on cohesion among the member states and on regulatory harmony at the level of the EU. As a major beneficiary of intra-EU trade, it was likely to place as much weight on internal openness as on high environmental standards. By contrast the small states, with no auto production, proved very willing to use unilateral measures to increase regulatory control regardless of the consequences for harmonization.

In summary, Germany and the United Kingdom were the pivotal member states, and the U.S. multinationals and VW the crucial firms, in the story that follows. Their overriding preference for harmonization was decisive; the fact that Germany set its interest in harmonization above its preference for a high level of regulation led to a low-level outcome in the first round of bargaining. The fact that the United Kingdom and some mass-market producers set their interest in harmonization above their preference for low-level regulation led to a high-level outcome in the second round. The difference was in the institutional arena.

The Legal and Institutional Environment

In the short account that follows, it will become apparent why EU policy-making in this area up until the middle of the 1980s privileged harmonization rather than high levels of regulation. All regulation of the automobile industry by the EU occurred within the context of a framework directive, agreed on in 1970 (Directive 70/156/EEC). This directive was supposed to lay the foundation for the harmonization of all standards in this sector. However, 3 of the 51 directives on type approvals remained unapproved by the Council of Ministers at the insistence of France.[4] This was a good example of the limits of intergovernmental bargaining over harmonization.

It may be wondered why product standards such as these could not, instead, be harmonized on the basis of the *Cassis de Dijon* ruling, which encouraged negative integration through mutual recognition (what follows relies in part on Rehbinder and Stewart 1985). In fact, centralized bargaining over standards had been the dominant mechanism for the integration of environmental laws in the EU. The reasons, partly practical and partly legal, have continued to shape EU policy in this area to the present and were reflected in some of the provisions of the SEA.

In the first place, there was no basis for EU policy-making in environmental matters under the terms of the Treaty of Rome. As a result, environmental regulation very often adopted as its legal basis the provisions of Article 100 of the treaty, which relate to the free movement of goods.[5] Sometimes, often at the same time, the provisions of Article 235 were also used, this article being something of a "catchall" article that could be used to justify almost anything, as long as a link could be made with the functioning of the common market (Vandermeersch 1987, 411). Hence the goal of EU regulation was not so much a high level of environmental protection, at least at the outset, as the reduction in barriers to the free movement of goods consequent upon divergent levels of national regulation in this area. Second, the question of barriers to trade was especially sensitive in the auto industry. Some member states were fearful of unilateral choices by others in environmental matters. As noted above, variation in national standards was believed to privilege some producers over others. Since "negative" integration would not result in harmonization, and "positive" integration through an EU directive could only have that as its goal, the pattern of policy-making up until the mid-1980s was of increasingly centralized regulation at a low level.

For example, there was considerable disagreement over regulating the amount of lead in gasoline in the 1970s—on the surface, at least, a relatively uncontroversial subject. The debate was dominated by Germany, which had instituted, unilaterally, its own reductions in lead (in two stages, to reach .15 grams per liter by 1976) (Vogel 1995). Britain had less severe standards; other countries, none. However, there was fear that the German position would serve to limit auto sales by non-German producers in its domestic market. The outcome resulted in the establishment of both a maximum permitted level of lead and a minimum. The adoption of a minimum was designed to prevent further unilateral choices, downward, by states in this area.

The EU's record in regulating auto emissions exhibited the same pattern. Beginning in 1970 it set maximum standards, which meant that any auto meeting those standards could circulate freely. The standards were revised in 1977, 1978, and 1983. But each member state could also permit the sale of autos that did not meet those standards in its domestic market. Of course, as intra-EU trade in autos grew, the effect was that of centralized harmonization; however, the EU's standards did serve as a ceiling, rather than a floor, preventing unilateral increases in standards on a national level (Rehbinder and Stewart 1985, 376–77; Vogel 1995). Indeed, as will be seen, the Commission would challenge in the European Court of Justice (ECJ) a member state who wished to impose, unilaterally, higher standards.

It may be said, therefore, that the status quo at the beginning of the 1980s was characterized by "optional harmonization" at a low level (that is, with a ceiling that set an upper limit on standards but that did not prevent lower standards from being applied domestically). The agreement on new standards in 1985 reflected this European pattern of centralized harmonization at a low level.

Agreement at Luxembourg

On 6 March 1983, in the German federal elections the Green party obtained 5.6 percent of the vote, passed the 5 percent threshold required by Germany's electoral system, and entered the Bundestag for the first time.[6] The new Free Democrat (FDP) and Christian Democrat (CDU/CSU) coalition government moved suddenly to improve its green credentials. At the beginning of 1984, without the customary consultation with industry typical of German regulation, the government demanded that cars meet U.S. emissions standards by 1985, a requirement that would have meant the immediate introduction of CATs.[7]

This radical departure resulted in a nasty and unusual public dispute between the VDA—the German auto industry association—and the ministers of the interior and the environment, a dispute that was costly for the VDA's public image and political credibility (interview with Achim Diekmann, VDA, 15 June 1992). What proved even more embarrassing was that the technical problems of operating CATs at the high average speeds common in Germany proved much easier to surmount than had been anticipated. At the moment when the German industry minister Martin Bangemann, the future commissioner of Directorate General (DG) III, was compromising Germany's proposed regulation in favor of Europe-wide regulation at Luxembourg, the German auto industry performed a political turn worthy of its best products and became supporters of US 83 standards, with specialist producers, as noted above, being in the forefront.

It was these developments in Germany that were to give impetus at the European level to serious emissions control regulation, which resulted in what has been called the "Luxembourg agreement" (not to be confused with the well-known "Luxembourg compromise"). In this agreement Germany proved to be the crucial player. It had encouraged the Commission to make its proposals, and it made enough concessions in order to obtain a compromise, one that clearly tended to the interests of the mass-market producers. On the other hand, it did obtain a concession for itself—an agreement on a program of introducing unleaded gas on a Europe-wide basis, necessary for cars with CATs. The outcome is presented in table 6.

Automobiles were divided into three categories based on engine size and different emissions levels, and target dates were set for each. New models, which could have the requisite controls introduced at the design stage, had shorter deadlines than new cars from existing models. As can be seen from the deadlines imposed on medium-sized autos, enough time was granted for the development of lean-burn engines to remain viable. Another crucial feature of the agreement is that for small cars there were to be two stages, with a second standard to be decided upon at a later date. This element of uncertainty was to frustrate the producer interests, who were now aiming at a moving target.

TABLE 6.   The Luxembourg Agreement: Directive 88/76/EEC

Category	Implementation Dates (new models/new cars)	Emissions Standards (grams/test)
>2 liter	1 October 1988/1989	CO 25; HO + NO_x 6.5 NO_x 3.5
1.4–2 liter	1 October 1991/1993	CO 30; HO + NO_x 8
<1.4 liter	1 October 1990/1991, Stage 1 Stage 2 to be decided later (before end of 1987)	CO 45; HO + NO_x 15 NO_x 6

Germany had retreated on its goal to introduce US 83 standards unilaterally and, furthermore, had agreed to limitations on its right to introduce fiscal incentives that encouraged the sale of autos meeting higher standards (Vogel 1995). Such incentives were perceived by many as a potential nontariff barrier to trade. But the outcome also fell short of the goal of true harmonization, for the standards were only voluntary. Countries were permitted to keep lower standards domestically, even if their producers had to adhere to higher standards when trading in other European markets. EU regulation continued to serve as a low ceiling rather than a universal requirement.

Environmentalists and the small, clean member states were very disappointed by the outcome. Denmark, in the event, refused to agree to the compromise and "reserved" its position. In other words, it blocked the measure for the next two years because such a directive needed unanimity in the Council of Ministers to become law. The agreement was passed only after the SEA was in place, at which point Denmark became the first country forced to submit to the preferences of a qualified majority. But, as will be discussed below, this proved to be a Pyrrhic victory, for the SEA also introduced rule changes that were to work to Denmark's advantage.[8]

Apart from the environmental interests, sentiment in favor of the compromise was widely spread, as is revealed by testimony before the European Parliament's Committee on Economic and Monetary Affairs and Industrial Policy (EP 1985, 2–19). The main anxiety expressed by Ford, GM, and the Comité de Constructeurs d'automobile du Marché Commun (CCMC), the transnational industry association, was that the agreement failed to reduce the fragmentation of standards in Europe. They also all felt that the standards were too demanding, naturally. However, Germany had agreed to keep the value of fiscal incentives well below the cost of CATs, and the Dutch and Danes did not, in fact, pursue their own incentive schemes until after the institutional environment had been altered by the SEA. It is fair to say that the compromise was a move, albeit an imperfect one, toward centralized harmonization at a low level, and that producers and member states had strong preferences over such harmonization.

Finally, it is worth noting that some elements in the EP were as sympathetic to the interests of the industry as the Commission was supposed to be. While the Committee on the Environment, Public Health, and Consumer Protection was in favor of increased emissions control, it also supported "lean-burn" technology, as did the British Consumers Union (EP 1985, 5; EP Doc. 2-1149/84/final, 16–17). The Committee on Economic and Monetary Affairs, which produced a general report sympathetic to the interests of the industry, also placed a high value on the degree of harmonization as much as on the level of regulation (EP Doc. 1-1505/83, 8–9).[9]

Overall, the major producing countries and the mass-market producers were able to act in concert to limit the regulations imposed on mid-sized and small vehicles. This ability reflected nicely their general interest in harmonization and emissions control discussed above. In particular, Germany's willingness to come to an agreement with its major partners indicates the relatively high value it placed on harmonization, which is in keeping with the importance of exports for its producers. The higher standards imposed on large vehicles—for which Germany may have had a strong preference, being sensitive to the claims of the VDA and its specialist constituents, who saw in them a technical advantage—were less controversial. In short, this round of European-level regulation was "produced by the bosses" (interview with Dr. Glatz, Daimler-Benz, 6 October 1992).

For environmental interests and the small member states, no institutional avenues were available to change the outcome. A small state had only the power to block such regulation with a national veto, which meant accepting the low regulatory levels of the status quo. The EP also reflected to a degree the concerns of the producers. It considered harmonization and long lead times important and could not be considered an arena favorable to those actors opposed to producer interests. But the institutional environment was to change in important ways before the next round of EU bargaining. This change had dramatic consequences for subsequent outcomes, altering the trade-off between harmonization and the level of regulation.

The SEA and Environmental Regulation

The institutional changes incorporated into the SEA made unilateral actions by some of the member states much easier and so changed the character of the status quo. The Luxembourg agreement, inasmuch as it was a move to centralized harmonization, was doomed to be eroded from the moment it went into effect as a result of the changes discussed below.

As noted above, Denmark was outvoted in the Council of Ministers as soon as the SEA came into force. The Luxembourg agreement was approved as a directive concerning the free movement of goods, based on Article 100 of the Treaty of Rome. But under the terms of the SEA there were new, specific provisions for environmental legislation where none had existed before. Furthermore, Article 100 itself was to be modified in significant ways in order to address the concerns of some member states, notably Denmark, over the environmental consequences of the 1992 project (what follows relies, in part, on Vandermeersch 1987).

The SEA inserted a new Title VII, called "Environment," into Part 3 of the treaty, the new provisions being numbered 130R–130T. The objectives, enumerated in Article 130R, make no mention of the internal market or of any other specific economic purpose for environmental regulation. Protection of the environment and of the health of the citizens of the Community now became an end in itself for the EU. Yet any directive taking this section as its legal basis would require unanimity in the Council of Ministers (Article 130S). This unanimity would be difficult to accomplish; any such measure would have to be accepted by the member state with the weakest interest in environmental protection. However, Article 130T provided an escape clause for member states with strong environmental preferences:

> The protective measures adopted in common pursuant to Article 130S shall not prevent any Member State from maintaining or introducing more stringent protective measures compatible with this treaty.

What the phrase "compatible with this treaty" means precisely was left unclear; presumably, the ECJ would have had to rule on it. The likely implication was that any such unilateral measure should not represent a barrier to trade; however, this article certainly appeared to leave a member state plenty of latitude.

Yet the agreement at Luxembourg, of course, was not passed under the terms of these articles, nor were further regulations proposed under them. The second stage in emissions control, proposed by the Commission in July 1987, was still characterized as an internal market measure and therefore subject to the terms of Article 100. But there had been important additions to this article in the SEA. The best known, of course, relate to the introduction of qualified majority voting for internal market issues and the role of a new legislative rule known as the cooperation procedure (for a description see Fitzmaurice 1988). But there were also important additions relating specifically to environmental matters. Article 100A(3) stated that "the Commission in its proposals . . . will take as a base a high level of protection." It is not clear what a "high level of protection" means, but it is evidence that the member states wished to check any tendency for directives aimed at completing the internal market to give environmental regulation less weight (in other words, avoid regulation based on the lowest common denominator).

A more important addition to the treaty is Article 100A(4). The implications of this article are significant enough that it is worth reproducing here in full.

If, after the adoption of a harmonization measure by the council acting by a qualified majority, a Member State deems it necessary to apply national provisions on grounds of major needs referred to in Article 36, or relating to protection of the environment or working environment, it shall notify the Commission of these provisions.

The Commission shall confirm the provisions involved after having verified that they are not a means of arbitrary discrimination or a disguised restriction on trade between Member States.

By way of derogation from the procedure laid down in Articles 169 and 170, the Commission or any Member State may bring the matter directly before the Court of Justice if it considers that another Member State is making improper use of the powers provided for in this article.

This article was agreed upon at the highest level in bargaining over the SEA (Moravcsik 1991, 43–44). While it seems to confer power, in the last instance, on the ECJ, that institution could act only at the behest of others; monitoring occurred on a combined self-reporting/fire-alarm principle. The Commission, historically, has proved reluctant to bring states before the Court on matters of compliance, when and where it does so being a strictly political question. Article 100A(4) does also allow for other member states to bring suit, in what is an accelerated procedure. However, it is very likely that the Court would look on the Commission as plaintiff with much greater favor than on a member state, who might be suspected of harboring a strictly parochial interest in the outcome rather than the interest of the community as a whole. In short, unless the Commission took energetic legal action, unilateral environmental regulation by a member state would be seen as consistent with these articles.[10]

Taken together, Articles 130T and 100A(4) presented a conundrum for the Commission, given the overall purpose of the SEA. The treaty was a framework for completion of the internal market; the qualified voting provisions of Article 100A(1) were a crucial element in that framework. Only with a mechanism of that kind could the difficulties of intergovernmentalism be avoided. The agreement on emissions at Luxembourg had been subject to such difficulties for nearly two years. However, the escape clauses in Articles 130T and 100A(4) surely eroded the possibility for harmonization, at least in environmental matters. In effect, these particular provisions of the SEA risked moving policy outcomes away from centralized harmonization and toward a patchwork of regulations across Europe.

The Commission could choose to propose low new EU standards and use the ECJ to restrain those governments seeking unilaterally their own national standards. Or it could propose high standards that would require no appeal to the ECJ but would surely run the risk of being blocked in the Council. The second option depended upon the spread of preferences among firms and the governments of the member states. In the event, there existed a winning qualified majority that included a coalition of firms and governments willing to trade their preferences over the level of regulation for increased regulatory harmonization. The uncertainty created by a Commission strategy that depended upon the ECJ contributed substantially to the formation of this coalition.

New Standards

A decisive factor in what followed was that the small, clean countries now attempted to pursue their own course unilaterally. In June 1987 Danish officials announced that they would seek permission from the Commission to apply higher emissions standards than those in place generally in the Community. Since judicial review was subject to the discretion of the Commission, bargaining over the next stage of emissions control regulation turned on the trade-off between certainty and regulatory harmonization as opposed to low levels of regulation under significant uncertainty. The preferences imputed to the states and firms above suggested that they shared an interest in harmonization but were divided over emissions control. This contrast between unity on the one hand and division on the other determined the observed outcome.

The Commission's Proposal

In February 1988 the Commission sent a proposal to the Council of Ministers for a new set of standards for small cars. This began the second stage of regulation promised in the earlier agreement (what follows relies, in part, on Kim 1992). The levels suggested were for 30 g of CO and 8 g of HO + NO$_x$, to be implemented on 1 October 1992 for new cars and on 1 October 1993 for new models. In effect, the standards for medium-sized autos were now to be applied to small autos. The standards were also to remain optional. They represented a ceiling. While these standards were at a higher level, they still permitted the use of lean-burn technology, although relatively expensive electronic engine controls would be needed.

This proposal was as friendly to the industry as was possible, given the increasing political salience of environmental questions. In 1987 the Greens in Germany had increased their share of the vote to 8.3 percent. In one state government, Hesse, they had already entered into a governing coalition. By 1986 protecting the environment and fighting pollution ranked third overall among Europeans as a priority issue for debate in the European Parliament. (In Germany and Denmark it ranked first; *Eurobarometer* 25, June 1986, table 42.) The Dutch government had chosen green issues as the basis for a major political offensive (*Financial Times*, 14 October 1988, 2).

To understand why these proposals were relatively lax, it is necessary to understand how proposals were authored and subsequently altered; for, once the agenda was set in EU policy-making, it could only be altered under very specific conditions. In short, the discussion that follows will show how cohesion, or the lack of it, within the industry had a decisive effect on the position taken by the Commission, which, under the cooperation procedure, had power as a conditional agenda setter, as will be discussed below.

The Commission was at the core of the process as an actor because it had the power to propose (for a description of the Commission's responsibilities and powers see Ludlow 1991). Furthermore, its representatives chaired the technical committees, a role that might be a source of significant power, as I argued in chapter 2 (see also Eichener 1993, 50–53). Yet the Commission was itself an arena for political struggle, within which national and interest group representatives participated. The Commission was relatively small and lacked the institutional capacity to make expert choices or develop an autonomous position where the issues were complicated and technical. It therefore relied on outside sources of information and actively solicited the participation of industry (this discussion relies on a variety of interviews with officials and interest group representatives in Brussels; see the appendix).

This pattern of industry involvement was repeated in the technical committees of the Council. However, by the time a proposal had got that far no completely new arguments or positions were considered. The "bracket" of possible outcomes was already set (the last "plastic" moment was at the level of "Chef du Cabinet" within the Commission). Because making preferences known at an early stage was crucial, and industry representatives were always present at an early stage, the auto producers were generally perceived as very influential in Brussels. They were involved in the very beginning of the process and stayed involved at every stage, in informal as well as formal ways. Everyone was in constant touch with everyone else, and position papers and confidential documents circulated at a high speed in a process described by some as "anarchic," by others as "opaque."

This shows how the level of coordination among groups of member states and the firms concerned was a vital determinant of the Commission's position. In its absence, or in the event of a breakdown, the Commission found it difficult to take a position, and when that happened, the opportunity arose for the political arena to widen. Given that the auto industry had nearly always succeeded in presenting a united front, chiefly through its transnational association (the CCMC), the tendency of the Commission to look after the interests of the industry was to be expected. The divisions between the member states in the Council had always been resolved on the basis of an initial proposal shaped in important ways by the auto producers themselves. However, the industry was deeply divided over the issue of emissions control, as were the member states.

The low level of the Commission's proposal led Holland into a confrontation with the Commission and other member states. On 19 July 1988 it notified the Commission that it was going to begin a program of fiscal incentives that would encourage consumers to buy automobiles with CATs. The Commission at first asked Holland to suspend its regulation while it was evaluated. While the Danes were also threatening to use fiscal incentives, and the Germans seemed interested in doing the same, it was Holland that was first to be taken before the ECJ.

Meanwhile, in the Council the German, Dutch, Danish, and Greek delegations at first formed a blocking minority opposed to the Commission's proposals. It was felt that they would still not bring Europe up to US 83 standards. In the technical working groups of the Council that considered these proposals the German, Dutch, French, and British delegations were the most active. The British had suggested an alternative even weaker than the Commission's proposal, a plan that was backed by the French, Italians, Spanish, and Portuguese (Kim 1992, 10–12). However, the significant development, as it was at Luxembourg in 1985, was the movement of Germany away from its opposition to the Commission's proposal. It renounced fiscal incentives on the condition that the norms adopted would not be final. In the end the Commission was to promise a proposal for a "third stage" of reductions, to be agreed on before the end of 1991. By the beginning of July the Council had approved the Commission's proposal by a qualified majority, which, under the new cooperation procedure, was now sent to the Parliament for its first reading.

The Auto Industry in Disarray

However, before the reading occurred, the French government disowned its own environment minister, Lalonde, and rejected the compromise. This dramatic turn was perceived to be a response to intense lobbying by one of the major French producers, Peugeot, under its controversial chairman Jacques Calvet. Indeed, the attitude of Peugeot was to put both the French government and the producers' association in a very difficult position at a critical moment. What was

Peugeot's objective in lobbying the French government so intensely? The French government gave as its reason for abrogating the agreement the announced Dutch intention to introduce fiscal incentives for encouraging the strictest emissions requirements, regardless of the other member states. This departure made it likely that some others would follow suit, unless a ruling from the Court could be obtained. But while both France and Britain were concerned about harmonization, as much as about the level of regulation, I suggest that Peugeot's preference reflected a peculiar strategic position that set it apart, both from its government and its fellow producers. In short, it preferred optional harmonization (in which France and others could adopt low standards) over centralized harmonization at some higher level.

If some governments preferred high standards and they could not be constrained by the institutions of the Community, then from Peugeot's perspective it would be better that the other countries, such as France—in which, coincidentally, it had a significant market share—could choose lower standards. Its strategic situation fostered this preference for a variety of reasons. It was, in important ways, the least internationalized producer. The comparison with the other French automaker is instructive. By the late 1980s Renault had begun the long process both of cutting its connection to the French government and establishing a new one with Volvo of Sweden (although ultimately the marriage broke up on the steps of the altar). This was to be an alliance with a producer that, as a matter of course, adhered to U.S. standards, which meant that harmonization assumed even greater importance in Renault's eyes, evidenced by the comments of Renault spokesman Patrick Bessy at the time: "Presently we are living with five different definitions of a clean car. It will be more practical for us to have only one" (*International Environment Reporter,* August 1988, 440). Furthermore, while the French government was eager to extricate itself from its relationship with Renault, it continued to stand behind it as lender of last resort until the beginning of the 1990s. Access to these deep pockets would surely help Renault overcome the technological hurdles imposed by emissions control.

By contrast, Peugeot was a private firm that had played a lone hand in the marketplace. In part this role was forced on it as the opportunities for strategic alliances or takeovers, such as Renault-Volvo, GM-Saab, or VW-SEAT, were very limited in such a concentrated business. Furthermore, the takeover of Citroën by Peugeot in the 1970s took longer to digest than anticipated (interview with Tristan D'Albis, Peugeot, 19 June 1992). Finally, Peugeot had also, secretly, made a serious commitment to lean-burn technology, which it saw placed in jeopardy by the Commission's proposals. This lack of resources and allies put Peugeot in the weakest position of all the carmakers.

However, the rules of the Europe-wide industry association, the CCMC, worked to its advantage. All positions had to be adopted unanimously, and Calvet used this requirement to paralyze decision making in an attempt to drag the other producers toward his point of view. This obstruction provoked a crisis in the ranks of the producers. A firm such as VW, for whom harmonization was a very important issue, as argued above, saw it being sacrificed in a hopeless attempt to block a compromise that had the backing of a powerful majority of member states. Of course the two U.S. multinationals were not even members of the industry association, while specialist producers of large autos (such as Daimler-Benz), for whom the stakes were not important, were much more influential. In short, underlying divisions among firms were exacerbated by the institutional peculiarities of their industry association.

The timing of this crisis could not have been worse; it occurred at the moment when the terms of the cooperation procedure now granted the European Parliament the power to consider and amend proposals.

First Reading in Parliament

Even before the Parliament began considering the substance of the report of the Committee on the Environment, Public Health, and Consumer Protection (Doc. A 2-0132/88), there was sentiment, for institutional reasons, in favor of challenging the proposal sent down by the Commission and the Council. As the chair of the committee complained:

> I feel that, now that the Single Act has been passed, the Council would do well to show the respect for Parliament that is appropriate and necessary under the rules of this European Community. . . . I want to protest very formally against the preliminary decision taken by the Council in June and its announcement throughout the Community that a decision had been taken. The Council cannot formally have its first reading until Parliament has taken its decisions. (*Debates of the European Parliament,* 13 September 1988, 82–83)

In short, the Parliament was eager to flex its institutional muscle because the Council had conducted its business without even soliciting an opinion from it, as was required under the terms of the cooperation procedure.

The committee's report proposed radical amendments to the Commission's proposal: 20 g CO and 5 g CO + NO_x per test. It was adopted by the Committee 16-10, with one minority holding that the report went too far, and another that it didn't go far enough. An interesting element was the change of opinion by consumers' representatives. In 1985 they had supported lean burn as an economical solution to the problem of emissions; by 1988 they became persuaded that CATs were the only immediate solution to the problem of costly pollution (EP Doc. A 2-0132/88, 13). Lean burn enjoyed some support in the debate that followed, but the crucial factor seemed to be the demonstration effect of US 83 standards, which were already in place not only in the United States, but also in Sweden, Switzerland, and Austria (a country that had threatened to boycott French cars after France withdrew from the Council agreement) (*Debates of the European Parliament*, 13 September 1988, 84, 85; *International Environment Reporter*, September 1988, 491).

Clinton Davis, the Commissioner for the Environment, rejected the Parliament's amendments summarily. His reasons are illuminating. First, he feared that such amendments would break up the consensus that had been reached in the Council over the Luxembourg agreement; he observed that he was in the process of coaxing the French into cooperating once again. He went on to say:

> if we fail to adopt (this proposal) within the next few months member states will be tempted to apply their own measures and that could well lead to a fragmentation of the market, to protracted litigation and, worst of all from the point of view of an industry that needs to advance on this front, uncertainty about the future parameters of policy. (*Debates of the European Parliament*, 13 September 1988, 88–89)

He clearly valued harmonization and was doubtful of the Commission's ability to ensure it through the courts. What is more, he also signaled the strong preference of industry for certainty, as well as uniformity, in regulation. He went on to say that the Parliament's proposal would eliminate lean burn as a possible technical choice and impose excessive costs on industry. On the whole, this position was one aimed at pushing through a proposal that would, at one and the same time, foster cooperation in the Council and limit unilateral policies by individual states.[11] The crucial change by the time of the second reading in Parliament was that it became apparent that these two objectives could no longer both be accomplished at a low level of regulation.

The proposal returned to the Council, where every effort was made to recapture the support of the French, while retaining the support of the Germans. This feat was achieved by the Commission when it agreed, reluctantly, at the urging of the French, British, and Italians, to take the Dutch government to court. It then also agreed to introduce proposals for a third stage of reductions in emissions before the end of 1991. Holland, Denmark, and Greece were, again, outvoted by a qualified majority.

The Dutch fiscal incentives were introduced on 1 January 1989. On 10 January the Commission, using its powers under Article 93 of the treaty, ordered the Dutch government to suspend the plan, pending investigation, which it was going to conduct on the basis of Article 30 as well as Article 93 (*International Environment Reporter*, March 1989, 112). Article 30 relates to restrictions on trade, while Article 93 applies to state aids. It would seem that the Commission would have a better case if it was based on trade restrictions as opposed to state aid. After all, while there were significant investments in commercial vehicle production in Holland, there was much less in the way of auto assembly, mainly a small Volvo plant. However, only by invoking Article 93 could the Commission order Holland to suspend the rule. The Dutch government then applied to the ECJ for an immediate decision against the Commission, arguing that it was not yet proven that the regulation was against European law. By July officials in Brussels were openly admitting that the court case had been instituted for "blatantly political" reasons, and legal experts doubted that they could convince the judges of the ECJ (*Financial Times*, 25 May 1989, 3).

There was another significant development at the beginning of 1989. A new Commissioner for the Environment was appointed, to begin a four-year term, Carlo Ripa di Meana. He was a member of the Italian Socialist party and a former member of the EP and had just completed a four-year term as commissioner responsible for cultural affairs. His appointment by Jacques Delors was (at first) seen as a defeat for environmentalists, who had hoped for the appointment of a Belgian, Karel Van Miert, who was a member of the antinuclear lobby (*International Environment Reporter*, January 1989, 6). Whatever Delors's purpose, Ripa di Meana's subsequent actions suggest that he wished to start out by taking a stand designed to bolster his green credentials.

Second Reading in Parliament

At the beginning of April, the parliamentary Committee on the Environment, Public Health, and Consumer Protection had issued its second report on the emissions proposals for small cars (EP Doc. A 2-26/89). In it all the amendments rejected by the Commission and the Council at the end of 1988 were proposed once again. Under the terms of the cooperation procedure, on the second reading, any amendments proposed by the Parliament and accepted by the Commission might be adopted by the Council by qualified majority, but amended only by unanimity. However, and this is a crucial element of the power of the Parliament as a conditional agenda setter, any blocking minority—for example, two large countries and one small one—that prefers the status quo over the amendments proposed by the Parliament can simply prevent passage of the directive. Therefore, for the Parliament's proposals to pass, not only must the Commission accept them, but they must also be preferred by a qualified majority in the Council over the status quo.

On the eve of the parliamentary debate, Ripa di Meana, in consultation with Delors and Transport Commissioner Karel Van Miert, decided on a turnabout in the Commission's position (Kim 1992, 13). The Parliament's proposals were going to be accepted. How could this be explained? Ripa di Meana's role as political entrepreneur was an important one; no doubt he was aware, as were all the other actors, of the rising tide of public sentiment in favor of environmental issues. But the most important point was that failure to move to high standards would increase divergent national patterns of regulation, as a dissatisfied minority of member states introduced unilateral measures and sought to fight matters out in the court. In this regard the position of Germany was crucial, and there is evidence (see below) that fear of fragmented regulation was causing Germany to shift away from the hard-won compromise. It too might now be willing to set its own standards to US 83 levels without waiting for the Community. The question of harmonization was also most likely to weigh heavily with Delors. His name was associated above all with the internal market program, and its completion had to be his priority. Given that the status quo meant its delay in a very-high-profile sector, it is no surprise that he would prefer, instead, harmonization at a high level.

In short, therefore, taking into consideration the rise in environmental sentiment, the element that must be added to the story of the EP as a conditional agenda setter in this case is the tyranny of the new status quo after the passage of the SEA. The agreement at Luxembourg represented a certain amount of harmonization at a fairly low level. This was a good outcome for a qualified majority of the member states and for the industry. But the SEA altered the legal and institutional environment in a decisive way, allowing the status quo to drift toward regulatory uncertainty and a decline in harmonization. In that event, for the Commission, and for a critical coalition of member states and firms, guaranteed harmonization at a high level was preferred to uncertainty at any other level.[12]

The industry, as described above, was in disarray. None of the choices before it were very palatable, and its ability to speak with one voice was being held hostage by one recalcitrant member. The situation of Ford, although it was not a member of the producers' club at that time, is illuminating. It had made a significant commitment to lean-burn technology. However, the concession by the Commission to Germany, promising a third stage in reductions, guaranteed that small-car standards would be raised too high too quickly for anything but CATs to be effective. On the other hand, as a regionally integrated producer Ford also had a very strong preference for harmonization. For it too, and for others such as VW, the post-SEA status quo with continued uncertainty about future standards was unacceptable. In short, the issue of harmonization was one on which there was much more industry agreement than on the issue of emissions control. Finally, high-level standards were more likely to be acceptable now than at times in the past because of the recent boom in auto sales.

For these reasons the turn by the Commission was not actively opposed by the industry, nor was the reexamined proposal (that is, a proposal to which the Commission has accepted parliamentary amendments) voted down once it was submitted to the Council in June 1989. European Parliament elections were only a week or so away, and green issues featured prominently. In the end, the standards agreed upon by the Council were somewhat greener than those proposed by the Commission and the Parliament. US 83 standards were to be introduced in 1992, a year earlier for new models than under the proposal, and were to be mandatory—in other words, true harmonization rather than a ceiling (the first-stage standards, due in 1991, were dropped, which gave the industry more leeway in the period prior to introduction).

The bargaining behind this outcome assumed a classic intergovernmental pattern (Kim 1992, 17–20). Germany staked out a relatively extreme position on the timing, urging that the standards be adopted in 1991. Britain, which had wished for 1993 as the date, was persuaded to settle on 1992 as a compromise. With the eclipse of lean burn as a viable technological alternative, its position became flexible. This also meant that the Dutch fiscal incentives were now a moot issue, since they would be quickly overtaken by the mandatory requirements. Italy also weakened, as FIAT was now prepared to introduce CATs. Indeed, it transpired that FIAT was to be given, in effect, side-payments by the Italian government. In Germany and France also, emissions controls on small cars were to be the subject of tax relief or subsidies (*International Environment Reporter,* July 1989, 345, 346; October 1991, 553). Mandatory harmonization was established, and all the national fiscal incentives noted above were limited to 85 percent of the cost of the converter. The shorter lead time meant that the incentives would quickly cease to be an issue (*Financial Times,* 10, 11 June 1989, 1). The defection of Italy and Britain left France isolated. Rather than go it alone, the French government agreed to adopt the directive on the basis of unanimity.

This "greener" outcome at the level of the Council reflected the high salience of harmonization. This issue clearly came to dominate the agenda, reflecting not only the preferences of a core group of the member states, but also those of some of the producers. The institutional changes represented by the environmental escape clauses in the SEA meant that this preference for harmonization could most easily be realized by a high level of regulation. The "power" of the Parliament as an agenda setter merely reflected this constellation of political preferences in the context of the post-SEA status quo.

Conclusions

It is not easy to do a simple accounting of the forces that shaped the outcome. Because of the rising tide of environmental consciousness the change in policy was, in a sense, overdetermined; it could be argued that all other considerations were submerged by popular sentiment. The fortuitous change in the person of the environmental commissioner also had an effect. However, the core of the story seems to be as was argued throughout: the ability of states and firms to coordinate their responses to proposed regulation, as conditioned by the spread of their preferences, interacted with the institutional environment to determine the outcome.

Important elements in the analysis were consistent with expectations yielded by the analytical scheme presented in chapter 2. As expected, variation in the costs of regulation across issue areas led to variation in coalitions among states and firms. For example, divergent technological capacities would be the kind of element to inhibit interfirm cooperation; this factor clearly played an important part. I also suggested that a vital precondition for institutions to mediate outcomes was a spacious "Pareto surface." The divisions over the level of regulation satisfied this condition, allowing the EP and the Commission together to set the agenda in a way that played to that coalition of firms and governments closest to their ideal point.[13] A final element that is worth noting was the direct links that clearly persisted between major auto producers and their national governments. In this case a pronounced role was played by bilateral firm-state relationships. It is possible that such connections matter most when the industry is in disarray.

Finally, I noted in the analytical framework that the member states would have more control over outcomes where only a qualified majority was required. In this story, once the Commission had accepted an amended proposal by the EP on the second reading, unanimity was required from the member states if they wished for some different outcome and found the status quo unacceptable.

That cooperation problem, in the context of this very divisive issue area, was insuperable.

Did the member states foresee this kind of outcome, or did the significant influence over the level of regulation enjoyed by the EP, and environmental interests working within it, come as a surprise? The EP was an institution that was believed to be poorly organized; it may well be that the power to set the agenda that it deployed on this occasion was the result of several contingencies: the salience of environmental issues across party lines, the desire for institutional recognition, the character of the status quo, which the framers of the SEA may not have fully anticipated. If so, it may be imagined that firms and governments reacted accordingly at a later date—the former turning their lobbying activities toward the EP, the latter seeking new institutional change that had the effect of clipping the Parliament's wings. This important issue is revisited in the concluding chapter, in which the implications of the outcomes observed in these case studies for institutional innovation and adaptation are drawn out.

CHAPTER 5

The Politics of External Trade

Introduction

In July 1991 the European Union and Japan adopted a "voluntary trade agreement" on automobiles, which has been characterized as "one of the most unusual understandings in modern international economic diplomacy" (Mason 1994, 427). It represented a singular departure from the principles governing the completion of the single market, and it was at odds with the rules governing trade among the member states of the General Agreement on Tariffs and Trade (GATT). Why did the establishment of a common external trade regime fall so short of free-trade principles? Were the institutions of the EU ineffective? The explanation is a simple one: the mass-market auto producers, in direct contrast to the policy outcome in emissions control described above, were united by a very strong interest in the outcome. This political weight was decisive.

In the analysis that follows I show how the distribution of firm and government preferences fostered cohesion among them and gave rise to influential coalitions. I also show how the weak institutional environment allowed an outcome far short of external openness. The absence of a formal, rule-governed process had two significant consequences: it limited the set of actors who had influence on the policy-making process, and it allowed for an expanded set of possible outcomes, some at odds with the objectives of the single market program. The united front presented by the producers in combination with these two elements gave them significant control over the outcome.

I begin by discussing the preferences of governments and firms. The preferences imputed to them in chapter 3 are assessed in greater detail, and the set of choices before them are specified. In particular I show how the issues of external trade and transplant production were closely linked. The analysis continues by looking at the history of EU relations with Japan, and the legal basis

111

for the trade regimes practiced separately by the member states before the passage of the Single European Act. I show how the passage of the SEA ended these regimes and forced the issue of external trade onto the agenda.

Of course, once national restrictions were to be submerged by an EU-wide regime, then EU institutions were bound to play a significant role in international bargaining. However, such was the informal character of the bargaining process that industry interests were privileged, due to their cohesion and influence over the Commission, while the formal procedures established by the SEA, which in other issue areas structured outcomes in ways favorable to openness, played no part.

A crucial question is why those interests favorable to greater openness were not able to shelter behind the institutional structures of the EU. How was it that an informal process governed this outcome? I return to this question at the end of the chapter. However, worth noting here is the perverse way in which the very absence of escape clauses in EU and GATT rules, in a situation in which a blocking minority was opposed to a pure liberal outcome, pushed the bargaining outside the institutional environment and so expanded the set of possible outcomes. The fact that new trade barriers were accompanied by a liberal investment regime reveals divisions among producers and governments, rather than the effects of institutional constraints.

The analysis concludes by giving an account of the bargaining behind the agreement. I show how crucial changes that occurred in the auto producers' transnational industry association during the negotiations increased their political weight. These changes reflected the forces, identified in chapters 2 and 3, that shaped interfirm cooperation and had the effect of increasing the power of the industry over the outcome. I also show how this power was unmediated by a formal institutional environment, which condition was endogenous to the cohesion among producer interests.

The Preferences of Governments and Firms

As noted in chapter 2, the preferences of governments for radical integration would be shaped by the degree to which they imagined it would foster even greater rationalization in industry. That is to say, if greater openness further divided national producers into winners and losers, then the preferences of governments would, likewise, diverge. It was certain that *overall* all the member states would gain something from integration; the problem was that the gains would be asymmetrically distributed. While there would be some significant winners within the ranks of the producers, to say nothing of the general welfare gains to consumers and the possibility of long-term gains in per capita income (which gains would, of course, translate into more auto purchases), other producers might simply go out of business. In other words, as argued in chapter 2, although the aggregate economic gains from openness would outweigh the costs, the asymmetric distribution of those gains would lead to wider political divisions among governments.

But the issue was much more problematic when internal openness was married to external trade, in particular trade with Japan. Here too the gains outweighed the costs, but the balance of economic benefits was less absolutely favorable, while the asymmetric distribution of the political costs, in keeping with the discussion in chapter 2, was even more pronounced. Any member state home to significant production facilities of mass-market autos was likely to face acute adjustment costs from unrestricted Japanese imports. The fear was eloquently stated by a French member of the EP:

> [The] application pure and simple of the large internal market of 1993 will offer the Japanese . . . the opportunity to submerge Europe in the same way as they have submerged the American market. (*Debates of the European Parliament*, 11 June 1991, 112)

In short, it was feared that the Japanese would be the ones to gain from the internal market project, rather than European industry. There was good reason for this fear; the experience of the U.S. auto industry in the 1980s was a salutary one. Japanese market share in the United States had reached almost 30 percent by the end of the decade. The possibility that the Japanese might make the same gains in Europe in the 1990s was strongly indicated by the results of a large and widely publicized study on the relative efficiency of the various world automakers (Womack, Jones, and Roos 1990). This study was often cited in Commission and other documents addressing the future of the EU auto industry. In chapter 3 I argued, based on that study and on other productivity figures presented in table 5, that the preferences of all the producing countries, and the mass-market producers, for external openness reflected this lack of competitiveness and fear of an uncertain future.

External Trade

The picture of firm and state preferences was, at first, somewhat more mixed than is suggested above. There certainly existed a core group of member states who feared external openness: these countries—Spain, Italy, Belgium, and

France—were home to those producers most exposed to adjustment difficulties, of the kind suggested by table 3 in chapter 2. In this table dependence on one national market is taken as a proxy for exposure to adjustment costs. All of the production of Renault, Peugeot, and FIAT was concentrated in these countries (for a complete picture of the distribution of production facilities of the major producers across Europe see Salvadori 1991, 43). It was this concentration that determined their preferences, rather than the past performance of each country in international trade in this sector, which varied significantly between the states under consideration. Italy's balance of trade was certainly poor, but France had maintained its position, and Spain and Belgium had enjoyed a steady improvement in performance (see figure 7 in chapter 3). The key elements were future prospects: all these countries were host to those firms that were at a decisive disadvantage in comparison to Japanese producers. Not only were they less efficient, but they specialized in mass-market models, a market segment in which the Japanese could be expected to make the most severe market inroads.

British preferences present a contrast: the performance of the British auto industry had been even worse than that of the Italian. However, the government's strategy in response to this crisis, already being pursued on the eve of the SEA, was to rely on foreign direct investment (FDI), in particular the establishment by Japanese firms of significant production facilities in the United Kingdom. As noted in chapter 3, this reliance gave it an incentive to maintain a liberal investment regime, but also to permit protection and so foster tariff-jumping investment. However, the Japanese producers were still a long way from being able to supply the EU market entirely from their plants in the United Kingdom and elsewhere in Europe, and if the U.K. government was to play the part of a good partner to these producers, it could not appear to be a supporter of the protectionist position of the core group of producing countries. This tension was reflected nicely by the industry association in the United Kingdom, the SMMT. It had a very diverse membership; the Japanese firms themselves belonged, as did parts producers, retailers, and so forth. For that reason Ford, GM, and Rover, who were likely to face the fiercest Japanese competition, found themselves members of an institution that welcomed Japanese investment but, at the same time, accepted the need for limitations on EU imports (interview with Michael Stedman, SMMT, 22 May 1992).

Germany, at first, was inclined to pursue much more of a free-market strategy. This reflected both superior performance in this sector and the specialized interests represented by the VDA (the German industry association). As in the British case, the way interests were aggregated nationally was important. While Germany was home to significant production by three mass-market producers—

Ford, GM (Opel), and VW—it was also the location for a globally competitive, specialized set of assemblers and parts producers (as noted in chapter 3). The specialist producers were both confident that they could make significant progress in the Japanese market and fearful that any restrictions would drive the Japanese producers up-market into their segments. Parts makers such as Bosch could be confident that they would benefit from the arrival of Japanese investment in Europe, which required local, high-quality suppliers. These firms, members of the "inner circle" of German industry, dominated the VDA; and their preferences were reflected in the preference of the German government, which favored openness, even at the expense of its own mass-market producers.

The small open countries of the EU, of course, had an interest in the welfare gains that would accrue to their consumers as a result of radical openness, both external and internal. However, their role in the bargaining to follow was to be very limited, a position that contrasts dramatically with their ability to upset the status quo, as discussed above, in the emissions control episode. The difference in this case, it will be apparent, lay in the character of the rules and institutional arena, or rather the lack of either, that governed the bargaining over the agreement with Japan.

In discussing the preferences of the states, the interests of the firms in question have also been suggested. In particular the mass-market producers were all fearful of the competitive strength of the Japanese, even if some governments were less disposed to take their part. The preferences of the firms involved were clearly evidenced by a set of hearings held by the House of Lords (U.K.) Select Committee on the European Community (1990). In these hearings the specific policy to be adopted by the EU in response to the threat of Japanese competition was under discussion. While it was impossible for the EU to establish permanent, Europe-wide legislation in place of the various national limitations that had existed in the past, the automakers did want the EU to permit a significant derogation from the principles of the single market and of GATT. As will be discussed below, the existing national regulations were rendered impotent by the passage of the SEA. European producers wanted a lengthy "transitional" period (perhaps indefinite!), during which Japanese producers would be subject to a limitation on their market share.

Firm preferences over the market share granted to Japanese imports were inevitably linked to the question of FDI. The important question was whether transplant production would displace Japanese imports and so be subject to some EU-wide limitation, or whether any such limitation would apply only to imports, while transplant production could reach any level the Japanese producers were able to accomplish. Taking the question of imports in isolation, the evidence from the House of Lords hearings is quite clear. FIAT, Ford, Renault, and the transnational industry association, the CCMC, all favored a transitional period to extend at least until the end of the century (House of Lords 1990, 44, 45, 52, 61). By contrast, the representative of Daimler-Benz indicated his own firm's preference for no transitional period, although he felt that five years would be acceptable to others, that is, 1 January 1998 (House of Lords 1990, 26).[1]

In contrast to the unity displayed by the mass-market producers, there was a split down the middle of the EU member states, as reported by British government testimony before the committee, with the United Kingdom, Germany, Denmark, and the Netherlands opposed to EU-wide controls. However, the circumlocutions of C. Roberts, deputy secretary at the Department of Trade and Industry, betrayed the fine differences that existed between the United Kingdom and the other states favoring openness. He admitted that the U.K. government had not taken a position on ending the existing voluntary export restraint (VER) between the United Kingdom and Japan, although he later indicated support for its replacement by EU control of some national markets, but not for an EU-wide limitation. Of course, select national limitations might divert Japanese products into markets that did not have them, such as Germany, which would be opposed to any such outcome.

Foreign Direct Investment

The truth was that the U.K. government cared about a VER, whether national or EU-wide, only inasmuch as it had consequences for inward Japanese FDI. The issue of FDI was very sensitive, and even mass-market producers were less united on it than on the question of simple imports from Japan. To understand why, it is necessary to specify the character of the competitive advantage of the Japanese producers, and the way in which investment in the EU might have mixed results for EU industry.

Japan's competitive advantage, which made its imports so threatening, was based on three important elements: an advantage in the cost of capital, in the cost of labor (allowing for significant differences in productivity), and in "X" efficiencies (i.e., they knew how to do things better, faster, and cheaper). When they came to operate transplants, their advantages seemed to persist: they still had access (at that time) to cheap capital, they still knew how to make better cars faster and for less, and they enjoyed a "greenfield" and "green labor" advantage. That is to say, their new plants were able to incorporate the latest advances in manufacturing technologies and practices. Furthermore, they could selectively recruit a young, largely male workforce without experience of large-scale manufacturing who were willing to be socialized into Japanese working routines. In northern England the workers were drawn from an area of very high unemployment and were therefore likely to be grateful and energetic. The Japanese were also, especially in the case of the Nissan plant in northern England, the beneficiaries of subsidies aimed at assisting depressed areas (see Dicken 1987).

The role of component makers is crucial here. Wage rates on the assembly line were not very different between Europe and Japan, but the gap widened considerably when comparing the first and second tier of suppliers (see Boston Consulting Group 1991, 21). This was the main source of the Japanese labor cost advantage. The relationship between the assemblers and suppliers was also, in part, the source of Japanese manufacturing efficiencies. The co-development of parts and systems, just-in-time inventory control, and flexible production schedules—all of these being some of the constituent elements of so-called lean production—were made possible as a result of the effective way in which suppliers and assemblers were entwined legally and operationally. The strength of these relationships allowed the Japanese producers to be less vertically integrated than their American and European counterparts (see de Banville and Chanaron 1991).

The Japanese would wish to reproduce these relationships between supplier and assembler in their European transplants. While many Japanese suppliers, therefore, would follow the big producers to their new locations, there would also be an opportunity for European suppliers to become more efficient as a result of doing business with the new arrivals. These beneficial "externalities" accruing to local manufacturers as a result of exposure to Japanese business practices were a primary reason for the British government's encouragement of Japanese investment. The other reason was the effect large-scale auto assembly by the Japanese would have on the balance of trade in automotive products for the United Kingdom. While nothing was set down in writing, the British government "encouraged" the Japanese to use a high level of domestic/EU content in their cars—80 percent once production exceeded 100,000 units annually—and to export a "majority" of the finished product (interview with Thoss Shearer, Department of Trade and Industry, 27 May 1992).[2] This was an obvious and effective strategy for the United Kingdom to pursue, but one likely to discomfort its partners in the Community. The improvement in the balance of trade that the U.K. government was seeking had to come, in part, at the expense of other member states. This meant that interstate divisions on this matter were likely to be intense.

From this it also follows that the extent to which the European auto producers could share in the "externalities" created by Japanese investment, either

because of joint ventures with Japanese producers or as a result of increased efficiencies in their suppliers, would determine their willingness to insist on strict
limits on transplants.

This willingness would be further moderated if European producers were
able to obtain comparable "greenfield" advantages of their own. By coincidence
the opening up of Eastern Europe increased these kinds of opportunities for the
European producers. Although Spain's low-wage advantage became eroded
quickly following its entry into the EU, a pattern of investment in the European
periphery had already occurred as part of a "regionalization" of production (see
Diekmann 1992a, 3). If the EU encouraged, and funded, the location of plants
in the periphery, this should have the effect of leveling the playing field and
so moderate further the opposition of European automakers to Japanese FDI
(of course, such a move to the periphery would have a negative effect on the
balance of trade in what are at present the major producing countries).

Certain automakers were best situated so as to benefit from the arrival of
the Japanese. Because of the small number of assemblers, and the ever increasing costs of playing in all, or most, market segments, there was an increasing
tendency for all the players in the industry to participate in a variety of limited
cooperative enterprises. In other words, while competing head-to-head in many
market segments, automakers might agree to cooperate over specific products
or parts that could not otherwise be funded. For example, Ford and VW cooperated in the production of an all-purpose vehicle (APV) in Portugal (this will
be discussed in greater detail in chapter 6), and Honda and Rover shared output from an engine plant. Clearly, those firms with the most experience in these
kinds of operations were least likely to object to Japanese FDI. The U.S. multinationals were just such firms, while both VW and Renault had some experience (if not always good experiences, to be sure) of international cooperation.
However, FIAT and Peugeot were, by comparison, the most isolated—especially
Peugeot, which had spent its energies digesting other French producers rather
than forging links with producers further afield.

In short, while the mass-market producers were united on the subject of
imports, their preferences over the issue of Japanese transplants were more divided. By contrast, the member states were more divided on both issues. The
relative positions of all are illustrated in figures 14 and 15. In figure 15 it can be
seen that, while all the producers are clustered together when it comes to trade
openness, the multinationals, necessarily, are more inclined to be amenable to
a liberal FDI regime. While Ford felt "somewhat betrayed" by the British government's policies over external trade (interview with David Hulse, Ford, 25
June 1992), in its testimony before the House of Lords committee it merely in-

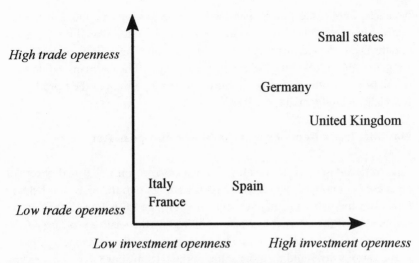

Fig. 14.   Governments: trade and investment

sisted that Nissan U.K. (for example) be held to a very high standard in local content (House of Lords 1990, 52).[3]

Figure 14 reveals the divisions between the member states on both issues. Clearly, the positions taken by Germany and the United Kingdom would be decisive. It is to be expected that the Iberian countries and Belgium, as significant

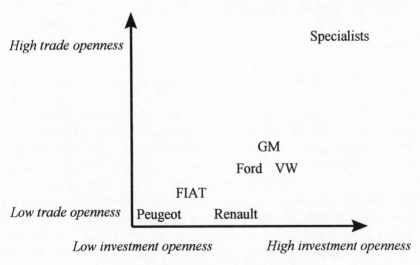

Fig. 15.   Firms: trade and investment

beneficiaries of inward investment, would have to support a more liberal investment regime. But all were willing to restrict imports. Would the Germans and the United Kingdom move toward this position? The position of the United Kingdom on trade was soft, while the preferences of the Germans would turn out to be a function of changes in the competitive position of their producers, especially the influential specialists.

National Trade Regimes and the Single European Act

This section describes the various national trade regimes that had governed Japanese automobile imports in the years leading up to the SEA, thus helping to explain the pattern of market segmentation that existed on the eve of the completion of the internal market and indicating the relative exposure of the various national markets. It should be no surprise that the preferences imputed to the various firms and member states in the section above were mirrored by the trade regimes adopted by each member state; an uncompetitive industry is typically associated with tariffs and nontariff barriers.

The section goes on to describe the early stages of EU regulation in this area and shows how the changes implied by the SEA spelled the end of national restrictions and so required either perfect external openness or some replacement at the level of the EU. It also shows that, since the former option was politically impossible, and the latter was inevitably at odds with many of the rules and norms governing international trade, any new trade agreement at the level of the EU with the Japanese would have to be informal.

National Trade Restrictions in Europe

Each of the producing nations of Europe dealt with Japanese competition in characteristic ways. By 1977 the Japanese share of the British market was roughly 10 percent, and informal talks seeking "a gentleman's agreement" on voluntary restraint had the effect of limiting future increases in Japanese sales in the United Kingdom (*Financial Times*, 2 November 1977). This never became a legal agreement—which would, of course, have been contrary to GATT rules—but remained an informal one between the SMMT and the Japanese Automobile Manufacturers Association (JAMA). Subsequently Britain began to actively solicit inward investment, in a pattern similar to Spanish policy, from Japanese automakers. As a result, the "big three"—Nissan, Honda, and Toyota—all had plants, or plans for plants, in the United Kingdom by 1990 (see *Financial Times*, special section, "Japan in the UK," 20 September 1991).

The Japanese slowly built up a 15 percent share of the German market, which is the largest share they have in any of the domestic markets of the major producing countries. Yet many commentators claim that even the Germans had some kind of tacit agreement with Japanese producers that limits their sales. These claims are, of course, denied by representatives of the German auto industry. As will be discussed below in greater detail, Europe-wide monitoring of Japanese auto sales, along with several other categories of goods, was begun in the early 1980s. The Japanese Ministry for International Trade and Industry (MITI), in conjunction with JAMA, announced at the beginning of every year a "target," and Japanese sales would invariably reflect that figure at the end of the year. As Smith and Venables point out, given that there existed national restrictions in all the other major markets of the Community, this Community-wide voluntary restraint must have operated as a de facto limit on Japanese sales in Germany.

In France an understanding with the Japanese limited them to 3 percent of the market, an understanding backed up by the regulatory instrument of type approvals. Furthermore, an attempt by Subaru to invest in a plant in Tours in 1988 was rejected by the French government, indicating its attitude to FDI as well as to trade (Mason 1994, 419). In Italy (as noted in chapter 3) Japanese producers were limited, technically, to only 3,000 imported units every year. Spain (also as noted above) had very high import barriers before its entry into the Community.

In the smaller member states of the EU (except Portugal), in which Japanese cars faced few restrictions, they captured an average of 29.3 percent of the market. In the five EFTA countries of Sweden, Switzerland, Austria, Finland, and Norway the Japanese captured an average of 33.7 percent of the market. By contrast, under the patchwork of restrictions in place in Europe as a whole the Japanese had only 10 percent of the market (CCFA 1991, 13). Therefore, most estimates, based in part on the success the Japanese enjoyed in the markets of the small open member states and the members of EFTA, supposed that the ending of all these various national controls would result in the Japanese increasing their share of the overall European market from 10 percent to 25 percent. This would not only mean that they captured all the increases in demand for new cars that might follow from the SEA, but also that they would cut into the existing level of sales enjoyed by the European producers.

Protection was costly for European consumers, because it allowed European producers to set higher prices for their cars. Smith calculated the costs as follows:

Restrictions on Japanese car imports cost consumers in France, Italy, the U.K., Spain and Portugal around ECU 6 billion per year in total (or over 4% of the value of consumers' expenditure on cars in Europe). The gain to

European producers is only half this sum; and the gain to Japanese producers is around ECU 1 billion a year. (1992, 3)

Thus the deadweight costs ran to ECU 2 billion a year. These distortions were a powerful incentive for the Community as a whole to end protectionism. Another incentive was that, since the protective mechanism was a quota, the Japanese earned rents from those cars that they did sell. This made Nissan especially fortunate; having earned rents from the cars it sold, it was at the same time given subsidies in order to invest in new plants! (An important effect of the new regime on state aids was to limit the access of other Japanese producers to such incentives, as will be discussed in chapter 6.)

Because of the economic distortions caused by trade restrictions, those national markets most closed to Japanese autos would, perforce, face the greatest adjustment costs. In that case the character of any new agreement at the level of the EU would be very important. If national restrictions were lifted suddenly, then severe dislocations might be expected.[4] On the other hand, a partial lifting might cause diversion from the more protected to the less protected markets—also unacceptable.

Another important factor would be the role of the rules, or lack of them, that would govern any new arrangement. It is to this institutional and regulatory environment that this study now turns.

EU Regulation and the SEA

In this section I show how completion of the internal market would inevitably mean an end to national restrictions. In the past some member states had effectively blocked internal harmonization until an external trade regime at the level of the EU was installed. By that means, national restrictions existed under conditions of regional free trade. With the move to qualified majority voting, the ability to block required a (small) coalition, not merely one vote. The need to resolve the problem of external trade was, therefore, even more acute.

The patchwork of limitations noted above in place at the national level before the passage of the SEA consisted of two kinds. Spain and Italy were allowed to restrict imports under Article 115 of the Treaty of Rome, which exempted certain national policies from the requirements of the Treaty of Rome where they were in place prior to a country's accession. In France and the United Kingdom the restrictions were informal. The completion of the internal market would have the effect of ending both kinds of limitation and of imposing on the Commission (and others) the necessity of either moving directly to openness or of somehow establishing EU-level restrictions. Section 36 of the White Paper specifically recognized this problem, and its implications. It is worth reproducing in full:

> If Article 115 were no longer to be applicable, any import restrictions would have to be applied on a Community-wide basis. The enforcement of such quotas, which relies to a large extent on the administrations of Member States, would require intensive cooperation between national administrations and the Commission. Should it prove impossible to eliminate all individual quotas for member states by 1992, internal frontier controls could no longer be the instrument of their application. Alternative ways of applying quotas would need to be found. (Com 85 310, final, 14 June 1985)

The problem was that the principle of free internal circulation of goods could not permit an exception to be made for the auto sector.[5] Nor could GATT rules allow discriminatory treatment of Japanese products. The perverse consequence was that any attempt to accomplish less than full and immediate openness, which was politically unacceptable, would have to occur as the result of an informal bargain.

The member states were well aware that the completion of the internal market would necessarily end national restrictions (Hanson 1998 argues otherwise). That was the reason for the failure of the EU to accomplish the harmonization of type approvals (as discussed in chapter 3). Without type approvals, limitations by one national government could be easily circumvented through the establishment of "parallel markets" in which, for example, Japanese cars entered Holland and were then reexported to France. However, it transpired that there was a mechanism for the informal control of auto sales readily available as a result of an entirely separate derogation obtained by the auto industry from the principles of radical market openness. This was the exemption from EU competition policy granted to automakers in their contracts with their dealers (OJC L, 15, 18 January 1985). This exemption allowed carmakers to grant their dealers an exclusive territory in exchange for exclusive representation. The importance of this agreement in the context of EU competition policy will be addressed in full in chapter 6. In the case of external trade it meant that should the Japanese automakers agree to some kind of voluntary limitation, following the completion of the internal market, the mechanism was in place whereby Japanese producers could monitor and control not only the overall level of their sales in the European market, but also the sales in each national market, notwithstanding the end to internal border and customs controls.

In fact (as also noted in chapter 3), Japanese sales of autos in the EU were already subject to monitoring by MITI starting in 1982. This control was the result of the efforts of Commissioner Davignon, with the result that several categories of manufactured goods from Japan began to be "monitored." The "announced" goals by which MITI signaled the market share likely to be garnered each year by Japanese imports proved to be an effective mechanism for governing what both sides referred to as "prudent marketing." Clearly, in conjunction with the restrictions on dealer contracts that gave close control over sales to the automakers, this precedent could form the basis for some "informal" arrangement after the passage of the SEA that stood apart from the EU's own rules on free circulation, and from GATT.

Although the Commission had begun to take a strong interest in the question of external trade with Japan from the 1970s, it had never had a central role to play. The Japanese preferred to take advantage of the wide variations in preferences over external trade that existed among the member states and negotiate separately with each. In the event, the passage of the SEA not only ended the effectiveness of national restrictions but also made the EU a plausible negotiating partner for the Japanese for the first time. This also, therefore, gave the transnational association of automakers a strong incentive to coordinate their position and lean on the Commission as hard as possible.

It is to the story of intra-European coordination, and international bargaining, that this account now turns. The outcome would not only settle the immediate future of Japanese-EU relations, but also permit the completion of the internal market for autos. The acceptance of the three remaining type approvals was an internal market issue, of course, subject to qualified majority voting in the Council. But the deciding factor was not the formal proposal itself—that is, harmonization of type approvals—but the linked issue of external trade. The crucial question was whether the winning coalition in the Council of Ministers on this issue would be a liberal or a protectionist one.

Since the proposed agreement on external trade was bound to be informal, the member states in this issue area were not subject to agenda control by EU institutions, or other interests such as consumers operating within the European Parliament. For that reason the controlling coalition of member states, reflecting the preferences of united producer interests, proved to be a "minimalist" one: the degree of external openness accomplished was minimal. While a permanent regional quota at the level of the EU was removed from the set of possible outcomes by the SEA—Germany, among others, would not have accepted it—nevertheless, regional market-sharing between European and Japanese producers established by the agreement was not far from the same thing.

It is worth noting how the national restrictions that constituted the status quo could not be reproduced at the level of the EU. However, political influence ensured that informal restrictions took their place.

The EU-Japan Trade Agreement

This agreement has been described in detail elsewhere (see Vigier 1992; and Mason 1994).[6] The purpose in what follows is to enrich existing understanding of the agreement by showing how the preferences of the various actors over the two crucial, linked issues of trade and FDI fostered cohesion among them, and how, given the anomalous institutional environment, this cohesion determined the outcome.

The Commission Begins Bargaining

The Commission—led by DG III, the directorate responsible for industry under the leadership of Martin Bangemann, together with Sir Leon Brittan of DG IV, one of the most influential commissioners—began a series of consultations in early 1989 intended to establish the basis for an EU-level response to this issue (*Financial Times*, 19 May 1989, 2). The divisions that existed between DG III and IV, and their respective heads, mirrored the divisions among the member states (see *Financial Times*, 10 July 1991, 6). By the end of 1989 the preferences of the member states had been solicited and internal research completed. This research formed the basis of two documents: a Commission staff working paper, "The Future of the Motor Industry (Sectoral Analysis)" (SEC, 89, 2275); and a communication from the Commission, "A Single Community Motor-Vehicle Market" (SEC, 89, 2118, final).

Familiar issue areas featured prominently in these documents: technical harmonization (i.e., type approvals), taxation, state intervention, R&D, training, and quantitative restrictions. The opening section of the communication from the Commission, which discussed the overall outlook for the industry, concluded by noting the great increase in competition that would result from the phenomenon of transplants. This led in turn to the proposal for a "transitional phase" in which Japanese market penetration should grow slowly in order that European producers might have a chance to adjust. More precisely, the Japanese should share any growth in the EU market, predicted to be modest in the 1990s, with European producers and actually reduce their imports, and by implication market share, in the event of a market downturn. As it happened, the EU market turned down in the very next year, providing a clear test of the degree to which such an arrangement could be made to stick.

The bargaining, therefore, would be over the nature of this transitional phase. There were two specific issues: whether the transitional phase was to be of fixed duration; if so, for how long, and whether transplant production should be included in the limits on the growth in Japanese market share. There was also the possibility that the EU would coordinate side-payments, in the form of re-structuring grants and other subsidies, in order to moderate the costs to EU producers of the move to increased openness.

At the beginning of 1990 the Commission—led by Frans Andriessen, commissioner of DG I, which was responsible for external affairs—began negotiations with MITI. What is most suggestive is that the Council of Ministers could not bring itself to write down a formal mandate for the Commission to work with. Only an "oral" one was granted. The various reasons were "remaining differences between the member states, worries that an official . . . position would weaken the EU's bargaining position, and fears that any official agreement . . . might violate GATT rules" (Mason 1994, 422). This statement reveals two crucial aspects that governed the process: it was inevitably going to be highly "informal," deliberately aimed at avoiding the constraints of the existing rules that governed trade (the EU's own rules as much as those promulgated by GATT); and the member states lacked cohesion, thus leaving the Commission exposed to the influence of industry, should it be better positioned to forge a united front.

Indeed, just as the EU settled on its position and began its negotiations, in early 1990, direct pressure from EU producers on their various national governments and on the Commission began to grow. By the time a preliminary agreement, known as "the elements of consensus," was reached in August 1990 between the EU and Japan, the automakers were thoroughly mobilized. The preferences, and the cohesion, of the mass-market producers are indicated by a meeting they had with Commissioner Bangemann (Mason 1994, 423–24). He had deliberately excluded the chairman of Peugeot from the encounter in the hope of obtaining a more friendly hearing but was disappointed. The producers found the content of this preliminary agreement to be unacceptable.

In this first attempt at an agreement a transitional period was adopted; it anticipated the eradication of national limitations on 1 January 1993, and their replacement at the level of the EU by a VER for a period of five years. However, the major automakers thought that this was too short a time for them to adjust. They were also dissatisfied because it did not include any specific basis for adjusting the respective market shares of the Japanese and Europeans in the light of changes in the overall level of the EU market. Finally, it made no mention of the role of Japanese transplant production. As a result, in the meeting with Bangemann and elsewhere, the European producers began to actively seek changes in the EU bargaining position; they did so as individual firms, working to shape the positions of various national governments at the level of the Council, but they also set about improving their ability to work in concert at the level of the Commission, through their transnational industry association.

The Producers Reorganize

Even within the mass producers there had been a range of opinion on openness, illustrated by figure 15. Peugeot, as noted above, under the control of its noisy chairman, Calvet, was opposed to any opening without reciprocity.[7] GM, on the other hand, while accepting the need for a transitional period, believed that adjustment was inevitable and ultimately in the hands of the producers themselves (*Financial Times*, 5 October 1990, 4). However, the threat of external openness was combined with important changes in those factors I specified in chapter 3 that tended to foster cohesion. The competitive position of the auto industry in general, and the specialist producers in particular, had declined further. Whereas the specialists had looked upon the Japanese threat as aimed at the mass market, the sudden and successful descent of the Japanese onto the luxury market in the United States in 1990 dramatically altered their calculations. Furthermore, in the four major markets of Europe—apart from Germany, because of the bubble in demand created by unification—registrations fell in 1991 for the first time in several years. I argued in chapter 3 that poor economic times should increase the willingness of firms to cooperate. Finally, due to dramatic changes in the character of the transnational auto industry association, the majority of the mass-market producers, including the U.S. multinationals, achieved effective control for the first time over the position articulated by the auto industry to the Commission.

The existing industry association, the CCMC, had been subject to a rule of unanimity. Furthermore, the U.S. multinationals were not represented, while national industry associations played a significant role. In short, the CCMC sought to articulate very different interests within the European auto industry and was likely to be paralyzed by the outlying preferences of a single member (as reported in chapter 4 in the case of auto emissions regulation). In late 1990 a group of automakers attempted to change the rules on voting toward a form of qualified majority voting. There was also talk of admitting the U.S. multinationals. However, Peugeot refused to accede to this change, at which point the other members, apparently by prior arrangement, exited the organization and set about establishing a new one under the leadership of the chairman of BMW, von Kuhnheim (*La Tribune de l'Économie*, 29 November 1990). The satisfaction of the Commission, in particular officials of DG III, was barely concealed. All this occurred just as the automakers were trying to apply the greatest possible pressure on national governments and the Commission over the elements of consensus.

At the beginning of 1991 the Association des Constructeurs Européens d'Automobile (ACEA) was established, in which the national industry associations had only an auxiliary role, and to which the U.S. multinationals were invited as members (see McLaughlin and Gordon 1994, for a good overview of the changes in lobbying institutions by the European auto industry). While the head of BMW, von Kuhnheim, wrote the association's new constitution, it was understood from the start that the mass producers would have "special weight." Although the association was governed by a form of qualified majority rule, issues rarely came to a vote, because, as the representative of a major producer commented in a private communication with this author, "either you are a member of the club, bound by the club consensus, or you aren't in the club."

The transnational interest group thus formed was effectively the instrument of those producers for whom the incentives and conditions for cooperation were favorable, that is, the mass producers. The market was soft, their factor costs were converging, and their products were becoming increasingly less differentiated. The gains from concerted action, therefore, had risen. Furthermore, I would expect that VW and the U.S. multinationals played a particularly important role in the new industry group. This is because the character of their national industry associations had the effect of diluting the impact of their views by including them with the views of many other kinds of interest (see the discussion in chapter 3). By contrast, in this issue area mass-market assemblers across Europe had more in common with each other than with the various elements that went to make up each of their particular national auto industries. Even if Ford and GM weren't "German" or "British," they were "good Europeans." Indeed, the complete regional integration of their R&D and production was held up as a model for the Japanese to follow. VW, by the same token, had less in common with the German specialist producers than with the other mass producers. It was therefore Ford and VW, in particular, who acted as entrepreneurs in the creation of ACEA. The distinctive difference between this and the earlier transnational industry association was the much increased control of these mass-market producers. (The preceding discussion was based, in part, on interviews with David Hulse, Ford, 25 June 1992; Dr. von Hülsen, VW, 16 June 1992; and John Wilson, DG I, 3 June 1992.)

At its first meeting ACEA produced a common position to serve as the basis for the bargaining between the Commission and MITI on the subject of Japanese auto sales in the EU (see the press release from ACEA, 20 March 1994, "The European Manufacturers Agree on the Opening of the EU Automobile Market"). It was at this point that the Commission and the member states started to shift position (interview with Dr. Hanns Glatz, Daimler-Benz, 10 June 1992). In short, once the mass-market producers overcame their collective action problem, their influence over the outcome increased significantly. The role the producers played is clear from this remark of Commissioner Frans Andriessen to the European Parliament, during a debate on EU-Japan relations and the auto industry: "The position taken by the Commission in its talks with Japan is largely the same as that adopted by the European car industry" (*Debates of the European Parliament,* 11 June 1991, 112).

In his testimony taken a year and a half earlier before the House of Lords, Dr. Glatz, Daimler-Benz's representative, noted that while his firm was not in favor of any restrictions, other producers were willing to accept five years, from 1992—that is, until 1 January 1998. In its conclusions the report of the committee also assumed that five years was a median position (House of Lords 1990, 11). By 1992 Glatz's views had changed; indeed, he can be seen as a bellwether for the views of the industry. He had new convictions: the transition was a necessary mechanism in order to get to the free market, transplants had to be counted with imports, and merely setting a limit to the transitional period was a victory for those interests favoring greater openness. (There was already talk among the others of a second "transitional" stage [interview with Dr. Glatz, 10 June 1992].)

The crucial question is the degree to which the shift of preferences within the auto sector toward a harder line and the increase in their level of cohesion were reflected in the character of the actual outcome. Given the "opaque" institutional environment and the high level of interfirm cooperation, my analytical approach suggests an agreement that favored the producers. It is to the nature of the agreement, therefore, that this analysis now turns. It will be apparent that while the agreement eventually established between the Commission and MITI was a compromise, in many ways the producers obtained the best outcome available. It reflected their interest in a long transitional period, the interest of a coalition of member states in a liberal investment regime, and the fact that bargaining occurred outside the EU's formal institutions.

The Agreement

The actual bargain made on 31 July 1991, unusual by the standards of most international agreements, is contained in the four documents that go to make up the agreement. First there was the so-called elements of consensus, the core of the agreement; this was announced in the context of two written statements, one by Andriessen and one by the Japanese minister for MITI, Mr. Nakao. In addition there was an "internal declaration" by the Commission putting a further gloss on two points in the agreement; and finally two "oral" declarations, one by each representative, which succeeded in highlighting the differences between the parties involved. This lack of clarity was deliberate and subject to numerous interpretations, even at the very moment the agreement was accomplished. Reinterpreting the agreement after the event became something of a minor industry, to be reported on below. The crucial question was whether transplant production was to be included in a global ceiling on Japanese sales in European markets (what follows relies, in part, on the report in *Financial Times*, 23 September 1991, 4).

The terms were as follows: the transition period was to end, definitively, at the end of 1999; this represented a seven-year period, longer than the one originally contemplated by the Commission when the bargaining process began. I argue that this shows the influence of the combined power of the automakers. Article 115 of the Treaty would no longer apply after the end of 1992, and all type approvals would be accepted throughout the Community by the end of 1992.

In addition, Japanese exports were to be limited in 1999 to 1.23 million units, more or less the same level as in 1992, given an agreed assumption over future levels of total EU demand. However, total sales of Japanese products would rise on the basis of an increase in transplant production to 1.2 million units. These estimates of Japanese capacity in Europe were exactly the same as those made in the internal staff paper of 1990 and seem to be deliberately conservative. The commission's estimates (SEC 89, 2275, 20) were at odds with reports published in the United Kingdom at the time of agreement, which (wrongly) put total output of cars and light trucks by transplants at close to 2 million by 1999 (*Financial Times*, 5 July 1991, 1). Whether the Commission's assumption about Japanese transplant capacity was in any way binding is a crucial question. In his "oral" remarks Andriessen indicated the importance of this working assumption about the level of transplants, but nothing explicit was stated anywhere else, and the Japanese merely reiterated their interest in open investment and free circulation.

However, the logic that tied many of the elements of the agreement together tended, of necessity, to imply restraint in the growth of Japanese transplant production. The crucial element was the agreement to "share" changes in the overall level of European demand according to some formula. In the "elements of consensus," section 4b, the level of exports was to take into account market variation. This was specified more closely in the "internal declaration" by the Commission, in which Community manufacturers were expected to benefit from at least a one-third share in any growth in the market. What was a Community manufacturer? If that meant non-Japanese manufacturers, then this market-sharing formula led to de facto limits on increases in the output of transplants. This was what was implied by Andriessen's oral declaration, in which a specific link was made between the overall share in increased demand to be enjoyed by European producers and the level of transplant output.

The question of national targeting was another area in which restraint was specified by the "elements of consensus" and also implies overall limits on Japanese market share. A regional market share figure—that is to say, the total share captured by Japanese products wherever they were made—was used by the Commission to calculate the future market share of the Japanese in those national markets that formerly had restrictions (although the Japanese never publicly admitted to the existence of such a figure). Of course, this calculation also implied limits on changes in the level of transplant output. The British, of course, rejected the idea that the global forecast represented such a ceiling (interview with Thoss Shearer, Department of Trade and Industry, 27 May 1992). For a more detailed discussion see Mason 1994, 430–32.

The critical aspect of what was a deliberately murky deal was the issue of monitoring. What the Japanese were *actually* willing to accept would be revealed through time. Indeed, in a sense the bargain represented only the beginning of a series of bargains, which might well extend beyond the official deadline. MITI and the EU agreed to meet twice a year, make estimates about future demand, examine the degree to which past estimates were accurate, and make adjustments accordingly. The overwhelming sense was that, being a VER, the agreement would be subject to continual reinterpretation. Raymond Levy, the head of Renault and the president of ACEA, stated soon after the agreement that "monitoring of the understanding by the Commission becomes of key importance. It will allow effective achievement in a factual way of the interpretation of the understanding as it was communicated to us."[8]

The deliberate uncertainty that surrounded the agreement and post hoc arrangements to manage it probably had several reasons. As noted above, an informal deal was the only kind of outcome possible in the light of the constraints imposed by GATT rules. That such a deal was realized was due to two factors. First, historically the Japanese preferred agreements that were not specific but that prescribed norms, such as prudent marketing. The JAMA had proved itself in the past to be an extremely reliable partner, for example in the agreement with the SMMT.[9] Second, instead of being a one-shot deal, the agreement took the form of an iterated game. We know that a characteristic effect of iteration is that it elicits cooperative behavior from the parties involved.

What cooperative behavior could the Japanese producers offer, what interest did they have in offering it, and why would the Europeans have accepted it?

As discussed above, inward investment by the Japanese would increase the efficiency of the European components sector. This was already happening by 1992 (see *Financial Times*, 17 January 1992). That would eventually help the European producers. The Japanese might also pursue joint ventures with European producers on specific projects from which the Europeans could learn. In short, the agreement was a mechanism by which the Japanese producers were admitted to the "club" of European mass-market producers. The implication of this agreement, even if an unstated one, was that their share of the market was contingent upon cooperative behavior.

What were the characteristics of this agreement that made it acceptable to some subset of the member states, such that the remaining type approvals could be agreed upon? From the point of view of the member states, side-payments that would enable some to gain from an open investment regime could form the basis of a coalition in support of it. In this regard Spain was a crucial player (see figure 14). Especially in the auto sector, its economic growth and exports depended on FDI, although it was EU firms who were the most important investors (on the structure of Spain's FDI see Stephen 1994). While a surge in Japanese auto sales in its formerly protected market would have caused significant dislocations, the prospect of future investment, by the Japanese among others, would be very attractive; after all, at some point Japanese investment in the auto sector in the EU was bound to be dispersed beyond the United Kingdom, and in that event Spain would likely be a significant beneficiary.

One way in which the Commission could enhance the prospects for intra-EU investment in Spain, among others, and lower the political costs to the member states was through side-payments to the European producers. In order to restructure, the European producers had to exchange old plant and old workers for new plants and new/retrained workers, often in the economic periphery of Europe. Funds provided by the EU could lower the cost of this adjustment. The industry was very interested in getting this kind of assistance. This was reflected in an ACEA position paper on restructuring in which the Community was asked to play a role in training and general restructuring through the regional development fund and social fund (see ACEA 1991). In response to this, in May 1992 the Commission produced a new communication on the future of the auto industry that indicated a willingness to play the role sought by ACEA (Com, 92, 166, final).

In short, the EU agreed, in principle, to subsidize the producers' adjustment costs, which would enable EU producers not only to obtain a "greenfield" advantage of their own, but to participate in new joint ventures with other automakers, especially the Japanese. The coalition of member states likely to support this outcome—liberal investment regime and subsidized adjustment—

were those on the "periphery" (Spain and the United Kingdom) and those confident in their competitive advantage or home to genuine multinationals (Germany). Significantly, France was home to the producer least likely to value this outcome, Peugeot. It had few links with other producers by way of joint ventures and therefore was the least able to "learn by doing" in association with others. The other "Mediterranean" producers were not much better off. Renault was in the process of merging with Volvo, but, apart from a joint venture in Colombia with Toyota, had no connection with a Japanese or U.S. firm. FIAT made trucks in conjunction with Ford and had extensive relationships with firms in Poland and the former USSR, but no relationships with Asian or U.S. competitors. By contrast, VW was on its third generation of co-production with a Japanese partner in Europe, with Toyota making trucks in Hanover, and shared the Brazilian auto giant Autolatina with Ford. The U.S. multinationals, of course, had the most extensive series of relationships of any producer anywhere.

The Political Endgame

It is not possible to give a blow-by-blow account of the bargaining that led up to the agreement—such was the informal nature of the process. A blocking coalition in the Council of Ministers was led by the "Mediterranean" member states (Spain, Italy, and France). From March 1991 onward they responded directly to the producers by insisting on a seven-year transitional period, two years longer than proposed in the existing tentative agreement (Mason 1994, 425). The crucial dimension, as always, remained the issue of FDI. Germany and the United Kingdom were, tacitly at least, willing to accept that kind of transition, as long as no numerical limits were set on the overall level of Japanese transplant production. German preferences over FDI reflected not only the presence of U.S. firms within its borders, and the possibility that the Japanese would wish to invest in a high-skill, technologically advanced region, but also its increasing role as a source of *outward* foreign direct investment. The crucial question, therefore, was whether the agreement would remain blocked over the issue of FDI.

In the event, it was predictable which member of the blocking coalition proved susceptible to side-payments. The last three type approvals were ratified after Spain withdrew (*Financial Times*, 8 November 1991). Spain no doubt expected to be a beneficiary from an open investment regime, as argued above. The Japanese may even have quietly indicated as much, and EU structural funds were perhaps promised by the president of the Commission, Delors. France, on the other hand, held to a hard line under Prime Minister Cresson, who had been active in mobilizing the producers the year before (interview with Christian

Mory, CCFA, 22 June 1992), although Mason (1994, 426) notes that even within France, divisions between Renault and Peugeot may have helped Mitterrand accept the compromise at the last. Overall, therefore, the "winning coalition" was that of the most internationalized producers—remembering that even they wanted a long transition period—and those member states sensitive to an open investment regime, that is, a coalition that shared preferences over restraints on trade and openness to FDI.

Conclusions

The mass producers accomplished much of what they wanted, short of a permanent regional VER, which would have actually represented a retrograde measure over the status quo (it would have effectively caused small-country markets to be restricted for the first time). Indeed, it could be argued that the market-sharing arrangements discussed above had much the same effect. The Japanese producers entered an iterated game in which they traded restraint and know-how for membership in the producers' club. The European automakers had a substantial breathing space in which market growth—or decline—would be explicitly shared with their Japanese competitors (there were even dark hints of a second transition period to follow the first).

The distinguishing characteristic of this episode is that rules played no part in the outcome. The agreement contravened GATT and the Community's own norms and regulations, and the political power behind it was sufficient to brush aside such institutional limitations. In short, the institutional arena, or lack of one, was endogenous to the political forces at work. For this reason also the arena was very small, restricted to the representatives of the member states, the producers, and the Commission.

The process was very typical of Brussels at its most opaque. Actors would make known their public positions (more often than not to Kevin Done of the *Financial Times*) and then "confess" their real preferences in a series of telephone conversations among themselves. The fact that type approvals were governed by qualified majorities did introduce a rule-governed procedure that allowed division among the member states to be overcome. But the proposal that mattered was the informal one establishing the length of the transitional period and the role of Japanese transplants. Agreement on harmonization was linked to agreement on very modest external openness. The control of the agenda in that case fell to the well-coordinated producers, who had a strong incentive to bully the Commission.

CHAPTER 6

Competition Policy in the European Union

Introduction

At the heart of the single market program was the idea that heightened competition, on a "level playing field," would yield welfare gains to consumers and efficiency gains to European industry. However, even after tariff and nontariff barriers had been eliminated, other distortions of the marketplace persisted, and these had to be carefully policed. For example, practices in restraint of trade and state subsidies would have to be monitored and sanctioned. But the difficulty of converging on a common antitrust policy, for example, is a classic coordination problem. A single policy was desirable in principle, but deep divisions were likely to exist over any particular choice; this made any common policy hard to adopt.

Furthermore, the logic of the legal framework that governed competition policy suggests that the auto industry, often suspected of collusion and the beneficiary of large amounts of state aid, should have felt the full force of EU regulation. Yet while the industry was restricted somewhat in matters of antitrust, I observe generally permissive treatment of the automakers. This requires explanation.

Answering these questions sheds new light on the role played by the legal and institutional character of the EU. The power to regulate antitrust and state aid was delegated to the Commission by the member states, and it enjoyed considerable discretion, sheltered by a well-developed legal order. Why did the Commission enjoy such a high level of discretion, and what outcomes did this institutional arrangement foster? Were the outcomes congruent with the interests of the member states, or was institutional "drift" of some kind at work?

I divide my analysis of competition policy into two parts, separating antitrust from state aid because of the significant variation that exists in the institutional and strategic environment of these two issue areas. In the second part of this chapter, state aid is examined. I begin with an analysis of antitrust policies. First I compare the approach so far adopted to law-based accounts of EU competition policy. I then analyze the preferences of the states and firms and go on to specify the legal basis for EU competition policy and the administrative mechanisms by which it was enacted by the Commission. Having laid out the institutional arena, I then report the outcomes of EU policy on antitrust as it was applied to the auto industry.

I find that the preferences of states were mixed. In general, this mixture accounts for the design of the institutional arena that governed competition policy. This point will be developed much more fully in the discussion of state aid. In the case of antitrust and the auto industry the governments of the member states had only a limited interest in, and so little influence over, particular policy outcomes—that is, specific antitrust legal proceedings. But they had some interest in an EU antitrust framework that deferred to the existing regulatory regimes of individual member states. By contrast, firms shared a strong preference for a level of tacit collusion, reflected in a formal legal exemption from some antitrust requirements. Beyond that I discover that the precise legal regime that governed antitrust, generated by European Court of Justice (ECJ) rulings, did give the Commission a degree of political autonomy and so served to moderate the influence of the industry.

Analytical Approach and Expectations

The preceding chapters analyzed policy-making in politically sensitive areas. These episodes were resolved by bargains at the highest levels within EU institutions. In particular, the Council of Ministers played an important role. I have argued that outcomes were shaped by the strategic interaction between firms and governments, as mediated by the institutional environment supplied by the EU. However, where rule making and rule enforcing had a less politically salient character, it might be supposed that the role of the governments of the member states was less significant and the role of supranational institutions and their legal processes, more important.

The Logic of EU Law

The EU is a *Rechtstaat*, in which the rule of law, including administrative law, is an important instrument in forwarding the purposes of the Treaty of Rome. For this reason, when issues of low political salience were subject to a technical and quotidian regulatory process, it could be argued that the inherent logic of the law, founded upon the Treaty of Rome, determined the character of policy outcomes. This kind of reasoning, as noted in the introduction, is found in standard accounts of the role of the Court of Justice (see, for example, Green 1969); it could be extended, without difficulty, to encompass the administrative law discharged by the Commission. According to this approach the character and extent of the EU legal order were *teleological necessities,* the inevitable results of court activity that had to fill in the gaps left by legislative inactivity. Other theories of this legal order explain the observed pro-integrationist slant of ECJ rulings by identifying factors external to the logic of the law (see Weiler 1991; Rasmussen 1986; and Burley and Mattli 1993).

Yet, taken all together, these approaches, while offering an explanation for the overall role of law in the integration process, cannot explain why judicial findings might vary from case to case. In other words, these kind of approaches cannot answer the question posed above: why was the auto sector privileged where it should have been punished?

I argue here that the mass of policy outcomes that made up EU competition policy were shaped by quite conventional political forces, that is, by underlying structures of interest, as mediated by institutions and strategic opportunity. Competition law, as it was applied to the auto sector, was shaped both by the preferences of the member states, who established the controlling legal regime, and by the interests of the major automakers. These preferences and interests were powerful to the extent that they converged, as I have argued repeatedly.

However, while governments and firms could act directly to shape policy outcomes, the member states also had the power to adapt the relevant institutional arrangements. I argue that the member states delegated power to the Commission in a way designed to serve particular political purposes, and the fact of this delegation had systematic consequences for outcomes.

The Logic of Delegation

There is an increasingly sophisticated literature on the politics of delegation by a legislature (or presumably an executive) to a bureaucracy (for a good discussion of this literature in the context of the EU see Pollack 1997). There are two plausible reasons, which apply in this case, why a bureaucracy is given a measure of effective discretion, or independence. The transaction costs of discharging directly the administrative minutiae associated with regulation are prohibitive for any busy legislative body; therefore it may delegate such responsibilities and devise instruments of effective monitoring. This kind of monitoring is discussed by McCubbins and Schwartz (1984) and McCubbins, Noll, and Weingast (1987).[1] Delegation may also have the effect of minimizing the political costs associated with the regulatory program (see Fiorina 1982).

I suggested in chapter 1 that these considerations may have played a significant part in the general institutional design of the EU. The role of these elements is nowhere better illustrated than in the specific case of competition policy. Clearly, regulating competition policy could not be accomplished on any intergovernmental basis; on the other hand, mutual gains—that is to say, the completion of the internal market—were available if the member states could coordinate this kind of Europe-wide regulation. In the event, law served as a "mask for politics" because the legal order that emerged from ECJ rulings supplied a prominent solution to the coordination problem at the heart of a regional antitrust regime, a solution that was legitimate and credible, albeit restricted in its purview.

At the same time, antitrust regulation was bound to be costly for privileged political clients within many of the member states. However, a useful consequence of delegation was the lowered political costs associated with subsequent administrative action. Full delegation had the effect of a credible commitment ex ante to realizing a competitive market. Those injured, therefore, would be deflected toward the transnational institution. The government of a member state could, at any particular moment, avoid the blame for some specific outcome. Indeed, it might make gallant, if ultimately ineffective, attempts to oppose it.

However, while these properties of the EU's institutions could suit the political purposes of the member states, delegation leads to agency "slack." There is a trade-off between obtaining the desired benefits of delegation and enduring the possibility that the agency might displace the goals formally assigned to it and supplant them with others. Of course, the procedures established by the principals, the member states, constrained the agent. For example, private interests could have been deliberately empowered in order to shape outcomes in a particular way (McCubbins 1985; Moe 1990). But inevitably the Commission had a degree of autonomy that, as I argue below, was at its greatest in the area of antitrust.

If and when the institutions of the EU enjoyed relative autonomy, then the preferences of the Commission could come into play—this institutional interest is examined below. However, those transnational firms likely to encounter EU regulation were potentially a countervailing political force. In other words, the relative autonomy of the Commission would be determined not only by the legal and institutional powers it was granted by the member states, but also by the extent to which it was able to enlist other interests in support of its rules, or deflect them where they were opposed.

All this taken together leads to the following argument. It is to be expected that the institutional design and evolution of competition policy in the EU reflected the desire of the member states to reap benefits from delegation. They needed a coordinated solution to the problem of competing national regulatory regimes. They found it by delegating power to the Commission, which discharged a liberal regulatory regime that had emerged through a process of legal precedent-setting by the autonomous institution of the ECJ. This delegation had several virtues: given a modest degree of agency slack, the Commission and the ECJ were inclined to choose pro-integration precedents, but the specific distributional consequences were uncertain ex ante, a circumstance that made acceptance by the member states easier. What is more, by establishing a strictly legal regime the member states were partly successful in insulating the Commission from private interests.

However, the desire of the Commission for legitimacy, and its modest capacity, gave mobilized interests a continuing degree of influence. This, too, suited the member states. By deflecting the political claims of private interests the member states reduced the political costs to themselves of greater integration. Yet at the same time, since the institution forced to address these claims was politically frail, it would never impose excessive costs on the powerful. In other words, the most mobilized private interests were able to mitigate the consequences to themselves of EU competition policy.

From this, and in conjunction with the analytical approach so far adopted, it is possible to summarize expectations about the outcomes to be observed. In the case of antitrust, given shared preferences among the firms involved, I expect to observe that the automakers enjoyed some power over policy outcomes, but that the strict legal regime acted as a check on them by granting the Commission a degree of autonomy.[2]

The Preferences of Governments, Firms, and the European Commission

In the discussion of the logic of delegation above it was suggested that some agency drift—independent action by the Commission—might be likely in this issue area. Therefore, in discussing the preferences of the various actors it is important, for the first time, to develop an understanding of the institutional preference of the Commission in addition to the preferences of governments and firms.

The Preferences of the Member States

The member states had divergent views on the subject of antitrust. This reflected their different national styles of regulation and different views as to the gains available from high levels of industry concentration, whether orchestrated by the state or not. Whereas France had traditionally seen government's role as that of a facilitator, bringing about marriages of convenience in order to create world-class enterprises (for example, the fusion of Citroën with Peugeot), Germany, through the Bundeskartellamt (BKA, or Federal Cartel Office), had a postwar tradition of much more stringent, pro-competitive regulation.[3] In effect, the member states were involved in the coordination problem known as the "battle of the sexes." While agreement on one standard was the efficient solution, which standard was to prevail carried with it distributional consequences. In each country interests were clustered about the status quo. For example, the *Mittelstand* in Germany was, to a degree, sheltered by the watchful eye of the BKA. This made the promulgation of an EU regulation on mergers and acquisitions very difficult, Germany being one of the most recalcitrant member states.

However, as far as any collusive practices by automakers were concerned, the governments of the member states were not directly affected. All the costs of such behavior were borne by consumers. Indeed, to the extent that producers were able to employ their market power to extract rents from their consumers, so they would be less inclined to ask their political masters for more direct economic assistance. The governments of the member states, therefore, had a preference for a single EU policy on antitrust to the extent that such a policy maintained a level playing field in the internal market. However, this shared interest was set against divisions over the specific character of the policy, and perhaps individual interests in sheltering a politically sensitive industry. These mixed motives are congruent with a regulatory regime that was applied uniformly, if only over a limited range of issues, but that gave formal exemptions to powerful players.

The Preferences of Firms

There is some evidence that suggests that collusive practices already existed in this sector on the eve of the SEA. Needless to say, no auto industry executive interviewed by this author ever admitted their existence. Furthermore, it is fair to say that automakers would like nothing better, as a general rule, than to design a better product than their competitors and "move more metal" than anyone else. However, these elements of this industry are significant: it was highly concentrated, with a long product cycle, large sunk costs, and increasingly similar cost structures and products. The benefits to the group of a collective policy of "live and let live" would be considerable and evenly shared.

The empirical record of firm market share in Europe (as noted in chapter 3) suggests such collusion. Between 1980 and 1986 the six major producers all had (roughly) between 8 and 12 percent of the EU market (CEC 1990a, 54). Of course, such tacit coordination would have always been subject to tremendous tensions. The automakers were involved not in some game against nature, but in a long-running mixed-motive game with each other. The industry was an oligopoly in which the main firms cooperated and competed by turns. By 1991 it would be fair to say that nearly *all* the main automakers of the world were involved in some kind of cooperative enterprise with *all* of their main competitors. Such activities might range from equity investments (by Ford in Mazda, for example) to technology-sharing agreements (between Renault and Volvo on engines, for example) to shared assembly or distribution agreements (between VW and Toyota over van production, for example) (see McLeod 1992). The general point is that in this kind of environment, where the shadow of the future was pushed back by repeated interactions in the management of shared projects over a long period of time, tacit cooperation in other areas, such as prices, was facilitated.

There was, however, a significant element in the situation that could have undermined such behavior. The automakers entrusted the final sales and servicing of their products to agents, the auto dealers. Given the different strategies available to dealers, and therefore the "slack" that existed in their relationship with the automakers, pricing practices would not be transparent, and tacit cooperation, therefore, could not be easily monitored. The way out was for the automakers to write strict, exclusive contracts with their dealers and so obtain a measure of control over their behavior. However, any such contracts, as will be seen, could fall foul of the provisions of the Treaty of Rome governing exclusive dealing. This issue, therefore, will serve as a convenient guide to the treatment of the automakers by the Commission.

In summary, the automakers found themselves in a strategic environment in which the returns from concerted practices were significant and evenly distributed. The major producers were few in number and accustomed to interacting in cooperative ventures, while their products and costs had converged over time. In short, they shared preferences over collusion and only needed the opportunity to realize them.

The Preferences of the Commission

Of course, in the event that the Commission enjoyed a degree of autonomy, what were its institutional preferences? It may be, given slack in its relationship with the member states, that it merely became the prey of whatever organized interests were able to seize it. However, I have argued that there may have existed an institutional bias within the Commission (as well as the ECJ) that favored "maximalist," that is, pro-integration, policy outcomes. The Commission was specially charged with forwarding the purposes of the Treaty of Rome and so was more likely to favor integration and the "Europeanization" of competition policy than most of the member states. As an institution it would enjoy prestige and resources commensurate with any expanded role. On the other hand, it would be reluctant to move too quickly and have its authority checked by the member states and its legitimacy thereby eroded. From this I conclude that it would pursue stringent regulation except where sectors with strong political claims were concerned. The influence of private interests would also play a role if poor institutional capacity made the Commission dependent on its regulatory clients for technological expertise.

In summary, collusion and its regulation fostered shared interests among the producers, but some divisions among the member states. If the Commission, as the guardian of competition policy, enjoyed significant autonomy, then a strict regime, perhaps similar to the BKA, might be enforced. However, the need for legitimacy and/or the technical cooperation of corporate interests might lead to a (relatively) permissive, but harmonized, EU regime, its stringency a function of the balance between private interests and the institutional ambitions of the Commission.

The Legal and Institutional Framework

The legal provisions of the Treaty of Rome granted the Commission significant discretion, the extent of which must be carefully mapped before analyzing the details of policy.

The Institutional Background

The Commission is uniquely empowered in the area of antitrust regulation.[4] It can make binding judgments on firms without recourse to the Council of Ministers or the ECJ (although its decisions may be subject to appeal in that court). Refinements to this power have been supplemented by decisions of the ECJ. However, in spite of the important role played by the Court in defining these powers, and in ruling on procedural matters relating to their execution, it is a distinguishing characteristic of competition policy in the EU that the Court has had little or nothing to say about the *substance* of Commission rulings, thus granting the Commission significant discretion in any particular case.

In a sense, therefore, the Commission is the last institution in a chain of agents and principals. The member states, acting in concert, wrote and rewrote the Treaty of Rome. In doing so they delegated certain powers to institutions of their own making designed to complete and monitor the contract (see Milgrom, North, and Weingast 1990 for an interesting example of this kind of delegation). To the Court was delegated the power of defining the boundaries of legitimate administrative discretion, and the rules by which that discretion was to be exercised. The Court, in its turn, allowed the Commission the freedom to make its own findings, only subjecting it to occasional review, largely on procedural matters. This very general picture will be refined significantly when the details of antitrust policy are examined below. The evolution in the character of this institutional arena over time will also be discussed, but the basic institutional arrangements just described have interesting political properties from the perspective of the member states.

The arrangement is exactly congruent with the logic of delegation discussed at the beginning of this chapter. It excused the member states from the very great administrative task of regulatory harmonization. Power was delegated to institutions with an institutional interest in the internal market. At the same time, as will be shown below, the *specific* character of antitrust policy emerged only through a process of legal and institutional maturation; this process, therefore, over which individual member states had no direct control, supplied a legitimate, prominent solution to the coordination problem identified above. At the same time, the political costs of such a regime were lowered as the member states shifted the blame for the consequences to the institution holding the power.[5] These costs could be further moderated by limiting the legal purview of the appointed institution and starving it of resources, thus making it dependent on those privileged clients the member states may have wished to shelter.

Having so far spoken about the institutional arena in the most general terms, it is now necessary to present a nuanced and detailed picture of the legal and institutional elements that governed EU antitrust policy, which was subject to distinctive patterns of institutional and legal change in the 1980s.

Antitrust in the EU

The core articles on which the authority of the Commission and Directorate General (DG) IV rests when regulating antitrust are Articles 85 and 86. In Article

85 concerted practices that distort trade between the member states are prohibited. In Article 86 the abuse of a dominant position is prohibited. The procedures by which this authority was to be discharged are contained in Regulation 17 of the Council (OJ 13, 21 February 1962, 204). The powers delegated to the Commission by this regulation are extraordinary. In particular, in Article 9 of the regulation the Commission is given sole power to apply Article 85(1) and 86 and has sole power to declare practices covered by 85(1) exempt under the terms of the escape clauses in 85(3) (subject to review of the decision by the Court of Justice). Furthermore, the Commission was granted considerable investigating powers under Article 14 of the regulation. It was able to examine books, make copies, ask for oral explanations on the spot, and enter any premises, land, or means of transportation.

In short, DG IV was the policeman, prosecutor, and judge in matters of antitrust. Legal challenges to this state of affairs have been rejected by the Court (see Harding 1993, 12–13). Thus the Commission seemed to enjoy a significant measure of autonomy and discretion. However, both elements were limited in important ways. DG IV tended to follow very legalistic reasoning when giving judgments, so the logic of the law perhaps served to limit discretion (see Wilks and McGowan 1995). The extraction of rents from consumers would be limited only to the extent that the law itself was strongly pro-competitive. Also, high-profile decisions could lead to political conflicts between commissioners. While DG IV had effective control over day-to-day business, the College of Commissioners—a very political body—ultimately ruled on its recommendations. This power served to limit DG IV's autonomy in some cases.

To these constraints were added practical limits on the ability of the Commission to discharge its responsibilities. In general, monitoring was on a combined police patrol, fire alarm, and self-reporting basis (McCubbins and Schwartz 1984). But each of these mechanisms was subject to specific failings, all of which limited the institutional capacity of the Commission. Notwithstanding its significant powers of investigation (police patrol) under Regulation 17, DG IV has always been poorly equipped to monitor numerous and powerful transnational corporations. It had, until the passage of the merger control regulation at the end of the 1980s, no more than 200 officers directly working on cases.

Another limitation was that, while under Article 3(2)b of Regulation 17 any natural or legal person can make a complaint (fire alarm), it was inevitable that collusive behavior bound closely those involved and fostered secrecy. Consumers and other potentially injured parties might know little of the problem and might not be able to organize or pay for legal representation in Brussels.

Only where other firms were involved might this change. A review of cartels fined by the Commission in the 1980s shows a great increase in its willingness to impose truly painful penalties on firms (see Harding 1993, 104).[6] However, these were cartels of intermediate goods producers. Downstream firms who consumed them, therefore, had a strong interest in setting off the "fire alarm." Between 1985 and 1989 only one cartel with individual consumers as its main customers had been fined (Dutch dairies). In other words, Commission action was only likely when one set of firms was opposed to another.

Finally, under Article 2 of Regulation 17, firms may obtain a "negative clearance" (self-reporting) by informing the Commission about agreements before they went into effect. However, that depended entirely on the willingness of the firms in question to cooperate in their own regulation.

These disabilities were mitigated by the evolution of the *actual* practice of competition law over time. First, a body of appropriate case law was established. The legal environment on horizontal mergers became fully developed as a result of various Court rulings (Goyder 1988, 139), ex ante control over mergers was granted (by implication) to the Commission in the well-known Continental Can case (ECR 215, Europemballage and Continental Can Co. vs. Commission, 1973, Case 6/72; see also ECR 461, Hoffman La Roche vs. Commission 1979, Case 85/76), and procedural issues were clarified (Goyder 1988, 415). By the 1980s, therefore, the Commission had a body of case law that it could rely upon, and therefore good information about the (modest) constraints it faced from the Court.[7]

An even greater change had occurred in the economic and political environment in which the Commission operated. During the 1970s, as Europe struggled to deal with the consequences of the oil shock, slow growth, and inflation, it was no surprise that a regulatory program that imposed even more adjustment difficulties on firms was a low priority. Indeed, a suspension of "normal" competitive practices in favor of the stabilizing effects of cartels and state aid was the effective "nonpolicy" adopted. However, by the 1980s there had been a neoliberal response to the second oil shock, in which pro-market solutions to Europe's chronic economic difficulties were now pursued. The SEA and the completion of the internal market were logical free-market responses at the regional level, and the EU's competition policy was now at the center of the stage. In short, the preferences of the member states were now much closer to the purposes embodied in those articles of the treaty that defined competition policy.

Finally, with some internal reforms in the early 1980s, DG IV, although still seriously understaffed, was better able to manage its caseload. Its internal processes were streamlined, and responsibilities within the directorate were better defined (see Harding 1993, 12).

In summary, the Commission enjoyed significant formal autonomy over competition policy, but its discretion was limited by the strict legal framework, and its autonomy was limited by the role of the College of Commissioners and the limits of its enforcement mechanism. However, its autonomy and discretion were enhanced by the legal and economic changes that occurred in the 1970s and 1980s.

Implications

What kind of antitrust policy outcomes, therefore, should we expect to observe in the late 1980s? As the legal and political environment shifted, greater antitrust activity is to be expected. But patterns in the way DG IV used its discretion are also to be expected. These will reflect the cohesion of powerful firms and DG IV's own institutional weakness. In short, the Commission exercised significant control over industry, based on a strict legal order, but that control would inevitably be moderated in the case of the most organized and best mobilized. It might also be expected that the governments of the member states would conduct political struggles within the Commission in high-profile cases with important distributional consequences. However, in general the regime on antitrust would have the virtue of keeping these governments out of the way of the political costs associated with regulation.

European Competition Policy and the Auto Industry

In keeping with the discussion of firm preferences above, I expect the automakers, being few in number and so well organized, to be favorably treated by the Commission in comparison with other firms subject to EU regulation. But, given the strict legal basis of the antitrust regime, I would expect whatever rules were established to be relatively infrangible. In the event, it is fair to say that the formal regime was favorable to the auto industry, but not plastic.

Limitations of the Empirical Material

The analysis is based, in part, on the detailed annual reports on competition policy published by the Commission every year. I examine the decisions relating to the auto industry for the years 1986–92, the years at the core of my research project, being the period between the publication of the White Paper on the completion of the internal market and the target date of 1 January 1993 (CEC 1987, 1988e, 1989b, 1990c, 1991b, 1992b, 1993; the publication date for each report is always the following year). However, in spite of the apparent level of detail to be found in these reports, there are significant difficulties associated with using them.

Much of the Commission's work in this area is out of plain view. A categorization of the Commission's workload for a particular year will illustrate this point. In 1989, in antitrust, the Commission took 15 formal decisions, issued 46 administrative letters, and dropped 382 inquiries.[8] The reasons given for ending the inquiries were that the practice had stopped, or was considered unimportant, or did not contravene the relevant articles of the treaty (CEC 1990c, 56). The Court allows the Commission to drop inquiries, even when they are the result of complaints, without giving any formal, public statement of its reasons (CEC 1993, 189). As a result, only formal decisions and some of the details of administrative letters are reported by the Commission in its annual survey of competition policy. Observers are left with the strong impression that competition policy has something of the character of an iceberg: only one-tenth of it is visible, and possibly subject to analysis.[9]

Furthermore, those formal decisions that are reported by the Commission represent high-profile cases. Therefore they represent the "easiest" cases for any analysis that wishes to show the political patterns behind regulatory outcomes. This fact will detract from the analytical bite of the study presented here. It could be argued that the "logic of the law" applied in most cases, which were not reported, while politics and political influence played a role in those few cases that were reported.

Finally, many "exemptions," whether from antitrust or state aid regulation, were obtained as the result of a protracted period of bargaining and so represented compromises. If, for example, a state proposed an ECU 5 billion scheme of aid, and after intervention by the Commission that proposal was reduced by 50 percent, how can the outcome be characterized? Is this a victory for the Commission, or did the member state, anticipating a bargaining round after announcing its proposal, ultimately realize its sincere preference after surrendering what was only really a bargaining position?

However, these difficulties may themselves be subject to counter-objections. It is in exactly those cases where the stakes were high that the forces at work shaping policy would be most visible. Arguably, these cases are the best test of the efficacy of EU competition policy and reveal the most about its character. As for the patterns observed in bargained outcomes, a careful case-by-case analysis is the way to decide on the relative balance between winners and losers.

The Block Exemption

By far the most important element of antitrust regulation toward the auto industry in Europe was the "block exemption" granted to automakers in their contracts with dealers. This was no less than a legal exemption that permitted restrictive contracts that made cartelization of the market possible. This provision reflected, in large measure, the interests of the mass-market producers. However, attempts by specific automakers to avoid even this permissive legal framework were turned back. In other words, powerful interests had influence over the establishment of formal rules but could not subsequently bend them. A strict legal order served to insulate DG IV in any particular case from irregular appeals.

In the 1970s the Commission exempted BMW's attempt to legally restrict the number of its dealers in Germany from Article 85(1) of the treaty (OJL 29/1, 1975). Since all automakers in Europe subjected their dealers to contracts limiting their numbers and their autonomy, pressure grew for a general exemption to be issued by the Commission for the whole of the industry (Goyder 1988, 224–25).[10] Following protracted negotiations between the parties involved, principally the dealers and producers—the consumer voice being conspicuous by it absence—such an exemption was granted at the beginning of 1985 (Regulation 123/85).

This exemption was singular: the automakers were able to limit both the character of retail operations and their number. The exemption was even more permissive than that granted to the breweries in 1983 (see Goyder 1988, 209–11). This combination of qualitative and quantitative restrictions represented nicely the balance of power between the retailers and the producers, which, while still favorable toward producers, led to an outcome that was not as one-sided as that observed in (for example) the beer case. The key was selectivity and exclusivity (what follows relies, in part, on interviews with Neil Marshall, RMIF, 5 July 1992, 27 March 1995).

The producers imposed standards and set conditions under which a dealer had to operate, the most important of which was that no product from a competing producer could share the premises. In exchange, the retailer got exclusive rights to the product in a geographical area. The bargain favored the producers in a subtle way: as they insisted on more elaborate investments, so the exit costs to retailers rose, and their bargaining power fell, when the time came to renew contracts. The benefits to the dealers came in the form of relief from intrabrand competition. Thus the danger of unwelcome price competition in the same product was avoided. In short, the arrangement created a comfortable dependency of the dealer on the producer and so increased the power of the producer over the prices charged for their products.

The Commission, aware of the dangers inherent in this, incorporated several elements into the regulation designed specifically to limit market segmentation by the producers. The Commission permitted dealers to meet demand from outside their authorized geographic areas (Sections 3.8 and 3.9). Models sold in one area of the Community had to be available, after a reasonable wait, at the going price from any part of the authorized network (Section 13.10). Finally, the exemption did not allow the setting of minimum or maximum prices by suppliers. However, these provisions were crucially weakened by the rule against intermediaries (Section 3.11). Dealers could not sell to independent agents except where the agents were representing a named buyer from elsewhere. In other words, entrepreneurs who might seek to arbitrage price differences across the EU were legally excluded.

While the approval of used auto sales across national boundaries was made easier by a notice in 1988, and the role of intermediaries was further clarified by a notice in 1991, the exclusion of intermediaries except where they acted as agents for specific consumers had the inevitable effect of limiting "parallel sales" (Commission Notice, 88/C 281/08, 91/C 329/06).[11] This limitation must be remembered when later Commission action to protect such sales is examined. The individual consumer had to obtain information about price differences and endure the relatively high transaction costs of trying to take advantage of them. Agents were able to help, but they could not hold stocks of autos and were themselves subject to delays and other obstructions placed in their way by the producers and retailers.

While the Commission was aware of the anticonsumer effects of market segmentation, because it led to higher prices, the benefits to the consumers, it argued, came in the level and quality of service these selective networks would be able to provide. Autos, it was claimed, were a unique durable good, with a long lifetime that required constant, technically demanding maintenance. The effect of Regulation 123/85 was to guarantee to all consumers the availability of service at the appropriate level, since the automakers and dealers had an incentive to make the necessary investments. (For a strenuous defense of this point of view by an official in DG III see Vigier 1992, 83–86.) Another virtue, it was claimed, was that it maintained the number of dealers, thus ensuring good geographic coverage. The decline in the 1980s in the number of U.S. franchises was seen as retrograde (Vigier 1992, 96). However, another way of looking at this extensive dealer network suggests that selective distribution awarded rents to the producers and dealers, of which the overmanning in the distribution network is evidence.

Evidence of the presence of rents comes from the actual spread in prices. From the outset the Commission identified the importance of price differentials as a measure of the degree to which the exemption was anticonsumer. It had intended to include them as a test, failure being grounds for the withdrawal of the exemption in specific cases. However, strong opposition caused the Commission to drop all mention of prices in the regulation. The issue was merely addressed in a notice published at the same time (OJC, 17/3, 1 June 1985). In the notice the Commission identified under what conditions it *might* withdraw the benefit of the exemption. However, it went on to note that differentials of as much as 18 percent would be permitted for limited periods and that a member state's tax or price control policies would also be taken into consideration. In short, while paying lip service to the dangers of price differentials and market segmentation, no specific threshold or sanction was identified.

Added to this was an even more important difficulty—the proliferation of models, marketing techniques, and other elements in the selling of autos greatly reduced price transparency. The history of the struggle of the European Consumers Union (BEUC) against this exemption, and its consequences, is one of seeking to establish and publicize the real prices of autos as they varied across the continent. But even though they had some success in increasing the level of information in this area, it was not translated into much more influence over policy outcomes (interview with Laura Mosca, BEUC, 24 June 1992).

In addition to these efforts by consumers, and partly as a consequence, there were also official attempts to pin down the actual level of price differentials. One study by the EU suggested that on the eve of the SEA the price dispersion in autos was above average (compared with other consumer durables) and had risen over the period 1975–85 (CEC 1988b, 120). The Commission itself, after expressing doubts about the level of price dispersion over a period of some years—doubts shared by the European Parliament—and after having great difficulty getting data from the producers, acted in 1991 (see CEC 1988e, 245; 1989b, 26, 266; 1990c, 40; and 1991b, 47). It published in 1992 the results of its investigation, which suggested that price dispersion ranged as high as 45 percent for any one particular model across the various European markets (CEC 1992a). DG IV, in commenting on the report, observed "very large price differentials" and noted that "selective distribution systems, as they currently operate, contribute to sustaining such differentials" (CEC 1993, 168).

The report was greeted warmly by the BEUC, which noted that "at last the figures we have been sending to the Commission year after year have been officially corroborated." The Brittan report, as the study became known, and a report by the Monopolies and Mergers Commission (MMC) in the United Kingdom earlier in 1992 that focused on U.K. prices and that was much more favorable to producers were challenged by all the parties with an interest in publicizing the results, or in obscuring them. The MMC report was ridiculed by the

National Consumers Council (NCC), and the Brittan report was ridiculed by Ford of Europe (interview with David Hulse, Ford, 25 June 1992). (BEUC had published its own report in 1989.) Whatever the various parties believed, the end result was no action taken by the Commission.

In summary, therefore, Regulation 123/85 had the effect of allowing, if not actually encouraging, the cartelization of the auto industry. Mindful of the imminent threat from Japanese competition, and the increase in market pressures consequent upon the completion of the internal market, the automakers, in particular the mass-market producers, were given an exemption that allowed the consolidation of their "club." Those structural elements in their economic environment fostering tacit cooperation were now formalized in the legal order governing antitrust. Furthermore, in spite of a variety of evidence indicating price dispersion, and therefore market segmentation, the relevant regulatory authority, DG IV, did nothing.

Antitrust Rulings

The record of actual decisions taken by the Commission in the area of antitrust up until the end of 1992 somewhat moderates this simple claim. While Regulation 123/85 fostered segmentation and tacit collusion, attempts to restrict the market beyond the letter of its provisions were firmly resisted. Other practices in restraint of fair trade were also addressed by the Commission, in particular issues relating to joint enterprises and takeovers and the abuse of patent protection. In general, the Commission was very favorable in its rulings on these latter issues, and more mixed in its examinations of practices that pushed the limits of Regulation 123/85. In other words, greater legal certainty led to greater autonomy for the Commission from the claims of the powerful.

In 1986 DG IV ruled against distribution agreements adopted by Peugeot; it ruled in favor of VW in a dispute with a distributor; and found Rover, the British automaker, guilty of abuse of a dominant position (CEC 1987, 63, 111, 113). In 1987 it ruled against certificates of conformity used by Volvo to limit parallel trade, and against FIAT's attempt to impose oil of its own make on its distributors (CEC 1988e, 75, 77). In 1988 it compromised with Peugeot over promotional schemes in Belgium; in 1989 it ruled against VW over the supply of right-hand-drive autos and against AKZO (a major supplier of auto refinishing products) in its attempts to restrict the supply of its products (CEC 1989b, 68; 1990c, 61, 64). In 1990 it gave VW clearance for the way it controlled the kinds of motor oil used by its distributors (CEC 1991b, 80). In 1991 it gave a major ruling in the ECO System/PSA case, in which Peugeot was threatened with the loss of its exemption under 123/85 unless it ceased hindering parallel trade in its products (CEC 1992b, 78). In 1992 it ruled in favor of BMW in a dispute with a dealer, on procedural grounds, and reported that the ECO Systems/ PSA decision had had a good effect on the position of wholesalers (CEC 1993, 189, 168). In short, notwithstanding its pro-producer elements, regulation 123/ 85 had the effect of drawing a line in the sand that the Commission was then able to closely police.

In other areas the situation seemed to favor the producers more consistently, for example in the area of joint ventures. In 1988 FIAT and Iveco, a truck manufacturer, were allowed to proceed with a joint venture (CEC 1989b, 69). In 1990 Renault and Volvo received a "negative clearance" for their increasing cooperation, while VW had to compromise in its takeover of a car rental company, and Daimler-Benz was denied permission to buy a share of ENASA (a Spanish truck company) (CEC 1991b, 39, 92). In 1991 two big parts producers (Magneti Marelli and Bosch) had to compromise over takeovers they were involved in, while in 1992 Ford and VW received a negative clearance for cooperation in the production of multiperson vehicles (MPVs), notwithstanding the complaint by Matra, which was a producer of the leading product in that segment (the Éspace, with Renault) but not a bona fide member of the automakers' club (CEC 1992b, 84; 1993, 94).

Finally, in the area of property rights the automakers were permitted significant concessions. In 1988 national laws were permitted giving automakers proprietary control over the design of spare parts (CEC 1989b, 99). In 1990 Ford was allowed some patent rights over the design of body panels. Finally, in the regulation for the harmonization of property rights, the automakers ensured that the design of spare parts was not exempted, to the fury of BEUC (see comments by BEUC on the Commission Green Paper on Industrial Design, 3 March 1992, 2). The issue of "must fit"/"must match" is a low-profile one, but with significant consequences for consumers and producers. To the extent that the automakers have a property right in the design of spare parts, so can they extract rents from competing parts producers. In this the Commission has favored the automakers.

Summary

In summary, Regulation 123/85 set the stage favorably for the producers, albeit further practices in restraint of trade using the distribution system were more easily limited.[12] They were also favorably treated in the area of joint ventures and patents. It is suggestive that negative rulings and tough bargains were imposed on parts makers or on sectors outside of mass-market autos, such as trucks.

In order to substantiate the impression that the automakers received good treatment, it is worth comparing a (rough) total of the Commission's decisions in the area of antitrust with the overall picture. Those listed above are not exhaustive. I report decisions for the period 1987–92 because the Commission's report for 1986 adopted different reporting techniques, making it incommensurable. The totals are presented in table 7 and seem to confirm the privileged position of the industry—3:1 in favor of the auto industry as opposed to 3:2 in favor of industry as a whole. However, the problems with the data make ambitious claims based upon it very unwise. The coding of the cases is somewhat uncertain; the Commission reports exemptions positively in some cases (that is, in favor of firms) even after having extracted significant concessions. These figures should be regarded as tentative, designed to give a rough sense of the disparities involved.

Since the auto industry is one of the most concentrated in Europe, likely to engage in all kinds of dubious practices, greater control by the Commission would be expected (on concentration in European industry see the figures in CEC 1989e, 41, 65). However, the figures reported above suggest that the contrary is the case—the ratio of favorable to unfavorable rulings clearly favors automakers. I argue that the kind of political and institutional factors identified here played a crucial part in this difference.

Outcomes in Antitrust

The automakers were a powerful interest, well organized and able to shape the EU's legal order in their favor. This simple state of affairs was mediated by the strict legal administration of that order. Given the support of the ECJ, the well-defined procedures of Regulation 17, and the relative precision of Regulation 123/85, the Commission was able to take a stand on certain issues against the automakers. While the shared interests of the industry were reflected in, for example, the block exemption, the autonomy enjoyed by the Commission was able to check the industry on occasion. The section that follows will finish with a more thorough, comparative evaluation of competition policy, taking the regime on state aid into consideration. In it the role of the member states was much more prominent, and the institutional environment differed significantly.

TABLE 7. Antitrust Cases, 1987–92

	Positive	Negative	Ratio
Total rulings	78	52	3:2
Auto-related	15	6	3:1

State Aid

In the previous section I identified a strategic dilemma that related specifically to the member states: the coordination problem inherent in establishing a unitary regulatory regime. A different and more challenging strategic dilemma was present in the case of state aid. The member states faced more than a simple coordination problem because there also existed a danger of exploitation. One state, through the judicious use of subsidies, might capture rents or economic activity with desirable externalities attached to it. However, such activity would be inefficient for the EU overall if everyone pursued it. The institutional changes chosen by the member states in an effort to overcome this political challenge are at the heart of the story that follows.

There existed a further difficulty. All the automakers had received state aid of one kind or another in the past. They were among the most privileged elements in the European political economies. To deny these clients the benefits to which they were accustomed would be very costly politically. How were the member states able to accomplish collectively what they had been unable to achieve singly, and avoid the political costs associated with a reduction in these subsidies?

Again, the institutional design of the EU, as it applied to competition policy, is part of the answer to this problem. In addressing these two questions I explain how the institutions of the EU helped to resolve the adjustment problems faced by the member states. However, it would be surprising if these institutional arrangements proved to be completely effective, because the relationship between the Commission and the member states was especially complex and fragile in the issue area of state aid.

In the case of antitrust in the auto industry, I found that the member states did not attempt directly to influence specific outcomes, although, as I argued, the overall design of the legal order suited them for various reasons. However, in other areas of competition policy there had been cases that excited tremendous political conflict. The takeover of de Havilland by Alenia and Aérospatiale, which was denied clearance by the Commission on antitrust grounds, is one of the best-known cases. Yet it is in the area of state aid that rule making by the Commission impinged most strongly on the member states. In this issue area DG IV was regulating not only firms but also national governments. Failure by the government of a member state to cooperate could result in the Commission, its agent, bringing it before the ECJ. It is this power that placed the Commission in a very curious position, with significant consequences for the institutional mechanisms that were adopted.

I begin by rehearsing (briefly) the nature of the principal-agent problem as it related specifically to the issue area of state aid. I go on to specify the preferences of states and firms and then establish the character of the institutional environment—drawing out the differences that existed between the issues of state aid and those of antitrust. Finally, I report on EU policy outcomes directed at the auto sector in the area of state aid.

Regulatory outcomes reflected the shared interest of the member states in reducing the collectively inefficient level of public assistance that this sector had historically enjoyed, as long as the political costs of doing so could be minimized. Constraints were placed on the level of state aid, but only slowly. In this case the ability of the automakers to cooperate was much more limited, due to the inherently divisive nature of the issue area, and the producers tended to rely on their separate relationships with particular governments. The institutional order was much less legalistic than in the case of antitrust, and so less insulated. Progress was accomplished less by monitoring and sanctioning than by increasing the level of information.

Analytical Approach

As noted in the last section, the institutions of the EU served two useful purposes in the area of competition policy. The legal order was a legitimate, prominent solution to the coordination problem of regulatory harmonization, and the Commission also served to deflect the political costs of this regulation away from the governments of the member states. This second purpose was even more pronounced in the case of state aid. However, legitimacy or credibility was more difficult to establish in this area because of the acute strategic dilemma faced by the member states.

As discussed below, an institution designed to serve as a prominent solution to a strategic dilemma with multiple equilibria will be hard to adopt in the case of a "coadjustment problem" (of the kind discussed in chapter 2). Because of the danger of exploitation, the institution must earn credibility before it is in a position to impartially arbitrate outcomes and assign costs and benefits. By the early 1980s the regime on state aid was ineffective. The story of EU policies directed toward state aid in the auto industry will prove to be the story of an institution seeking credibility. It couldn't do this by suddenly sanctioning recalcitrant elements; such sanctions would have led to challenges it was too politically weak to resist. But it was nevertheless expected by its principals to address their *collective* need for a regime that fostered mutually beneficial restraint among them.

The member states were in a difficult situation. They wished, by delegating the power to regulate themselves to an external body, to escape from the dilemma identified above. However, they would inevitably be concerned that the institution they had devised was scrupulously impartial over every specific case. They would also fear the consequences of "agency drift." If they gave this institution too much autonomy, it might impose outcomes on them far removed from their ideal point, outcomes that would be politically costly. The legal order, therefore, had to be nicely balanced so that it gave the Commission enough autonomy to make it credible, but not so much that it pursued its own institutional interest or generated outcomes that varied wildly from what was politically acceptable in any particular case.

It will become apparent that the answer to this dilemma was only an imperfect one. There was steady change over time toward the kind of credible regime that the member states desired, a change accomplished at relatively low political cost. But while transparency was increased, effective control over outcomes was subject to a lengthy bargaining process. This (often murky) deal making succeeded in imposing change on subsidized enterprises, but the clear politicization of the process degraded the credibility of the Commission. The most significant area of improvement was in obtaining and circulating information about state aid through monitoring and self-reporting, which is the easiest, though very useful, role of any institution.

Government and Firm Preferences

Given that some firms were more likely to have political patrons than others, subsidies from national governments were inevitably divisive. Table 4 in chapter 3 gives a clear ranking of the major auto producers in terms of their past ability to obtain state aid.[13] As this table suggests, the U.S. multinationals were at a constant disadvantage and so were always critical of the level of aid given their competitors, even if they themselves obtained it where possible (interview with David Hulse, Ford, 25 June 1992). They were anxious for a "level playing field," which was the avowed policy of the Commission.

From this it follows that were the level of state aid to decline in the late 1980s, the ability of firms to cooperate would increase. Furthermore, should aid be allocated by the Commission, as opposed to national governments, it could be available to automakers on an evenhanded basis. In that event the producers were likely to share preferences—for more! All the firms in a sector have a dominant preference for any subsidy that gives them an advantage over all other sectors, as long as these firms are likely to share the bounty equally. Indeed, as reported in chapter 5, a move to external openness in trade was purchased, in part, with restructuring funds to be administered by the EU. In short, while firms had a dominant preference for aid whenever they could get it, those without a national government for a patron would prefer a strict set of policies controlling the availability of state aid. The industry would be divided over national subsidies, but not over aid available to all through an impartial agent, such as the Commission.

The situation facing the member states was much more complicated. Many who had been willing to subsidize national champions in the past were no longer willing to do so by the late 1980s. The desire to reduce budget deficits and master inflation now took precedence over maintaining full employment. However, it may be imagined that the political costs of shaking off old habits were potentially high, although the economic boom, and buoyant sales of autos, in the late 1980s must have helped. Furthermore, the strategic environment was a delicate one. Each member state might have had an interest in moving away from the collectively inefficient levels of assistance that had hitherto existed, but each was also fearful that another, by persisting in subsidizing its own producers, might "snatch" a greater share of the industry, a share that, due to barriers to entry, could not easily be recaptured.

The actual levels of state aid given to all industry by national governments in the past varied significantly, as can be seen from the EU's first survey, published in 1989 (CEC 1989d, 10). Over a five-year period, 1981–86, it is apparent that Luxembourg and Italy employed state aid at roughly four times the level seen in the United Kingdom, Denmark, and the Netherlands. While neoclassical economics supposes that one country should be indifferent to unwise political payoffs made by another (it should merely avoid them itself), international trade negotiations have increasingly focused on issues such as subsidies (in part, of course, because significant tariff barriers have been progressively eliminated). In the context of the EU, this wide variation in the level of subsidies employed by various countries, therefore, would inevitably be a source of division.

However, the most divisive aid is that spent on specific sectors. Here the mature, "sunset" industries of steel, coal, shipbuilding, and railways consume, on average, half of the funds so allocated (Gilchrist and Deacon 1990, 36). Three of these industries, of course, were subject to Community regulation from the start. It was in the other manufacturing sectors that regulation at the level of the Community was very underdeveloped, and it was here that there existed a danger that the economic adjustments imposed by the internal market project might lead to even greater attempts by member states to externalize the political costs with even higher levels of subsidies. Nowhere was this more likely to be true than in the auto industry.

In summary, the member states had a common interest in cutting off aid that inflated industry capacity without helping industry to become more competitive, as long as they could endure the political costs of doing so and were not exploited by their partners. The member states also shared an interest in a regime on state aid that could help the industry make "positive" (pro-market) adjustments and so be ready for intensified competition following the completion of the internal market. But these shared interests were subject to the danger of exploitation. One state might attempt to "buy" some kind of economic advantage over its partners, which, even if unsuccessful from the point of view of pure economic efficiency, would serve to shift the political costs of adjustment onto others. This was the reason why the best response of all member states—not to subsidize—was hard to accomplish collectively.

Expectations

These preferences and this strategic dilemma yield simple expectations about the kind of institutional arrangements adopted. If the Commission was to respect the sensibilities of the member states, while also seeking to perfect the internal market, then the steady imposition of an EU regime on state aid would have to occur slowly. The institutional interest of the Commission in pushing forward the integration project would always be weighed against the preferences of a core group of the member states. A slow rate of progress was inevitable anyway, because of the small resources available to the Commission for enforcement. From this it should be expected that new grants and schemes were subject to stricter controls than older ones. All this would minimize the political costs to the member states of detaching themselves from clients accustomed to state assistance.

As for the strategic element, the institutional environment would be a crucial determinant of the ability of the member states to avoid suboptimal outcomes and overcome their coadjustment problem. It would be expected, therefore, that restraint by national authorities would be a function of the credibility with which the Commission discharged its regulatory responsibilities and effectively enforced the rules governing aid. However, taken in conjunction with the political and institutional constraints identified above, this posed a "Catch-22" for the Commission. It could not move quickly to impose strict limits on state aid, but the more slowly it moved, the less credibility its actions would enjoy. One way forward, as will be seen, was for the Commission to make the most of its powers to obtain information and circulate it, thereby increasing transparency and making unauthorized payments public.

Finally, delegating the power to distribute aid to the EU, a possible long-term development following the steady expansion of the EU's "cohesion" funds and funds for technological research, was one kind of response that could meet the needs of the member states. State aid from national governments was a divisive issue for firms and the governments themselves, but less so where it was centralized and designed to encourage, rather than prevent, adjustment.

The Legal and Institutional Framework

Articles 92 and 93 are the main legal basis of the Commission's power to control state aid (in addition to the work cited above on competition policy, see also Gilchrist and Deacon 1990). This power has a contradictory element to it. Under the principle of "compensatory justification" aid must be aimed at some Community objective, rather than the interests of the state or firm in question (Evans and Martin 1991, 90–91). On the one hand, in Article 92(1) the treaty simply stated that "any aid . . . that distorts or threatens to distort competition" is incompatible with the common market. However, in 92(2) and 92(3) it goes on to list those aids that are, or could be, compatible with the common market. They are aid of a "social character," aid in response to disaster, aid granted as a result of the division of Germany, aid to promote economic development in poor areas (with high unemployment), aid to promote projects of common interest, and aid aimed at facilitating the development of "certain economic activities."

This contrast between what is forbidden and what might be exempted had the effect of giving the Commission tremendous discretion. Article 92 itself is not directly effective, that is, not subject to application or interpretation by the national courts. And the ECJ has limited itself to ruling on only procedural matters except in extreme cases (Evans and Martin 1991, 80; see, for example, Philip Morris Holland BV vs. Commission, ECR 2671, Case 730/79, 1980).[14] Therefore, while case law has served to provide the procedural framework for policy on state aid (there being no equivalent to Regulation 17), economic rationale is typically included in the Commission's evaluations of the actual effects of any particular project (for example, see CEC 1991a, 19–29). The economic rationale employed is known as the principle of compensatory justification and requires a separate analysis of each case, no general rule being useful. In short, it is up to the Commission to establish what *kind* of aid and what *level* of aid are acceptable. The legal order established by the ECJ only defined procedures, not criteria. (On the discretion of the Commission within the context of the law see Bluman 1992, 730–32.)

An attempt in the late 1980s by Italy (among others) to introduce the equivalent of Regulation 17 to cover the issue area of state aid was successfully resisted by the commissioner for DG IV at the time, Leon Brittan. It was a proposal clearly designed to limit the discretion of the Commission and so set in stone the existing permissive regime, which Brittan wished to steadily tighten (see Slot 1990). Procedural changes in the early 1980s, when state aid issues were no longer submitted to the Council of Ministers as "A" items on the agenda (requiring no debate), already meant that the institutional arena had become less insulated from the member states (Wilks 1992). By retaining the discretion derived from the "economic rationale" it used in each case, the Commission had some freedom to pursue its institutional interest in greater subsidy control, even if it could only be accomplished through a process of political bargaining.

Monitoring was done on a combined police patrol, fire alarm, and self-reporting basis. In Article 93(1) the Commission is required to keep under review all existing systems of aid. In 93(3) the member states are required to notify the Commission if they are about to grant aid or alter an existing aid program. However, the limitations of the Commission's institutional capacity and its lack of staff, noted above in the case of antitrust, applied even more strongly in the case of state aid in the 1980s. The customary anecdote was that there were 150 people involved in handing out aid in the Walloon region of Belgium and only three dozen monitoring it for the whole of the EU. The consequence of this was that by the middle of the 1980s the Commission was only able to keep up with new notifications (self-reporting), rather than being able to examine existing grants or projects (Gilchrist and Deacon 1990, 44).

Nevertheless, by the middle of the 1980s the existing regime on state aid in the EU had undergone an evolution similar to that described above in the case of antitrust. The procedures by which DG IV operated were clearly established as a result of a sustained series of legal challenges by the member states (Slot 1990).[15] Also, the political and economic environment was somewhat improved. Here the turn to neoliberal solutions by the member states, and the move to complete the internal market, had a contradictory effect. The recession in the early 1980s was very costly for those member states who had responded to the difficulties of the 1970s with public subsidies for politically favored firms. As noted above, this could no longer go on in an era when taxpayers were less willing to be taxed, and budgets harder to balance. This situation made a general move toward restraint more acceptable. On the other hand, the 1992 project was likely to impose adjustment costs that might, in the short run, provoke a greater demand for subsidies.

All this points to the most important element in the institutional arena governing state aid. Notwithstanding the divisions that existed between the member states over antitrust, the principal subjects of Commission initiatives in that issue area were firms. By contrast, state aid, by its very nature, put the Commission in the position of regulating and (perhaps) sanctioning the member states themselves. The institutional arena reflected this dilemma. The preferences of the member states had shifted toward the institutional interest of the Commission in limiting subsidies, and the institutional arena gave the Commission the discretion necessary to steadily increase controls. But this discretion also led to bargaining with the governments themselves and so intense politicization, which detracted from the credibility of the state aid regime.

State Aid and the Auto Industry

I begin the analysis of EU policy by focusing on the specific framework adopted by the Commission in 1989 that governed aid in this sector (89 C, 123/03). Its character reveals much about the political environment surrounding the regulation of aid by the Commission. I go on to analyze a few revealing episodes in which specific firms and states submitted to the scrutiny of the Commission. This approach was adopted because of the limitations of the Competition Reports, upon which much of what follows is based. These problems were identified in the case of antitrust and apply even more forcefully in the case of state aid. It is not reasonable to distinguish exactly between the winners and losers. Each case represented a bargained outcome in which the bargaining process was lengthy and opaque, and the outcomes themselves difficult to enforce. At the end an overall evaluation of the effectiveness of the regime is presented, but without the help of a formal scorecard of EU policy.

The State Aid Framework

The background to the framework on aid to the industry is familiar. The period 1973–85, a time of crisis in the industry, saw many major producers being subsidized by their governments because those governments were not willing to absorb the political costs of allowing such large employers to go out of business. This state aid had a distorting effect on the market, and it is quite possible that by the late 1980s there would have been only four major producers left had a free market been allowed to operate. (For a comprehensive analysis of state aid measures and the auto sector see CEC 1988c; and 1990a.)

As was noted in the discussion on overall levels of aid, sunset industries such as steel, shipbuilding, and textiles (not to mention agriculture) earned the lion's share. However, of the remainder it is estimated that the majority went to the auto industry (CEC 1991a, 38). It is this salience that accounts for the Commission's framework on state aid to the sector, which was the only industry not in secular decline to be treated in such a way. The truth was that the auto industry did resemble a "sunset industry" in important ways. It was characterized by a serious overcapacity and generally low profits (Wilks 1989, 170).

The framework, published after agreement among the member states' representatives, illustrates nicely the priorities shaping the policy toward aid in this sector and the strategy employed by the Commission (and, by extension, the member states) for getting it under control. When individual cases are examined in which the Commission bargained with member states, these are the criteria that operated.

It is important to remember that unlike Article 85(1), which stated that all collusion was, in principle, prohibited, not all state aid was prohibited—it was merely more or less desirable. The framework defined "good" and "bad" aid and established the underlying principle that even where aid was acceptable, the level had to be commensurate with the objective. The most straightforward issue was operating aid, which was declared unacceptable. Rescue and restructuring aid could only be approved in exceptional circumstances, as could aid for innovation, modernization, and rationalization. In that event it was to be accompanied by a "radical change" in the structure of the company—in other words, appropriate downsizing. On the other hand, aid for R&D, regional aid, and aid for vocational training was to be viewed positively.

Clearly, the member states agreed that there should be no money to sustain unprofitable capacity, and no money for new investment unless it was accompanied by dramatic rationalization. On the other hand, categories of aid that could serve as the basis for improving the competitiveness of the auto industry were welcome. Obviously, R&D fell into that category, and so did vocational training, inasmuch as it lowered the cost of adopting new techniques. Finally, regional aid, by giving firms access to greenfield sites with all their attendant advantages, could significantly help the industry adjust to heightened competition.

The shift from a rusty economic core to greenfield sites on the economic periphery of Europe, employing green labor, was seen by many as an inevitable industry development (interview with Dr. Achim Diekmann, VDA, 15 June 1992). This was especially likely because these were advantages enjoyed by

Japanese FDI (as reported in chapter 5). Ford and VW were the first to take significant advantage of the permissive approach of the Commission. They received an antitrust waiver for collaborating on a minivan project, and significant regional aid, acceptable under the framework because the plant was to be in Portugal. In short, aid aimed at restructuring or rationalization was seen as the route to competitiveness, a sentiment echoed by the commissioner of DG III, Martin Bangemann (1992, 368).

But this hierarchy of acceptable aid was not, perhaps, the most important part of the framework. It also required prior notification from the member states for the first time and laid out, in considerable detail, how such notifications were to be made. In other words, it represented a program to heighten the transparency of aid in the auto sector. Most of the framework is given over to two annexes, one in which a standard form for notifying the Commission about a new aid was presented. The form and amount of assistance had to be identified, as did its purpose, the share of the total invested (that is, the intensity of the aid), and the consequences for the marketplace. In the second annex a form was presented for the annual reporting of all state aid by each individual member state. As suggested in the discussion above, given the lack of credibility in the Commission's past regulation of this sector, one way to generate cooperation with reference to aid was to increase information, a role for which the Commission was well suited. These reporting requirements served just such a purpose.

In short, the framework was effective in two important ways but subject to one significant shortcoming. The member states delegated to the Commission significant discretionary power; at the same time, they provided guidelines for its use. While they agreed on the *outlines* of a policy in this area, the Commission enjoyed almost complete discretion in applying the principles to individual cases. The member states also agreed to reporting requirements that would restrain their behavior. Delegation made regulation on a daily basis easier and less politically costly for national governments because they could credibly deny responsibility. Higher levels of information would also serve to stigmatize backsliders among their ranks. However, the discretion enjoyed by the Commission, taken in conjunction with its weak political and institutional position, would inevitably lead to highly politicized bargaining over outcomes, which would harm its credibility. In the event, the Commission succeeded in slowly tightening the reins on the member states. In 1990 it actually moved beyond the regulation of new schemes and also began reviewing existing ones (CEC 1991b, 15). However, as I will argue shortly, some players would find the constraints much stricter than others, for political reasons.

Bargained Outcomes

I have already noted that many member states wished to shrug off old obligations to firms that had cost a lot of taxpayer money. One way to do this was to privatize them, where possible. The two cases of Renault and Rover present an interesting comparative example of how bargaining in high-profile cases occurred, and how the relative influence of the actors involved was reflected in the outcomes.

The problem was that both firms were technically insolvent, as a result of the monies owed to their respective governments. These sums had to disappear if privatization was to occur. The election of a conservative government in France in 1986 led to the plan to privatize Renault, but parliamentary opposition, primarily from the Communist party, delayed it. The plan called for an end to Renault's status as a *régie* (or public corporation), and its recapitalization with FF 12 billion, since the firm's liabilities had exceeded its assets since 1985. The French government then entered a series of protracted negotiations with the Commission, trying to establish the basis on which the recapitalization would be permissible. These negotiations, which had reached a compromise by 1988, were further complicated by another change of government, as a result of which the French were less willing to change the legal status of the firm. This increased recalcitrance inclined DG IV to force Renault to repay FF 9 billion in aid, which led to a new compromise in 1990 (CEC 1989b, 175; 1990c, 165; 1991b, 162).

The outcome was a mixture of aid in combination with reductions in capacity (including the closure of the plant at Billancourt) and an eventual change in legal status to a *société anonyme* (private corporation) (see *Financial Times*, 16 November 1989, 32). The change in legal status in fact suited Renault's management because they were now able to pursue closer links, including an equity swap, with Volvo. Two aspects of this outcome are significant. In order to ensure that its requirements were being met, DG IV found itself involved in the detailed questions of firm management and investment decisions. Second, the eventual outcome was not too burdensome politically for the French government; the effect of the legal authority of EU institutions made possible politically difficult choices, including shutting down one of the most politically sensitive industrial plants in the country.

The Rover case was simpler. The British Conservative government was, of course, eager to privatize the group. The government saw itself as having been "maneuvered" into providing £990 million in aid for British Leyland in 1981 and resented the fact. In 1988 a deal was made between the government and British Aerospace Plc (BA), of which the centerpiece was a cash injection of £800 million in order to write off Rover's debts. In exchange, BA was prevented from using Rover's accumulated debts as a tax write-off. The Commission modified the deal by reducing the size of the cash injection and insisting on a supervisory role in Rover's subsequent restructuring (CEC 1990a, 20). This very satisfactory deal, from the point of view of the British government and BA, was subsequently called into question as a result of revelations of side-payments that the British government may or may not have made to BA in its eagerness to be rid of Rover (even the European Parliament got involved in this; see OJC 284/56, 12 November 1990). In 1990 the Commission identified £44.4 million in illegal aid that it required to be repaid (CEC 1991b, 162). BA appealed to the ECJ, from which it received relief (on procedural grounds) in 1992 (CEC 1993, 235). The Commission then reopened proceedings against it under 93(2) of the treaty!

This episode reveals the problems faced by the Commission in monitoring deals. The preferential tax arrangement from which BA was said to have profited was a very difficult thing to discover. The arrangements were uncovered accidentally by the National Audit Office, a U.K. government institution. Furthermore, the case dragged on for many years—the sale occurred in 1988, and a new proceeding was opened in 1992. Finally, there is perhaps a suspicion that BA was sternly treated because it was not a member of the club (of course, the Conservative government in the United Kingdom was not a well-behaved member of the European club either). The very considerable sums written off by Renault make the advantage secured by BA appear small. In other words, policy was dogged by problems of low transparency, political influence, and procedural tangles.

The suspicion that club membership was important is given even greater weight by the comparative experiences of Daimler-Benz (DB) and Toyota in the matter of aid from a local authority. DB had planned an extensive new investment in Restatt and received from the enthusiastic state government of Baden-Württemberg significant promises of aid. The project attracted the attention of the Commission, which insisted on limiting, but not eliminating, the aid. The balance (over DM 100 million) was permitted on the basis that DB was going to "repay" it by virtue of all the taxes it would contribute to local authorities (CEC 1988e, 220). By contrast, Toyota, which opened a new plant in Derbyshire, to the delight of the local authority, received no cash incentives. However, the Commission decided that the local authority had sold property for the plant at less than fair market value, and Toyota was forced to repay ECU 6 million to the county council (CEC 1992b, 153). This episode occurred later, at a time when the Commission was generally exercising greater control. However, membership in the producers' club appears to have yielded benefits to DB.

It is not possible to discuss here all the cases reported annually by the Commission. However, before reviewing summary statistics for the period in question, the history of aid to FIAT should be quickly examined. Its record, after all, was spectacular even by the standards of the auto industry (see table 4, chapter 3). In 1987 the Commission opened a 93(2) procedure against Alfa-Romeo because of the capital infusion it had received and the sale price the Italian government charged FIAT when it purchased the firm, in spite of a competing offer from Ford, in 1987 (CEC 1988e, 168; see also Friedman 1989 and the discussion in chapter 3). Under the terms of the deal between the Italian government and FIAT, 66 percent of Alfa-Romeo's lire 2.1 trillion debt was to be written off, and FIAT would not begin paying the agreed price of lire 1 trillion until 1993. The Commission investigation was expanded in 1988 and decided against Alfa-Romeo in 1989. Over ECU 600 million was to be repaid. However, funds granted to FIAT to modernize the Alfa plants in the South were permitted, as the Mezzogiorno has always been an object of EU regional policy (CEC 1989b, 179; 1990c, 164). By buying Alfa-Romeo, a producer with plants in a regionally depressed area, FIAT increased its access to state aid, even after the passage of the framework agreement. How much of Alfa-Romeo's aid was actually repaid to the government remained a mysterious question. New procedures were opened in 1991 but dropped the next year (CEC 1993, 235).

The discussion above gives the impression that the regime on state aid was relatively permissive to all the members of the producers' club. The summary statistics reflect this fact. In addition to the decisions against Toyota and against Alfa-Romeo, only one other negative decision was handed down, against aid granted by the Belgian government to VW (CEC 1992b, 397). Many other cases were the subject of protracted bargaining. They cannot be easily coded into positive or negative ones, but an increase in rigor on the part of the Commission over time is apparent. Nevertheless, progress was slow, and the most progress has been in the area of increasing levels of information. Automakers, due to the bargaining encouraged by the Commission's discretion, were even better treated in this issue area than they were in matters of antitrust.

In the case of state aid, the divided preferences of the automakers mattered less than the power of the member states. They devised an institutional environment that attempted to strike a very fine balance; on the one hand, they successfully delegated some power to the Commission to regulate their behavior. This delegation of power resulted in a tightening of the rules, at low political cost to the member states, while those practices that were permitted had, it could be argued, "pro-market" consequences. On the other hand, the discretion granted to the Commission allowed for each case to be the subject of a separate bargain. This gave the member states the chance to moderate outcomes where necessary but at a cost in lost legitimacy to the regulatory regime, which stunted its development. In truth, the legal and institutional arrangements governing state aid could not entirely resolve the acute strategic dilemma identified at the outset that faced the member states.

Conclusions

The critical institutional difference between the issue areas of antitrust and state aid was the issue of discretion. In each case the member states had the ultimate control enjoyed by principals in a principal-agent relationship. But the rationale upon which the Commission discharged its delegated powers differed. In the case of antitrust it had little discretion and was constrained to apply a legal order forged for it, for the most part, by the ECJ. In the case of state aid it had much more discretion. The Commission had to apply a form of economic rationale in each case. This rationale opened the door to bargaining in many instances. In short, there seems to have been a paradoxical trade-off: a strict legal order limited discretion but increased autonomy, while greater discretion led to an erosion of autonomy.

The automakers fit into this picture in a reasonably simple way. They had a common interest in collusion, and that was reflected in a favorable exemption from some antitrust requirements. But they were unable to chisel at the edges of this legal arrangement; the legal order restrained them. In the case of state aid they were divided, and so the important relationships were much more likely to be between firms and national (or subnational) governments (where such governments were disposed to act on behalf of firms for political reasons) rather than among the firms themselves, with the exception of joint ventures.

The member states, who were in the curious situation of having to regulate themselves, were more successful in devising solutions to their needs in the case of antitrust. It is clear that the legal order, which emerged from rulings by the ECJ and the Commission, was a credible and legitimate prominent solution to the coordination problem faced by the national governments. The member states made no attempt to interfere in those cases that involved the auto industry. Indeed, even in other sectors complaints never resulted in action, such as changes in the rules, which suggests that the regime served their purposes. On the other hand, the strategic dilemma in the case of state aid was more severe, and the need for control led to a less autonomous and less credible regulatory regime. It was, in other words, only a moderately successful institutional design, at least in the short term.

CHAPTER 7

Economics, Politics,
and Institutions

Introduction

By 1995 the pessimistic views of the future of the European auto industry that seemed to be so widespread only a few years earlier had proved to be largely unwarranted. At one of its main showplaces, the Frankfurt motor show, an air of confidence reigned, notwithstanding the continuing effects of the recession. For Renault and FIAT in particular, companies that had faced some of the greatest adjustment difficulties, the show was an opportunity to roll out exciting new models in the important midrange segment of the market, to add to their recent triumphs in small-car design and development. What was more, the Japanese producers had failed, so far, to realize significant gains in market share even if imports and transplant production were counted together.[1] The European auto industry had exceeded its own expectations and now appeared to be much more competitive than imagined only a few years ago.

To what extent was this situation the result of a well-managed mix of policies pursued by the governments of the member states and the Commission, rather than the result of fortuitous market forces (the rapid appreciation of the yen, for example)? In other words, did the policy outcomes reported above foster the creation of an increasingly effective European industry?

It is important to remember that most of the "best practice" plants in the world auto industry continued to be found in Japan and North America (Womack, Jones, and Roos 1990, 85), and many European producers were still confined to one mature, regional market for most of their sales and still hobbled by some high-cost excess capacity. The industry was not yet out of the

169

woods. Nevertheless, the automakers had risen to the challenge of 1992 and avoided some of their own dire predictions. What was the impetus behind this response?

A consistent impression obtained by this author through a range of interviews was that the single market program was fully credible. Because integration in this sector was part of an overarching project realized through the institutions of the EU, to which all the national governments were committed, everyone in the industry knew that the status quo was no longer available. One way or another, adjustment was going to be forced on them. Truth to tell, there were numerous benefits from "1992" for the industry. But the short-term costs were to be feared. This was the dilemma at the core of the research reported above. Adjustment may have been inevitable, but the manner in which it was accomplished, its timing, and the way in which EU policy assigned the costs and benefits would be crucial to the survival of the individual firms that made up the industry.

This mixture of political compromises, across a range of issue areas, that governed economic adjustment was the product of a specific set of political processes, embedded in a rich set of institutions. The overall result was that some increases in openness and harmonization were achieved at moderate political costs. The member states of the EU were able to obtain a politically efficient solution to the problem of economic integration, even if this meant limiting the gains in economic efficiency. It is clear that the institutional environment of the EU helped, in part, to bring about this outcome.

Analytical Expectations and the Evidence

In the review that follows I will evaluate the extent to which the evidence discovered in the case studies is consistent with the expectations discussed in chapter 2. This is a measure of the effectiveness of the analytical framework. In particular I will seek to isolate the role played by the institutions of the EU. Once there is some understanding of the consequences for outcomes of the institutions of the EU, I can engage in informed speculation as to how and why these institutions were adopted and adapted in the first place. I argue that on occasion, modest alterations to the long-established structures of the EU resulted in an increase in their effectiveness as mechanisms for realizing economic liberalization. But in other respects even existing institutional arrangements were subject to those conditions that constrained the role of all institutions, new and old—that is, the spread of preferences among the relevant principals.

The Preferences of Governments and Firms

It is certainly true that France and Italy, governments that were home to those automakers most exposed to adjustment, acted vigorously to moderate the impact of policies on emissions control, external trade, and state aid. Indeed, while the governments of other member states exhibited variable revealed preferences over different issues, as did the U.S. multinationals and German producers, the evidence shows that the "Mediterranean" countries (France, Spain, and Italy) and the producers based in them (Peugeot, Renault, and FIAT) formed a bloc that did not vary across issue areas in its opposition to policies that would impose swift and/or costly adjustment. Therefore it is not exactly true that the composition of coalitions varied widely across issue areas.

As a result, the crucial players among the firms were the U.S. producers and VW. Where these producers showed a united front, it meant that the Mediterranean bloc was constrained to accept their leadership and preferences. For example, the length of the transition period finally agreed upon for Japanese imports, and the levels of those imports, reflected the ideal points of VW and the U.S. producers most closely (albeit ideal preferences for a somewhat illiberal outcome). Their divisions over emissions control reflected an element identified at the beginning: technological capacity.

Finally, as the market turned down, access to state aid dried up, and the necessary institutional arrangements were put in place (that is, the formation of ACEA), the level of cooperation among the mass producers steadily increased. A good indication of this was the ability of ACEA in 1994 to persuade the Commission to propose a straightforward renewal of Regulation 123/85, the antitrust block exemption. This generated howls of protest from consumer advocates, and a scolding from the editors of the *Financial Times*, but was successfully passed the next year.

While the British and German governments preferred more liberal policies in general, they were willing to overlook their principles in the case of the Japanese VER. The German government accepted a long transitional period because of the competitive shock VW and the specialist producers Daimler-Benz and BMW had received in the U.S. market from the Japanese (while making much less progress than expected in the Japanese domestic market), while the British were willing to use a VER to give the Japanese an incentive to ramp up production from plants located in the United Kingdom. As for preferences over environmental regulation, both Germany and the United Kingdom sought policies that played to the competitive advantage of producers located within each economy.

The most interesting finding is the change in the relationship between the U.K. and German governments and VW and the U.S. producers. I observe a steady separation between producers and governments (to the extent that it could be said that the U.S. producers had national patrons). For Germany and the United Kingdom the political maximum (to use the term employed in chapter 2) turned out to be increasingly further removed from the interests of the mass-market producers. This, of course, meant that these producers were the ones most likely to play an important role in transnational interfirm cooperation.

Cooperation among Governments and Firms

The governments of the member states, while the principals as far as the institutions of the EU were concerned, needed to agree (to a greater or lesser extent) if they were to accomplish any joint project. It was argued in chapter 2 that such agreement depended in part on the spread of preferences in each issue area. Furthermore, I suggested that the ability to cooperate would be shaped by the strategic dilemmas they faced and the structure of the institutional environment. What level of cooperation was accomplished might be endogenous to the institutional arena.

As suggested above, government preferences were consistent with the framework employed in this project. I would also argue that in the case of emissions control and state aid the strategic dilemmas identified in chapter 2 played a role. Emissions control regulation was a coordination problem with acute distributional consequences—the question was not whether to harmonize standards, but on whose terms. In a single play two equilibria were available; as reported in chapter 4, change in the institutional arena induced an outcome at a high level of regulation. In the case of state aid, the assurance necessary to avoid competitive subsidies could only slowly be provided by the Commission, due to the low institutional capacity and political influence of the governments themselves. In short, the coadjustment problem identified in chapter 2 could not be easily resolved, albeit some efforts were made to improve the effectiveness of the Commission with heightened reporting requirements.

The institutional arena also played a role in lowering the level of cooperation required in both the emissions control and external trade cases. In each case a qualified majority was required, rather than unanimity, thus isolating intransigent elements of the Mediterranean bloc. (Note, of course, that while a qualified majority could eliminate type approvals and so force external trade onto the agenda, the actual outcome reflected no such formal bargaining and so also allowed for the direct influence of firms.)

Firm cooperation reflected the degree to which they shared preferences, as discussed above. Furthermore, where joint action yielded group benefits—as in the case of the antitrust exemption and external trade—they were relatively united, as argued in chapter 2. Where political action yielded private goods—as in state aid—no cohesion was evident, notwithstanding the fact that all firms no doubt shared a taste for subsidies. Finally, I argued that those elements favoring firm cooperation became more pronounced over time and that increased levels of firm cooperation were the result, and indeed a private institution was devised—the ACEA—to make such cooperation even more effective. One consequence of the Single European Act was to bring about a far more coordinated club of "European" automakers.

The Institutions of the EU

The larger consequences for outcomes of the institutions of the EU can be best understood by considering the episode in which the institutional arena played the smallest part—the agreement on Japanese imports. Even in this case, in which the result was a failure to move far toward openness, there was never a possibility that there would be no change over the status quo. The issue linkage imposed by the centralization of regulation, specifically type approvals, meant that national trade regimes were ended by the SEA (however, although the new EU regime could never reproduce the effects of several national restrictions by imposing a global restriction, the market-sharing arrangement had, as an implied consequence, the restriction of the German market for the first time, a retrograde step). The informal bargain with the Japanese, if only a very small step toward openness, was possible because bargaining within a common framework, with the Commission coordinating the EU's position, inevitably meant an agreement beyond that desired by "minimalist" firms and national governments.

In general, therefore, an important consequence of the overarching bargain of the SEA, in which the status quo was removed from the set of possible outcomes, was that VW and the U.S. producers played a decisive role. When they wished to moderate outcomes, such as in the area of external trade, they found ready allies in the "Mediterranean bloc"; when they came to accept a deal on emissions as a necessary trade-off in order to obtain harmonization and regulatory certainty, their action forced the Mediterranean producers to seek the (ineffective) intervention of individual national governments. The institutional structure placed the more competitive, mass-market producers in the driver's seat, so to speak.[2] However, it is important to remember that along with an overarching bargain there was also an overarching side-payment—so-called structural funds—extracted by countries exposed to adjustment during the negotiations over the SEA. I return to this important topic below when discussing issue linkage in detail.

As for firms, so for the member states; the Mediterranean bloc was largely constant, allowing Germany, in particular, to play a decisive role. However, I do not argue that this was because of its economic power, or some kind of preeminent position. The explanation is simpler and more general and relies on the character of the legislative institutions of the EU. The location of German preferences in any spatial model of the preferences of the member states under qualified majority voting meant that it was usually a crucial member of any winning coalition. This is clearly true in the two rounds of auto emissions regulation analyzed in chapter 4 (see Garrett and Tsebelis 1996).

Of course, individual national governments were all willing to "go to bat" for client firms on occasion, but they obtained another kind of political advantage from an institutional situation—which they themselves devised—that limited the effectiveness of this response. The SEA inevitably placed a wide range of issues onto the agenda that would have painful consequences for numerous firms within many of the member states. To agree to it, as all member states did, meant that such consequences were accepted. It also meant that when the time came to resolve specific policies across a range of issue areas, these governments had tied their own hands, a situation that surely allowed them to avoid, in part, the political costs.

The French case is especially clear-cut. The government had favored Renault as a national champion in the past at great expense; one of the virtues of the SEA was that it now tied the hands of the French government and shifted the locus of political activity over to the institutions of the EU. The restructuring of Renault followed protracted bargaining over state aid with DG IV and was carefully monitored by the Commission. The French government held out for delay, and side-payments (or canceled debts), but ultimately was constrained to accept adjustment, as were the French producers. This development, very desirable from the point of view of the French consumer and taxpayer, would have been difficult, politically, without the external commitment to the EU, which acted as a constraint and political lightning rod.

The institutions of the EU served the purposes of the member states in other ways in other issue areas. The outcomes in the area of antitrust show how the emergence of a clear, legalistic institutional environment could foster competition and limit the rent-seeking activities of firms. It also shows how the member states, who had problems coordinating their responses to the issue of antitrust because of widely diverging national practices, resolved this coopera-tion problem by delegating the power to develop an appropriate if limited legal order to the institutions of the EU (DG IV and the ECJ). The auto industry was able, to a degree, to have its interests realized by means of an exemption from certain antitrust provisions. But, taken as a whole, these cases showed how the institutional environment served the purposes of the member states, by limit-ing market segmentation in the auto sector and insulating the Commission from the demands of powerful, private interests.

However, in the case studies reported above one possible expectation was not supported by the evidence. I do not observe significant agency drift on the part of the Commission, or an independent role being played by the European Parliament. The Commission's role was carefully circumscribed in the area of state aid by the member states, its powers were strictly defined in the area of an-titrust, and it was beholden to the interests of producers in both the external trade and emissions control cases. Rather than an autonomous actor, it was more an agent (with poor institutional capacity) over which different coalitions of states and firms sought to have influence. While sheltered by the legal order that governed antitrust, it also lacked discretion. Where it had discretion, it be-came subject to tremendous political pressure from firms and the governments of member states.

As for the Parliament, it too was circumscribed by the spread of govern-ment preferences (or "Pareto surface," as discussed in chapter 2). Some argue that in the emissions control case the Parliament was flexing its institutional muscle and so represents an example of EU institutions pushing a private, in-stitutional goal onto the member states and private actors. However, these ac-tions would not be possible unless some subset of each could accept them. Those were the conditions under which conditional agenda setting could occur. In fact, this was as much a story of EU institutions giving power to other actors, formerly excluded from the policy-making process—that is to say, environ-mental interests—as a story about the institutional interest of the Parliament.

In summary, the role played by the institutions of the EU is consistent with many of the expectations about the consequences of institutions discussed in chapter 2. By having the institutional framework of the EU within which to work out the details of the SEA, the member states were able to credibly com-mit themselves to a move away from the status quo, although substantial side-payments were required (see below). *Subsequent* efforts to resist change were doomed to failure; the agenda was—in a broad sense—already set. For exam-ple, the harmonization of type approvals forced the producers to face increased external openness, while the harmonization of emissions control also forced firms to face increased levels of regulation. The exact levels of openness and regulation, however, were contingent on the spread of preferences among all the relevant actors.

The institutions of the EU contributed in other ways. As expected, the Commission was able to play the part of honest broker and so facilitate political exchange and the coordination of policies. The institutions of the EU also lowered the political costs of adjustment by deflecting the political blame. Finally, pro-integration firms and member governments were placed in an advantageous strategic position; under the cooperation procedure minimalist coalitions could be broken up by more liberal proposals. Of course, none of the major actors sought purely liberal outcomes. Their rhetoric tended to obscure a straightforward pursuit of preferences determined by those elements I identified at the beginning—the distributional costs. The result was that the transition to a comprehensive pattern of EU-wide policy-making was accomplished at low political cost, although the actual pattern of policy-making clearly fell short of a purely liberal outcome.

Issue Linkage and Side-Payments

The discussion so far has assumed that each issue area existed apart from all the others, and that the overarching side-payments noted above in the case of the SEA had no consequences for this sector. But the institutions of the EU were at the center of a network of payments and policy concessions that compensated producers in one area for costs imposed elsewhere.

For example, the willingness of Germany and the United Kingdom to grant the Commission a role, if only a limited one, in coordinating the distribution of funds to the auto industry for retraining and the adoption of new technologies helped to smooth the way for a transition to external openness, as well as begin the steady limitation of national subsidies. In the emissions control case, by contrast, individual governments who were constrained to accept the proposed legislation made their own side-payments to their national producers (subsidies for the adoption of CAT technology). But there was, at least, no question of counting such assistance as state aid that had to meet Commission requirements.

But beyond these specific examples of political exchange, it is often argued that the increase in structural funds promised to poor regions or regions in industrial decline when the SEA was being negotiated represented a grand, preemptive payoff that allowed consensus to be accomplished (for a nuanced discussion see Marks 1992). It is worth noting that the definition of such regions was elastic, even by EU standards, such that many regions in all the member states could end up benefiting. In short, as Marks suggests, the funds represented a pool of money that insured the most exposed regions against the uncertainties of liberalization (although the rewards as well as the risks may have been relatively greater for poorer, more sheltered areas).

More importantly for the implications of this study, there is a suspicion that the slow progress on state aid and, in particular, the exemption from antitrust requirements were linked to the costs of adjustment elsewhere. Inasmuch as these issue areas were opaque and more or less subject to bureaucratic discretion, it might have been expected that, far from observing any progress, the SEA would have actually led to backsliding: more aid, more permissive regulatory treatment. To the extent that the exemption from antitrust allowed market segmentation and cartelization, so the producers were awarded rents at the expense of consumers.[3] This was accomplished without most people noticing (in spite of the best efforts of BEUC) and so was politically cheaper than subsidies or tariffs. No one interviewed for this project described the antitrust exemption in those terms, but it could certainly be interpreted in that way. Yet automakers were checked by a legal order that set constraints on the exemption. At the same time, in state aid some progress was actually accomplished. In short, while liberalization may have slowed progress in the area of competition policy, it did not halt it.

In summary, side-payments and issue linkage supplied glue at important points in the process of liberalizing the auto industry. However, structural funds were never a really significant pool of money (roughly 0.3 percent of EU GDP in 1993), while competition policy, which was the area most likely to be disrupted by the costs of liberalization, nevertheless exhibited some progress.

Institutions as Outcomes

Given the foregoing, it is possible to think about EU institutions endogenously, as outcomes shaped by the governments of the member states in search of institutional solutions to the problems of economic and political cooperation. Why were changes in the rules incorporated into the SEA? How were other institutional characteristics adapted and deployed by the member states? Many of the answers to these questions have been suggested by the discussion so far. The purpose here is to make some fruitful speculations about the purpose of the institutional innovations observed in the research reported above. It will also be possible to pose new questions about the foresight of governments and firms, and the degree to which institutional innovation occurs under conditions of uncertainty.

The Single European Act

There are always distributional consequences attached to choosing one set of rules over another. Harmonizing regulatory practices in the EU (a crucial element in the internal market program, given that tariff barriers had disappeared by the early seventies) could be accomplished by either "mutual recognition" or bargaining. Under mutual recognition all member states must accept the product standards of all other members, a practice that could have significant distributional consequences. Mutual recognition was the approach established by the ECJ, the most autonomous of the supranational institutions of the Community, in its now famous ruling in the case of *Cassis de Dijon*. It effectively supplanted the earlier cumbersome bargaining that had characterized harmonization in the late 1960s and early 1970s and that had resulted in wretchedly slow progress.

I argue that the SEA represented an effort by the member states to more closely control the process of integration (in particular the harmonization of health, labor, and environmental standards) without slowing it down. While harmonization based on bargains between states does not, a priori, yield more or less economic openness than mutual recognition, it does allow for a more precisely calculated political struggle over the distributional consequences.[4]

The SEA comprised two institutional innovations. The first is well known and has played an important part in the analysis so far: qualified majority voting. The other was the "new approach" to technical harmonization, in which the Council of Ministers defined basic objectives and requirements and then delegated the details to impartial technical standards bodies (such as the European Normalization Committee).[5] The result was that in sensitive issue areas a new approach was adopted that supplanted mutual recognition but did not return to the old, impractical mechanism of pure intergovernmentalism. While technical issues with modest consequences could be harmonized without the member states playing a significant part, they reserved to themselves the right to intervene in issues of high political salience. In that event, it was qualified majority voting, rather than delegation, that would break the joint decision trap.

The problem is how to reconcile the argument that the member states were asserting their control over the process of integration with the claim that they were also able to use the institutions of the EU to deflect the political costs of integration and obscure their responsibility for its consequences. Were the innovations of the SEA a form of institutional sleight of hand? Why, given enough foresight, didn't firms and other interests, whose gains from integration might be at best uncertain, resist the overarching framework bargain, because they recognized the dangers implied by the constraints incorporated in it?

As far as the firms are concerned, there are several answers. First, the SEA was a classic example of peak bargaining between states; it did not address a thick web of midlevel political issues (the transaction costs of doing so would have been prohibitive, as noted above, quite apart from the political considerations discussed here) but confined itself to establishing a framework. For that reason it was a bargaining arena insulated from particular interests that might have wished to influence the outcome. Second, the amount of foresight necessary to predict the *subsequent* distributional outcomes is entirely implausible, given that such outcomes would be subject to variation in rules across issue areas, trade-offs between issues, and intensely strategic behavior by all the actors involved. Finally, over integration as a whole, the prospects and dangers for industry were asymmetrically distributed. The industry's reservations were no doubt concentrated among the Mediterranean producers, while the regionally integrated U.S. and German automakers largely welcomed an open internal market. In short, the SEA framework increased the relative autonomy of each government toward their domestic interests, under conditions of considerable uncertainty, and established a program of action whose benefits would be asymmetrically distributed across industry, so limiting its ability to respond in concert.

Unintended Consequences?

To what extent did EU institutions, in particular the cooperation procedure adopted by the SEA, yield outcomes that the member states themselves had not anticipated? One way to estimate the experiences of the member states is to examine their subsequent institutional innovations at the time of the intergovernmental conference at Maastricht. Did they, at that time, "fix" elements that they had earlier adopted under conditions of uncertainty, and about which they subsequently became dissatisfied?

In the Treaty of Maastricht, the cooperation procedure was largely superseded by the codecision procedure. There were two interesting political conflicts over this change: the Commission resisted strenuously any attempt to strip it of its power to accept or reject proposals by the Parliament (under the new codecision procedure). Clearly, it did not imagine that they and the Parliament were of one mind. Also, the Council of Ministers, the arena in which the member states operated, now placed themselves in the position of being, in the last instance, the one to make a "take-it-or-leave-it" proposal to the Parliament in the Conciliation Committee—over the objections of the Parliament (see Corbett 1993, 57–58; Tsebelis 1994b; and Garrett and Tsebelis 1996). In short, the power of the Parliament to set the agenda was not expanded at the expense of the Commission and may have been limited by new powers for the Council. The change suggests that the member states took advantage of the Maastricht treaty to adjust some of the institutional innovations first introduced by the SEA.

It may be that the emissions control case indicates what it was that they had misjudged about the cooperation procedure that they were trying to correct.[6] The procedure gave a significant (and, perhaps, surprising) amount of control over the outcome to any set of interests who were able to obtain a powerful coalition in the body of the European Parliament—in this case, environmentalists. It follows from this that the change from the cooperation procedure to the codecision procedure at Maastricht may have been an attempt to limit the possibility of that happening again. Such a coalition, where it appeared, would be on the receiving end of a take-it-or-leave-it proposition and so have less power to shape the outcome. However, if environmentalists within the Parliament were more willing to endure inaction—the persistence of the status quo—than the governments of the member states, then the Parliament would continue to enjoy a measure of bargaining power over the Council of Ministers by threatening to let legislation die.

In short, the story is one of experience, innovation, more experience, and subsequent adjustment. This seems to be a sensible account of the way institutional innovation operates, somewhere between the two limit cases of perfect foresight on the one hand and perfect naïveté on the other (in which the consequences of institutional change are a complete surprise). It is also nicely congruent with the way institutional change has actually occurred throughout the history of the EU. The episodic character of EU integration is really a story of institutional experimentation, in which the member states move from arrangements that increase the pace of change to ones that protect the sovereign control of each government (and with it their ability to limit political costs), searching each time for the right balance between these conflicting goals. Inasmuch as the external environment is also constantly changing, driven by rising economic interdependence, it may be imagined that the perfect institutional recipe is doomed to be forever elusive. Any solution to yesterday's dilemmas will, inevitably, be somehow inadequate in the face of the future.

Conclusions and Future Questions

Perhaps the most important finding of this project is the straightforward, empirical one. I show how complex, interdependent industrial democracies were able to overcome a variety of cooperation and coordination problems and realize gains from the economic integration of a major (perhaps *the* major) economic sector. Simply on these terms, this is a story worth telling. By the early

1990s the European auto industry had changed dramatically from its situation 10 or 15 years earlier. It was much more regionally integrated and competitive, with reliable products from plants that were leaner and more efficient. As a result, its future was more secure. Indeed, with the fruition of various speculative joint ventures in Asia, especially China, in the 1990s, and the recovery of the South American market for autos, the major failing of the industry—its dependence on one regional market—is, perhaps, in the process of being overcome.

The political and regulatory change was even more profound. Separate and contradictory national policies were now supplanted by somewhat effective, centralized regulation of the industry. As a result, inspection standards, environmental standards, rules on state aid, and rules on antitrust applied in a uniform manner throughout the region. This centralization made the EU market much easier to trade in, with fewer barriers and greater regulatory certainty. The difficulties of accomplishing this were, as reported, significant, and the knowledge of how it was done is valuable, because the politics of multilateral free trade will also increasingly address regulatory issues, and the problems of coordinating national regulatory regimes. However, one puzzle remains, which requires more research and for which no easy answer is supplied by this project.

Above I argued that firms who stood to lose from the prospect of openness and harmonization were unable to prevent the institutional innovations that ushered in these changes because they were part of a very general framework bargain, accomplished at a high level of interstate bargaining, about which the exact consequences were perhaps uncertain. However, it has been observed elsewhere that many very prominent multinationals were involved in a long-running political program aimed at bringing about the kind of reforms observed in the SEA (see Cowles 1995). If winners from such changes were mobilized early on, why weren't potential losers?

The failure of potential losers to mobilize is at odds with the standard finding of the political economy literature, which suggests that losers are mobilized first in the political marketplace. One possible explanation would center on the way in which political opportunities are distributed across national and international institutions. The "old," national regime—for example, in the case of the auto industry the established relationships between industry associations and individual firms and their respective national governments—favored "minimalist" interests. As a result it was proliberal interests—lacking national political opportunities—who were most likely to mobilize transnationally. In the case of the European Union, the consequence was that the most regionally integrated firms with the strongest transnational links—in other words, the best "Europeans"—were the U.S. multinational producers.

Appendix

A list of people interviewed and their organizations and/or associations is presented below. While experts and academics were also consulted on many aspects of the industry, only those people involved as participants in policy-making are noted here.

Beazley, Peter	Member of the European Parliament
Bergevin, Jean	Directorate General III
Bolian, Niall	Directorate General III
Casper, Christian	Peugeot SA
D'Albis, Tristan	Peugeot SA
de Castlenau, Béatrice	Comité des Constructeurs Français d'Automobile (CCFA)
Diekmann, Dr. Achim	Verband Der Automobilindustrie (VDA)
Gabola	FIAT SPA
Glatz, Dr. Hanns	Daimler-Benz AG
Hulse, David	Ford of Europe Inc.
Johnstone, Jill	National Consumers Council
Kalk, Dr. Motele	Comité de Liaison de la construction d'Équipement et de Pièces d'Automobile (CLEPA)
Lueders, Dr. Hugo	Association des Constructeurs Européens d'Automobile (ACEA)
Marshall, Neil	Retail Motor Industry Federation (RMIF)
Molitor, Dr. Bernhard	Bundesministerium für Wirtschaft
Mory, Christian	Comité des Constructeurs Français d'Automobile (CCFA)
Mosca, Laura	Bureau Européen des Unions de Consommateurs (BEUC)

Rampa, Dr. Gregorio	Associazione Nazionale Fra l'Industrie Automobilistiche (ANFIA)
Shearer, Thoss	Department of Trade and Industry (DTI)
Stedman, Michael	Society for Motor Manufacturers and Traders (SMMT)
Stover, Dr. Klaus	Directorate General IV
Tongue, Carole	Member of the European Parliament
Vigier, Pierre	Directorate General III
Vitiello, L.	Directorate General III
von Hülsen, Dr. Hans-Viggo	Volkswagen AG
von Mobelen, Dr.	Volkswagen AG
Wilson, John	Directorate General I

Notes

Chapter 1

1. Speech by Raymond Levy before a hearing of the European Parliamentary Committee on External Relations and the Political Affairs Committee on relations between the European Community and Japan, held in Brussels, 16 and 17 September 1991 (author's transcription and translation). The tone of the speech was moderate compared to some of the more apocalyptic (and anti-Japanese) statements made by industry representatives in private communications.

2. What is now known as the European Union has been known by other names. The original European Coal and Steel Community (ECSC), founded in 1952, was joined by the European Economic Community (EEC) in 1958 (together with Euratom, an unsuccessful attempt to regulate atomic power on a regional basis). These three entities came to be known as the European Community (EC) by the late 1980s. The name was then changed to the European Union (EU) by the Treaty of Maastricht, 1992. In the interest of maximum clarity, the term *EU* will be used throughout to refer to all the various European Communities, notwithstanding the fact that the term *EC* was in general use when many of the events to be analyzed below actually occurred.

3. On the rule changes adopted by the SEA see Garrett 1992; and Nugent 1994, 304–29; for an overview of the legislative processes within the institutions of the EU see also, among many others, Peters 1991; Lodge 1994; and Keohane and Hoffmann 1991.

4. It is important to note that while the new trade theory does call into question the role of comparative advantage, it has failed to yield insights as broad and robust as neoclassical trade theory—its models tend to be sensitive to turbulence in the underlying assumptions. It follows that while strategic behavior may help states and firms "snatch rents," there is no guide available as to what, precisely, such a policy might look like.

5. Of course some economies would have more exposed sectors than others—the Commission attempted to measure this sometime after the SEA was signed (CEC 1990b). However, ceteris paribus, greater adjustment is accompanied by greater potential welfare gains, and such economies should gain as much as, if not more than, others. The political trade-off, as opposed to the purely economic one, is addressed in much greater detail in chapter 2.

186   Notes to Pages 11–29

6. I make no attempt to rely on the extensive sociological and cultural explanations for institutions (see, for example, Dobbin 1994; and Finnemore 1996). The micro-foundations offered by economic theories of industrial organization are more in keeping with the rational actor framework generally adopted in this project. That is not to say that other theories have nothing to add to this kind of analysis, only that in the interests of parsimony I stick to one kind of approach with a view to discovering how much it can explain.

7. The ability to be an *informal* agenda setter is available to anyone—political entrepreneurs of all kinds can attempt to promote issues and solutions (see Kingdon 1984). However, at some point in the social allocation of resources actors must enter the appropriate institutionalized bargaining arena and submit to the constraints embodied in its rules. Who *formally* makes proposals within that context enjoys, ipso facto, significant power.

8. The principal-agent literature is extensive and cannot be addressed here to good effect. Suffice it to say that due to the difficulty of monitoring and credibly threatening to sanction agents, "shirking" or drift occurs when an agent pursues goals separate from those assigned to it (among many others, see McCubbins and Schwartz 1984; and Moe 1987). In the context of the EU, the Commission may have considerable room to maneuver due to the complexity of its tasks and the divergent preferences of its multiple principals (Pollack 1997). A considerable underlying problem with this literature is that given rational actors with perfect information it is impossible to distinguish between successful monitoring and perfectly calibrated shirking.

9. In a coordination game with distributional consequences coordination may not be realized due to an inability to agree on any particular solution. In this context a "focal point" or "prominent solution" can solve the problem, where it has credibility, and an impartial international institution, such as the EU, could be the source of the required credibility (see, of course, Schelling 1980; for a discussion in the context of the EU see Garrett and Weingast 1993).

10. Roughly half of the bilateral trade deficit between the United States and Japan over the last 20 years has been due to a lopsided trade in automotive products, leading to the "voluntary" export restraint of 1982 and the threat of punitive tariffs in 1995. Trade in autos has also disturbed the South American customs union (Mercosur) (see *Financial Times*, 21 June 1995, 7).

Chapter 2

1. In the concluding chapter institutions are considered as dependent variables, the product of strategic choice by powerful actors. Some tentative conclusions are reached based on the evidence presented in the case studies of the way institutions limited policy choices. I suggest that the institutions of the EU were adopted and adapted by the member states in order to lower the costs of common policy outcomes.

2. Ceteris paribus, small states will benefit the most from openness. Worth noting in the case of the auto industry is that the major producing states, with the exception of Belgium, were all roughly the same size.

3. This asymmetry implies, therefore, that there exists a different but optimum level of integration for each of the governments of the member states, an optimum at which the political costs and benefits, at the margin, are in balance—in other words, a political

maximum as described by Peltzman (1976). However, it is not my purpose to specify a comprehensive model of the relationship between the domestic political marketplace and the political consequences of economic integration. A well-known model (Magee, Brock, and Young 1989, 2), which seeks to "build the micro foundations of party behavior, lobby behavior, and economic behavior" as the basis for endogenous policy formation, is subject to numerous objections (see, for example, Austen-Smith 1991).

4. In this context a rent is simply supernormal profits that depend upon market power obtained from nonmarket barriers to trade.

5. Worth noting is that any member state's preference would always be for more integration than was preferred by the most exposed individual interests, and less than was preferred by the best situated individual interests. Of course, when bargaining over specific issues, the most exposed interest would weigh heavily on the minds of policymakers.

6. The degree to which *actual* interest activity occurs is determined, in part, by the institutions involved. What follows is, in a sense, a map of *latent* preferences; when and where these gave rise to politics is contingent and will be accounted for in the context of the case studies.

7. For a discussion of this see Krasner 1991, 351. With the congestion of the electromagnetic spectrum the coordination problem is no longer so easily resolved, but it has the self-enforcing character of all games of mutual aversion. Failure to coordinate automatically imposes cacophony on all.

8. On the potential value to a country of export subsidies see Krugman 1984; and Brander and Spencer 1984; for a critique see Markusen and Venables 1988; for an overview of strategic trade theory see Krugman 1986; and Helpman and Razin 1991.

9. Choosing one out of a continuous range of strategies is the functional equivalent of playing the pure strategies of H and L probabilistically in iterated play. The equilibrium strategies and payoffs are, in this case, simple and symmetrical—each player subsidizes at a level exactly halfway between H and L and earns a payoff of 2.5, less than if each practiced maximum restraint or, of course, successfully exploited the other.

10. It is also easy to show that, absent institutions, even if the players could agree to side-payments, they would continue to choose suboptimal strategies. If the game is specified slightly differently, and the payoffs made asymmetrical (while retaining the structure of the game), the equilibrium level of subsidy is different for each player. The use of a side-payment has the consequence of restoring convergence in the payoffs to the two players, although still at a collectively inefficient level.

11. A firm might defect in the other direction. Unable to compete if the public good in question were obtained by all firms acting in concert, it would seek to block such cooperative activity. For just such a case see chapter 4. Of course, where the gains from political activity may be privately enjoyed, then the effect would be to create divisions among producers. Worth noting is a competing argument in which heterogeneity fosters cooperation because it is associated with reduced economic competition. The point here is exactly the opposite: the threat of heightened economic competition raises the returns from political strategies, that is, from collusion.

12. This, therefore, represents a structural explanation for the appearance and effectiveness of transnational interest organizations not generally supplied in "neofunctionalist" accounts.

13. From this it may be inferred that the rise of transnational industry associations is not likely to *precede* political agreements on integration but rather *succeed* them. This is congruent with the observed pattern of association formation and turns the causal relationship posited by the neofunctionalists on its head. For a good discussion of the way in which firms and firm associations rose up in response to the SEA see Camerra-Rowe 1993. For evidence that firm lobbying was redirected toward the institutions of the EU following the SEA see Coen 1997. On the other hand, some producer activity *did* precede, and shape, the SEA (see Cowles 1995). I return to this question at the conclusion of the project.

14. Some have argued that the Parliament and/or the Commission set the agenda for the SEA (see Jacobs and Corbett 1990). Others have suggested that transnational interests, in particular U.S. multinational business interests, put the political process into motion (Cowles 1995). However, treaty-based change places the governments of sovereign states firmly in the center of the action, making the SEA (for example) a "best case" for intergovernmental explanations (see, of course, Moravcsik 1991).

15. While some matters were specifically exempted from qualified majority voting by the SEA (such as national tax policy), in areas not specifically exempted the Commission was given significant power in determining what was, or was not, an internal market issue (see Garrett 1992, 550).

16. This accounts, according to some, for the prominent role of the Committee of Permanent Representatives (COREPER), in which national expertise was provided by each member state in order to inform the business of the Council of Ministers (see Hayes-Renshaw and Wallace 1995), and the prominent role of the representatives of industry and other specialists in the process known as "comitology," in which the Commission developed proposals. But, as discussed below, the influence of outsiders in this process was moderated in systematic ways.

17. I distinguish between mediating variables and independent variables in the following way. As noted above, different rules impose different cooperation challenges on the member states. However, while the effects of different rules are systematic, the consequences for policy outcomes are contingent, depending as they do on the preferences of the member states in each issue area. I characterize this institutional role as that of a mediating variable. By contrast, I argue in what follows that the institutions of the EU, because of their powers to set agendas and resolve disputes, in conjunction with their own institutional interest, may systematically shape policy outcomes in a pro-integrationist manner. This effect is an independent one.

18. Divergent preferences between the Commission and the EP will limit the Parliament's power, but Tsebelis argues that the Commission, in general, accepts the EP's amendments in the second reading. It may be constrained to do so by change in the status quo away from its ideal point (see Stephen 1995). Whether it does or not is an empirical question.

19. These committees are defined by decision 87/373/EEC of the Council. This decision is seen by some as an attempt by the member states to limit the power of the Commission to make proposals. However, the decision has not accomplished its objective. Indeed, through a process of co-option, the Commission may have gained in legitimacy while surrendering little control (Eichener 1991, 50–53).

20. Because the institutions of the EU are relatively small and underdeveloped, monitoring takes the form of a "fire alarm" system as opposed to "police patrol." For a discussion of the difference and the reasons why one kind might be preferred over another, see McCubbins and Schwartz 1984.

21. The only way for the member states to gain control over the legal structures of the Community would be for them to make significant treaty revisions at an intergovernmental conference. This is possible but would, of course, be subject to the requirement of unanimity among the states—a difficult test. However, it is notable that the two new pillars of the Community established by the Maastricht treaty—Justice and Home Affairs and Foreign and Security Policy—are not subject to judicial review by the Court.

Chapter 3

1. It is impossible to examine the prewar history and early origins of the European auto industry in any useful detail without embarking on another, separate project. However, from time to time it will be necessary to explain some of the characteristics of the postwar political economies of Europe by referring to earlier political choices and institutions. It has been argued by Reich (1990), for example, that the divergent national experiences of the postwar European auto industry have their roots in the character of prewar political regimes. These issues will be addressed as they arise. (For a general survey of the early years of the industry see Laux 1992.)

2. The U.S. auto industry has always been subject to brutal cyclical movements in demand, while by comparison the Japanese domestic market (up until 1992) has been much steadier, a major factor in providing Japanese manufacturers with a reliable environment for long-term investment (see Womack, Jones, and Roos 1990, 248).

3. Wilks estimates that between 1975 and 1984 the government invested just over £1 million per working day in the combine (1989, 189).

4. Reich argues that Ford U.K. benefited greatly from equal access to stocks of steel in the crucial early stages of the postwar recovery, as well as from significant retained profits as a result of its important role in war production—so much so that it was able to quickly assume a dominant position in the U.K. market, from which it has never been dislodged (1990, 74–107).

5. This agreement was, eventually, the subject of a consumer lawsuit; struck down by the ECJ, it had already been superseded by an EU-wide agreement (see chapter 5).

6. This level of production is roughly 25 percent of the minimum efficient scale (MES) in manufacturing in this sector, while most European producers achieved levels of 50–80 percent of the MES (Owen 1983, 71).

7. Revitalizing the auto industry through FDI was similar to the strategy with which the (successful) Spanish auto sector was developed, although Spain relied on intra-EU FDI flows and the United Kingdom on extra-EU FDI flows (see Stephen 1994).

8. VW had been a public enterprise at its inception, owned by the Labor Front, a National Socialist labor organization, and funded in part by public subscription. Rejected as worthless by the occupying power (Britain), it was turned over to the Federal Republic. Although its legal status was to remain unsettled for many years, it was finally privatized. The state of Lower Saxony continues to hold 20 percent of its shares.

9. This is illustrated by the testimony of Dr. Glatz, of Daimler-Benz, before a House of Lords committee that conducted hearings on the European auto industry in 1990. He anticipated at that time that European producers (with Mercedes leading the way) would have a 7 percent share (by value) of the Japanese market by the mid-1990s, and perhaps a 10 percent share by the year 2000. With the decline in the European share of the Japanese market below 3 percent in 1991, these hopes were disappointed (House of Lords 1990, 25–35).

10. For a nuanced account of the differences among the German producers (and among British producers), see Camerra-Rowe 1993.

11. It has been suggested that the French ambassador to Germany in the late 1970s advised the German producers not to be too aggressive in marketing in France (interview with Dr. Achim Diekmann, VDA, 15 June 1992). It is quite possible that self-restraint was practiced by German producers (at least until the French automakers had restructured by the end of the late 1980s), given the overall value to Germany of the political relationship with France.

12. Value added tax (VAT) in Italy is charged at a higher rate on cars with larger engine sizes, which has the effect of a nontariff barrier for foreign producers whose products use engines that are on average larger (Smith and Venables 1990, 156).

13. One of the few detailed examinations of the complex relationships that exist between the Italian state and major Italian conglomerates is by Friedman (1989). On the Alfa-Romeo deal see also Bianchi, Cassese, and della Sala 1989.

14. This limit is the result of an agreement between Italy and Japan that pre-dated the Treaty of Rome and that was established at the request of the Japanese. Since Italy had a competitive advantage in the production of small cars, the Japanese wished to protect their then-fragile postwar producers from Italian competition.

15. One wrinkle, which will be apparent in the discussion in chapter 4, was that auto production at the low end of the model range tended to be concentrated in Spain. Small cars had very narrow profit margins, and the cost of wages, as a percentage of the whole, was relatively greater. Small-car production, therefore, benefited most from low Spanish wages. However, this factor would make Spain sensitive to EU-wide regulation that hurt small cars the most (i.e., emissions control). Any inflationary pressures on Spanish wage rates would also be quickly felt.

16. Belgium's preferences, in keeping with the logic so far adopted, would have been similar to Spain's; its production base was a function of geography, EU membership, and national government incentives and was controlled by multinationals (Maxcy 1981, 105–6).

17. Interview with Pierre Vigier, DG III, 23 June 1992. This point was also made by the representative for Fiat in Brussels, Signor Gabola.

18. The management of capital markets by the French state in the postwar period had an analogous purpose—the provision of a critical factor at low cost to privileged sectors (Zysman 1982).

19. The figures in figure 7 were drawn from the OECD (Organization for Economic Cooperation and Development) COMTAP (Compatible Trade and Production Data Base), in which trade for all categories of manufactured products is recorded for a 17-year period. The figures shown are for trade in the International Standard Industrial Classification (SITC) four-digit category 3843, "motor vehicles." These results apply to intra-European trade; trade between Europe and the rest of the world in mass-market

autos was relatively small. In this market, as opposed to specialist production, Europe was relatively isolated. This was even true for the U.S. multinationals, whose intrafirm trade was, at that time, regionally specific (very little crossed the Atlantic). It is likely that the important *distributional* effects, and therefore political effects, of the 1992 project were to be felt in intra-European trade (with the important exception of Japanese imports). The growth of the deficits and surpluses is exaggerated by the data because it is reported in nominal U.S. dollars.

20. Figure 8 was calculated from data drawn from COMTAP, following the method of Lloyd and Grubel (1974, 20–22). An index was created that captured the relative size of an imbalance in trade measured against the level of that trade. A score of 100 means that trade is in perfect balance; a score of 0 means that it is completely one-sided. The formula for intra-industry trade (IT) is as follows:

$$IT = [(X + M) - |X - M|] \times \frac{100}{(X + M)}$$

21. The discussion that follows (here and throughout this project) considers mainly the six major producers of autos in Europe: Ford, GM, Volkswagen (VW), Fiat, Renault, and Peugeot. Some of the reasons for this focus will be addressed below. One important reason is that they controlled over 70 percent of the market and may be supposed to have enjoyed commensurate political influence.

22. This measure may be skewed by variation in the level of vertical integration among firms, and by variation in the product range among firms. In column c, table 5, is an attempt to adjust for the first of these difficulties. However, the numbers reported allow only rough judgments to be made of the rank ordering of firms.

23. I argue that common costs and technological capabilities make the advantages accruing to all firms who seek some collective good (i.e., the benefits of collusion) evenly shared. This makes it easier for the firms to overcome their collective action problem.

24. Wilks, on the other hand, argues that in the early eighties, partly as a result of overcapacity created by myopic state aid strategies, the industry was harmed by "excessive" competition (1989, 170).

25. Interview with Neil Marshall, Retail Motor Industry Federation (RMIF), 7 May 1992. The role of the "company car" in Britain was unique and resulted in the segmentation of the U.K. market observed above. Nearly half of all cars sold were sold to firms, who very often grant them to employees as a benefit.

26. Honda's connection to Rover, which was to transform that company's products and processes, was radically altered when the majority holder, the British Aircraft Corporation (which had bought the firm from the government), sold its share to BMW.

27. Interview with David Hulse, Ford of Europe, 25 June 1992, and Michael Stedman, SMMT, 5 May 1992.

Chapter 4

1. Taken together with the subsequent investment in Skoda, it was clear that VW was determined to maintain a presence at the low end of the market. However, these plans were somewhat disrupted by the corporate crisis of the early 1990s, and these investments were significantly scaled back. This pattern of dispersing production away from

Europe's traditional (and expensive) producing areas will be discussed in much greater detail in chapter 5.

2. By 1992 VW had twelve assembly plants outside Europe and had spent roughly DM 35 billion since 1986 on new capital investment (interview, Dr. von Hülsen, VW, 16 June 1992). This level of spending meant that other costs imposed by regulation would have been especially unwelcome.

3. The importance of U.S. standards was made more acute because Sweden, which exported autos in significant numbers to the United States, also adopted them, and other EFTA members were to follow. This meant that within the geographic area of Europe, as many as three or more emissions standards could be applied to autos.

4. The three (relating to tires, windshields, and weights) were held up because France wanted limits on EU-wide Japanese imports before it was willing to give up control over registration. Otherwise the consequence of agreeing to EU-wide standards would have been the end of national import quotas (see chapter 5 for a full account).

5. In 1980 the European Court of Justice (ECJ) affirmed that Article 100 could be a basis for environmental action (Case 91/79, Commission v. Italy, 1980, ECR, 1099, 1106).

6. It is interesting to note that an element contributing to this victory was state funding for party activities, which first became available to the Greens when they participated in the European Parliament elections in 1979 (Hülsberg 1988, 122).

7. These standards came to be referred to as US 83 (being the federal standards for 1983). The debate that followed in Germany and throughout Europe in the 1980s was framed in terms of these and subsequent U.S. federal regulations.

8. One puzzle is why Denmark preferred a two-year delay, during which earlier, much weaker standards remained in place, to the compromise that was immediately available. One of Denmark's arguments in the next round of bargaining was that because of slow turnover in the stock of vehicles on Danish roads (due to the severe tax burden laid on autos) Denmark needed standards sooner rather than later (Kim 1992, 18). The Danes may have anticipated either that changes in popular sentiment, or future institutional changes in the EU, would work in their favor and so it would be worth waiting.

9. The Committee on Economic and Monetary Affairs produced two more reports on the auto industry, in 1986 and 1991, which reflected the interest of its members in the difficulties facing the automobile industry (EP Doc. A 3-0140/91; Doc. A 2-171/86). On each occasion the chair represented a constituency with significant auto-related investment.

10. It has been argued strenuously by Krämer (1987) that this provision only protected relatively high national standards that already existed from being eroded by harmonization at a low level. It was not an opening for the introduction of new regulations at the national level. He reads the Danish declaration at the end of the treaty as supporting this claim. The opposite is clearly the case: the bargaining behind this clause suggests that it is a weakened form of national veto, an "escape clause" for opting out, and the declaration by the Danish government is no more than its attempt to make clearer the meaning ascribed to it. The Danes observed that "the provisions of Article 100A(4) guarantee that a member state can apply national provisions. . . ."

11. The only amendment the Commission did accept was the first, which called for the necessity of abolishing different regional and national provisions relating to emissions.

12. Jacobs and Richard argue that the EP threatened to reject the Commission's proposal unless the Commission promised to accept its amendments, which then would have required unanimity in the Council to be reinstituted (Jacobs and Corbett 1990,

170). This, they suggest, would have thrown the industry into disarray. However, it might be difficult to extract a credible commitment from the Commission. Parliamentary suspicion of the Commission persisted in the debate itself (*Debates of the European Parliament*, 11 April 1989, 92). The problem for the Commission was that the industry was already in disarray, and the status quo was now unacceptable. The Parliament's proposal was the only one that promised renewed harmonization.

13. The institutional changes of the SEA, which made the harmonization accomplished at Luxembourg uncertain, had the effect of deepening existing divisions.

Chapter 5

1. It has been argued by Hanson (1998) that there was a broad-based and unintended shift to more liberal external trade as a result of the SEA. The argument developed in chapters 1 and 2 suggests that it was by no means unintended. However, the auto sector, contrary to Hanson's argument, proved to be an egregious exception in the issue area of external openness.

2. The issue of local content is highly politicized in the EU, North America, and many developing countries. The rule in the EU is apparently a simple one: any product subject to a significant "transformation" within its borders was declared to be of EU origin. However, this rule left the door open to the proliferation of "screwdriver" plants, so in 1987, in response to considerable pressure from various industries, the EU passed a regulation designed to limit the activities of these plants (OJ L167, 26/6/1987). Since the EU has no local content regulations, it approached this issue by modifying existing anti-dumping regulations.

However, although this matter has apparently weighed on the minds of Japanese executives (see Stephen 1994, 16), no rulings against such plants have actually been issued. The Japanese auto plants in the United Kingdom were perceived by the French (among others) as Trojan horses for the Japanese auto industry, but there was no attempt by the Commission to influence the amount of local content.

3. See Wilks 1989, 172; Smith and Venables 1990, 126; and the testimony of Dr. Glatz before the House of Lords Select Committee on the European Communities (1990, 27).

4. Some argued that limited dealer networks for Japanese autos would have the effect of giving the more sheltered markets a de facto breathing space, but this was at best an uncertain constraint (see House of Lords 1990, 32).

5. Martin Bangemann stated this very firmly in the debate in the European Parliament on EU-Japan relations: "There is absolutely no question . . . of the internal market applying to a whole range of goods . . . but not to . . . the car" (*Debates of the European Parliament*, 11 June 1991, 115).

6. The discussion by Pierre Vigier is especially interesting because of his personal role, within DG III, in formulating Commission policy. He was also very helpful to this author during the research on this project.

7. For the full flavor of his personality, see the interview with the title "Thank God for Quotas!" (*European Affairs*, December 1991, 68–72).

8. Speech by Raymond Levy before the European Parliamentary Committee on External Relations and the Political Affairs Committee hearing on relations between the European Community and Japan on 16 and 17 September 1991 (author's transcription and translation).

9. The issue of trade statistics for the sector is a revealing indicator of the confidence that the Japanese elicited from the Europeans. ACEA relied, in large measure, on work done by the CCFA for its estimates of the European market. The CCFA, in turn, relied on figures provided by JAMA for estimates of the Japanese share. These figures always proved to be "very fine, very precise" (interview with Béatrice de Castlenau, CCFA, 22 June 1992).

Chapter 6

1. By implication the agency to which responsibilities are delegated responds as the enacting coalition desires—its administrative procedures will be "stacked" to ensure just that.

2. The role of the member states was significant in many areas of competition policy, but not in the case of antitrust and the auto sector. State aid will reveal much more about the direct and indirect role of the governments of the member states.

3. For an overview of the economic literature on the value of firm concentration in the European context see Jacquemin 1990. For a characteristic German point of view see Neumann 1990. On the BKA see Wilks and McGowan 1995.

4. For a thorough overview of EU competition policy see Goyder 1988; and Green, Hartley, and Usher 1991, 197–307; on the role of discretion see Harding 1993; for a general statement by the Director DG IV see Ehlermann 1992.

5. There is a significant objection to this line of reasoning. As the consequences of the prominent solution became known to both states and firms, uncertainty was likely to give way, in some cases, to serious dissatisfaction. One should then expect to observe political struggles over change in the institutional arena. The joint decision trap may favor the status quo—but it may be that some changes could be made. At this point uncertainty returned, and the relevant actors waited to learn the character of the adjusted solution fostered by the changes in the institutional arena. This is a very interesting pattern of politics, in which institutions act as sticky elements in a series of punctuated equilibria.

6. For example, polypropylene producers and PVC producers were fined over ECU 50 million by DG IV (OJ 1986, L 230/1; OJ 1988, L 74/21).

7. It has been suggested that lawyers in DG IV would probably have regarded a failure to win cases in the Court as a greater threat to their legitimacy than any other kind of political challenge (Wilks 1992, 13). Goldstein (1996) shows how rulings by binational dispute settlement panels may be anticipated by an administrative agency, which therefore moderates its output to avoid being checked at the higher level.

8. Most startling of all was the backlog of cases: 3,239, including 359 complaints by private parties and 271 investigations initiated by the Commission. This represented a slight improvement over the previous year.

9. The BKA in Germany was criticized for its resort to administrative guidance rather than legalistic enforcement, yet its record was much less weighted in that direction (see Wilks and McGowan 1995, 52).

10. The power to issue group, or block, exemptions derives not from Regulation 17, but from Regulation 19/65.

11. Such a notice was not a regulation but "advice," which could, for example, be considered by the ECJ in making a ruling, but which was not binding or directly effective.

12. From this point of view the regulation could be seen as the best outcome available (for consumers), given that greater legal and institutional uncertainty might have led to greater abuse and less transparency.

13. Notwithstanding the quite high average level of state aid in the EU—3 percent of GDP—the figures presented do not capture many of the other ways the governments of the member states used to help firms: public procurement, tax policy, energy policy, etc., could all be structured so as to privilege certain firms and certain sectors.

14. However, Article 93(3) is directly effective; thus a complainant can obtain an injunction from a national court preventing the initiation of an aid scheme before the Commission has ruled.

15. The fact that the only profitable legal avenue for member states when challenging the Commission seemed to be a procedural one is revealing. On matters of substance the ECJ clearly allowed the Commission almost complete discretion.

Chapter 7

1. Japanese transplant production, while still projected to rise steadily, had not met its early goals. Nissan (due to a contractual dispute with a former distributor) actually lost share in this period, while Honda lost its connection to Rover after its sale to BMW. Honda and Toyota both had large, integrated operations in production, but output was still below 200,000 units a year in each case. There were also continuing complaints by the Japanese about the quality of local (U.K.) suppliers (*Financial Times*, 16 March 1995, 15). The rising yen, in addition to the introduction of a variety of competitive models by European producers, served to keep imports from Japan well below the agreed ceiling in 1994 and 1995 (*Financial Times*, 10 September 1995, 2).

2. This suggests that the pursuit of national governments as allies by individual firms was a sign of industry weakness and division. It was a less effective strategy, given the way the institutions of the EU after the SEA limited the opportunities of any single member state to prevent common decisions. Of course, an individual government might still be relied upon in an area such as state aid, where murky deals might be cut on a case-by-case basis away from public scrutiny.

3. An important aspect of the exemption from antitrust was that it allowed for the informal monitoring of the agreement with the Japanese.

4. It may be supposed that those states who favored mutual recognition merely believed that, absent the political bargaining, the consequences of harmonization on the basis of mutual recognition would be in their favor.

5. The "new approach" was given specific form by the model directive on technical harmonization (Annex II, Council Resolution on a New Approach to Technical Harmonization, OJ, 1985, C 136/1). For a full description and discussion see Lauwaars 1988.

6. Historically, the Parliament had trouble even obtaining a quorum. The member states may, therefore, have discounted the possibility that a coalition within that institution could surface that was seriously at odds with the interests of most of the member states, or of an influential industry. However, two elements in the situation served to make such a coalition possible. Environmental issues were the only ones that the largest group in Parliament were likely to agree on, and "green" issues were, by chance, especially salient at that juncture.

Bibliography

ACEA. 1991. *Position on Desirable Policy Measures in Support of the European Industry's Industrial Adjustment Process.* Brussels: Association des Constructeurs Européens d'Automobile.

Acheson, Keith. 1989. Power steering the Canadian automotive industry: The 1965 Canada-U.S.A. auto pact and political exchange. *Journal of Economic Behavior and Organization* 11:237–51.

Alt, James, and K. Crystal. 1983. *Political Economics.* Berkeley: University of California Press.

Alter, Karen, and Sophie Meunier-Aitsahalia. 1994. Judicial politics in the European Community: European integration and the pathbreaking *Cassis de Dijon* decision. *Comparative Political Studies* 26:535–61.

Amin, Ash, and Ian Smith. 1991. Vertical integration or disintegration? The case of the U.K. car parts industry. In Christopher Law, ed., *Restructuring the Global Automobile Industry: National and Regional Impacts.* New York: Routledge.

Anderson, Svein S., and Kjell A. Eliassen. 1991. European Community lobbying. *European Journal of Political Research* 20:173–87.

Assemblée Nationale. 1992. *Rapport de la Commission d'Enquête Chargée d'Étudier la Situation Actuelle et les Perspectives de l'Industrie Automobile Française.* Seconde Session Ordinaire de 1991–1992. Paris: Journal Officiel.

Aujac, Henri. 1986. An introduction to French industrial policy. In William James Adams and Christian Stoffaes, eds., *French Industrial Policy.* Washington, D.C.: Brookings Institution.

Austen-Smith, David. 1991. Rational consumers and irrational voters: A review essay on "Black Hole Tariffs and Endogenous Tariff Theory." *Economics and Politics* 3:73–92.

Baldwin, Richard. 1989. The growth effects of 1991. *Economic Policy* 4:248–81.

Bangemann, Martin. 1992. Pour une politique industrielle Européene. *Revue du Marché Commun et de l'Union Européene* 358:67–371.

Banville, Étienne de, and Jean-Jacques Chanaron. 1991. *Vers un Système Automobile Européen.* Paris: Economica.

Bawn, Kathy. 1995. Political control versus expertise: Congressional choices about administrative procedures. *American Political Science Review* 89:62–73.

Becker, Gary S. 1983. A theory of competition among pressure groups for political influence. *Quarterly Journal of Economics* 98:371–400.

Becune, Stéphane, and Claude Mathieu. 1991. The determinants of intra-industry trade: The case of the auto industry. *Welt Wirtschaftliches Archiv* 127:35–51.

Belassa, Bela, and Luc Bauwens. 1988. Inter-industry and intra-industry specialization in manufactured goods. *Welt Wirtschaftliches Archiv* 124:1–18.

Berger, S. 1981. Lame ducks and national champions: Industrial policy in the Fifth Republic. In Stanley Hoffmann and William Andrews, eds., *The Fifth Republic at Twenty*. Cambridge: Cambridge University Press.

Beseler, Ariane. 1991. La protection intracommunautaire à l'égard des produits importés dans la CEE (Articles 115 CEE). *Revue de Droit des Affaires Internationales* 8:1119–44.

Bhagwati, Jagdish. 1988. *Protectionism*. Cambridge: MIT Press.

Bianchi, Patrizio, Sabino Cassese, and Vincent della Sala. 1989. Privatisation in Italy: Aims and constraints. *West European Politics* 13:87–100.

Bluman, Claude. 1992. Régime des aides d'État: Jurisprudence récente de la Cour de Justice (1989–1992). *Revue du Marché Commun et de l'Union Européene* 361:721–39.

Boston Consulting Group. 1991. *The Competitive Challenge Facing the European Automotive Components Industry: Executive Summary*. Brussels: Commission of the European Communities.

Bourdet, Yves. 1988. *International Integration, Market Structure, and Prices*. London: Routledge.

Bowman, John R. 1989. *Capitalist Collective Action: Competition, Cooperation, and Conflict in the Coal Industry*. Cambridge: Cambridge University Press.

Boyd, Gavin. 1991. *Structuring International Economic Cooperation*. London: Pinter Publishers.

Brander, James A., and Barbara J. Spencer. 1984. Tariff protection and imperfect competition. In H. Kierzkowski, ed., *Monopolistic Competition and International Trade*. Oxford: Oxford University Press.

Bressand, Albert. 1990. Beyond interdependence: 1992 as a global challenge. *International Affairs* 66:47–65.

Burley, Anne-Marie, and Walter Mattli. 1993. Europe before the court: A political theory of legal integration. *International Organization* 47:41–76.

Camerra-Rowe, Pamela. 1993. The political responses of firms to the 1992 Single Market program: The case of the German and British automobile industries. Paper presented at the annual meeting of the American Political Science Association, Washington, D.C., 2–5 September.

Cassing, James, Timothy J. McKeown, and Jack Ochs. 1986. The political economy of the tariff cycle. *American Political Science Review* 80:843–62.

Caves, Richard E. 1976. Economic models of political choice: Canada's tariff structure. *Canadian Journal of Economics* 9:278–300.

CCFA (Comité des Constructeurs Français d'Automobile). 1990. *L'Industrie Automobile en France, 1990.* Paris: CCFA.

———. 1991. *Le Commerce Mondial en 1989: Les Produits de l'Industrie Automobile.* Paris: CCFA.

CEC (Commission of the European Communities). 1987. *Sixteenth Report on Competition Policy.* Luxembourg: Office for Official Publications of the European Communities.

———. 1988a. *Basic Statistics of the Community.* Brussels: Office for Official Publications of the European Communities.

———. 1988b. The economics of 1992: An assessment of the potential economic effects of completing the internal market of the European Community. *European Economy* 35:1–222.

———. 1988c. *Innovation in the EC Automotive Industry.* Brussels: Office for Official Publications of the European Communities.

———. 1988d. *Research on the "Cost of Non-Europe", Basic Findings.* Vols. 1–16. Brussels: Commission of the European Communities.

———. 1988e. *Seventeenth Report on Competition Policy.* Luxembourg: Office for Official Publications of the European Communities.

———. 1989a. *EEC Competition Policy in the Single Market.* Brussels: Office for Official Publications of the European Communities.

———. 1989b. *Eighteenth Report on Competition Policy.* Luxembourg: Office for Official Publications of the European Communities.

———. 1989c. *L'Évolution de la Situation Concurrentielle Consecutive a Certain Fusions dans les Secteurs de l'Automobile et des Communications.* Brussels: Office for Official Publications of the European Communities.

———. 1989d. *First Survey on State Aids in the European Community.* Brussels: Office for Official Publications of the European Communities.

———. 1989e. Horizontal mergers and competition policy in the European Community. *European Economy* 40:1–98.

———. 1990a. *The Effect of Different State Aid Measures on Intra-Community Competition.* Luxembourg: Office for Official Publications of the European Communities.

———. 1990b. The impact of the internal market by industrial sector: The challenge for the member states. *European Economy,* special edition, 1–340.

———. 1990c. *Nineteenth Report on Competition Policy.* Luxembourg: Office for Official Publications of the European Communities.

———. 1991a. Fair competition in the internal market: Community state aid policy. *European Economy* 48:7–114.

———. 1991b. *Twentieth Report on Competition Policy.* Luxembourg: Office for Official Publications of the European Communities.

———. 1992a. *Intra-Community Car Price Differentials Report.* Luxembourg: Office for Official Publications of the European Communities.

———. 1992b. *Twenty First Report on Competition Policy.* Luxembourg: Office for Official Publications of the European Communities.

———. 1993. *Twenty Second Report on Competition Policy*. Luxembourg: Office for Official Publications of the European Communities.

Cecchini, Paolo, et al. 1988. *The European Challenge 1992: The Benefits of a Single Market*. Aldershot: Wildwood House for the Commission.

CEPS. 1992. *Refurbishing the Automotive Industry: The Role of the EC*. Proceedings, CEPS Business Policy Seminar, no. 43, Brussels, 26 May.

Chanaron, Jean-Jacques, and D. A. Spagni. 1987. *The U.K. Car Industry in the 1980's*. Geneva: International Labor Office.

Coase, Ronald. 1937. The nature of the firm. *Economica* 4:386–405.

Cocks, Peter. 1980. Towards a Marxist theory of European integration. *International Organization* 34:1–40.

Coen, David. 1997. The evolution of the large firm as a political actor in the European Union. *Journal of European Public Policy* 4:91–108.

Coleman, William, and Wyn Grant. 1988. The organizational cohesion and political access of business: A study of comprehensive business associations. *European Journal of Political Research* 16:467–87.

Commissariat Général du Plan. 1992. *L'Automobile, les Défis et les Hommes: Rapport du Groupe de Stratégie Industrielle "automobile" Présidé par M. Gilbert Rutman*. Paris: La Documentation Française.

Corbett, Richard. 1993. *The Treaty of Maastricht: From Conception to Ratification; A Comprehensive Reference Guide*. Harlow, U.K.: Longman Current Affairs.

Corcelle, Guy. 1989. La "voiture propre" en Europe! Le bout du tunnel est en vue. *Revue du Marché Commun* 331:513–26.

Cowhey, Peter, and E. Long. 1983. Testing theories of regime change: Hegemonic decline or surplus capacity? *International Organization* 37:157–88.

Cowles, Maria Green. 1995. Setting the agenda for a new Europe: The ERT and EC, 1992. *Journal of Common Market Studies* 33:501–26.

Davenport, Michael. 1982. The economic impact of the EC. In Andrea Boltho, ed., *The European Economy: Growth and Crisis*. Oxford: Oxford University Press.

Del Monte, Alfredo. 1986. The impact of Italian industrial policy, 1960–1980. In P. Hall, ed., *European Industrial Policy*. London: Croom Helm.

de Nards, Sergio. 1992. *La Specializzazione delle Industrie Manifatturiere dei Paesi CEE nella Prospettiva del Mercato Unico*. Rome: Confindustria, Centro Studi, no. 60.

de Ruyt, Jean. 1989. *L'Acte Unique Européen: Commentaire*. Brussels: Editions de l'Université de Bruxelles.

Dicken, Peter. 1987. Japanese penetration of the European automobile industry: The arrival of Nissan in the United Kingdom. *Tijdschrift voor Economische en Sociale Geografie* 78:94–107.

Diekmann, Achim. 1992a. Foreign investment and trade policy. Paper presented at OECD meeting "Globalisation in the Automobile Industry," Paris, 3 April.

———. 1992b. Perspektiven der europaïschen Automobilindustrie. *Wirtschaftdienst* 2:1–6.

Dixit, Avinash. 1983. International trade policy for oligopolistic industries. *Economic Journal* 94:1–16.

―――. 1988. Optimal trade and industrial policies for the U.S. automobile industry. In Robert Feenstra, ed., *Empirical Methods for International Trade*. Cambridge: MIT Press.

Dobbin, Frank R. 1994. Cultural models of organization: The social construction of rational organizing principles. In Diana Crane, ed., *The Sociology of Culture: Emerging Theoretical Perspectives*. Oxford: Basil Blackwell.

Doner, Richard F. 1991. *Driving a Bargain: Automobile Industrialisation and Japanese Investment in Southeast Asia*. Berkeley: University of California Press.

Dunn, James A. 1987. Automobiles in international trade: Regime change or persistence? *International Organization* 41:225–52.

Dunning, J. 1988. *Explaining International Production*. Boston: Unwin Hyman.

Dunning, J., and P. Robson. 1987. Multinational corporate integration and regional economic integration. *Journal of Common Market Studies* 26:103–25.

Ehlermann, Claus-Dieter. 1992. The contribution of EC competition policy to the Single Market. *Common Market Law Review* 29:257–82.

Eichener, Volker. 1993. Social dumping or innovative regulation? Processes and outcomes of European decision making in the sector of health and safety at work harmonization. EUI Working Paper SPS No. 92/28, European University Institute, Florence, Department of Political and Social Sciences.

Erickson, Christopher, and Sarosh Kuruvilla. 1993. Labor costs and the social dumping debate in the European Community. Unpublished manuscript.

EP (European Parliament). 1985. *The Automobile Industry in the Community: Evidence Given on the Automobile Industry for the Hearing Organised by the Committee on Economic and Monetary Affairs and Industrial Policy*, 28, 29 October. Brussels: European Parliament Secretariat.

Evans, Andrew, and Stephen Martin. 1991. Socially acceptable distortion of competition: Community policy on state aid. *European Law Review* 16:79–111.

Finnemore, Martha. 1996. Norms, culture, and world politics: Insights from sociology's institutionalism. *International Organization* 50:325–48.

Fiorina, Morris P. 1982. Legislative choice of regulatory forms: Legislative process or administrative process? *Public Choice* 39:33–66.

Fitzmaurice, John. 1988. An analysis of the European Community's co-operation procedure. *Journal of Common Market Studies* 28:389–400.

Flanagan, Robert J. 1993. European wage equalization since the Treaty of Rome. In Lloyd Ulman, Barry Eichengreen, and William T. Dickens, eds., *Labor and an Integrated Europe*. Washington, D.C.: Brookings Institution.

Frankel, Jeffrey, Steve Phillips, and Menzie Chinn. 1992. Financial and currency integration in the European Monetary System: The statistical record. The Political Economy of European Integration Working Group, Working Paper 1.3, Center for German and European Studies, University of California, Berkeley.

Frankel, Jeffrey, and Shang-Jin Wei. 1994. European integration and the regionalization of world trade and currencies: The economics and the politics. Paper prepared for the project on the Political Economy of European Integration, University of California.

Frieden, Jeffry A. 1991. Invested interests: The politics of national economic policies in a world of global economic finance. *International Organization* 45:425–51.

————. 1994. Making commitments: France and Italy in the European Monetary System, 1979–1985. In Jeffry Frieden and Barry Eichengreen, eds., *The Political Economy of European Monetary Unification*. Boulder: Westview Press.

Frieden, Jeffry A., and Ronald Rogowski. 1996. The impact of the international economy on national policies: An analytical overview. In Robert O. Keohane and Helen Milner, eds., *Internationalization and Domestic Politics*. Cambridge: Cambridge University Press.

Friedman, Alan. 1989. *Agnelli, FIAT and the Network of Italian Power*. New York: New American Library.

Friedman, David. 1988. *The Misunderstood Miracle: Industrial Development and Political Change in Japan*. Ithaca: Cornell University Press.

Garrett, Geoffery. 1992. International cooperation and institutional choice: The European Community's internal market. *International Organization* 46:533–60.

Garrett, Geoffery, and Peter Lange. 1996. Internationalization, institutions, and political change. In Robert O. Keohane and Helen Milner, eds., *Internationalization and Domestic Politics*. Cambridge: Cambridge University Press.

Garrett, Geoffery, and George Tsebelis. 1996. An institutional critique of intergovernmentalism. *International Organization* 50:269–300.

Garrett, Geoffery, and Barry B. Weingast. 1993. Ideas, interests, and institutions: Constructing the European Community's internal market. In Judith Goldstein and Robert O. Keohane, eds., *Ideas and Foreign Policy: Beliefs, Institutions, and Political Change*. Ithaca: Cornell University Press.

Gatsios, Konstantine, and Paul Seabright. 1989. Regulation in the European Community. *Oxford Review of Economic Policy* 5:37–60.

Geroski, Paul A. 1989. European industrial policy and industrial policy in Europe. *Oxford Review of Economic Policy* 5:298–333.

Geroski, Paul A., and Alexis Jacquemin. 1989. Industrial change, barriers to mobility, and European industrial policy. In Alexis Jacquemin and André Sapir, eds., *The European Internal Market: Trade and Competition*. Oxford: Oxford University Press.

Gilchrist, Joseph, and David Deacon. 1990. Curbing subsidies. In Peter Montagnon, ed., *European Competition Policy*. London: Royal Institute of International Affairs.

Glatz, Hanns R. 1989. The other side of the coin: Potential shortcomings of the 1992 internal market program, exemplified by its impact on the automobile industry. In J. Schwarze, ed., *Legislation for Europe, 1992*. Baden-Baden: Nomos Verlag.

Golden, Miriam. 1988. *Labor Divided: Austerity and Working Class Politics in Contemporary Italy*. Ithaca: Cornell University Press.

Goldstein, Judith. 1988. Ideas, institutions, and American trade policy. *International Organization* 42:179–217.

———. 1996. International law and domestic institutions: Reconciling North American "unfair" trade laws. *International Organization* 50:541–64.

Golub, Jonathon. 1999. In the shadow of the vote? Decision making in the European Community. *International Organization* 53:733–64.

Goyder, D. G. 1988. *EEC Competition Law*. Oxford: Oxford University Press.

Grant, Wyn, William Paterson, and Alberto Martinelli. 1988. Large firms as political actors: A comparative analysis of the chemical industry in Britain, Italy, and West Germany. *West European Politics* 12:72–90.

Grant, Wyn, William Paterson, and Colin Whitson. 1988. *Government and the Chemical Industry: A Comparative Study of Britain and West Germany*. Oxford: Clarendon Press.

———. 1989. *Government and Industry: A Comparative Analysis of the U.S., Canada, and the U.K.* Brookfield: Gower Publishing Co.

Green, A. W. 1969. *Political Integration by Jurisprudence*. Leyden: Sijthoff.

Green, Nicholas, Trevor C. Hartley, and John A. Usher. 1991. *The Legal Foundations of the Single European Market*. Oxford: Oxford University Press.

Greenaway, David. 1987. Intra-industry trade, intra-firm trade, and European integration: Evidence, gains, and policy aspects. *Journal of Common Market Studies* 26, no. 2: 153–72.

Grieco, Joseph M. 1988. Anarchy and the limits of cooperation: A realist critique of the newest liberal institutionalism. *International Organization* 42, no. 3: 485–507.

Grubel, H. G., and P. J. Lloyd. 1975. *Intra-industry Trade: The Theory and Measurement of International Trade in Differentiated Products*. New York: Wiley.

Haas, Ernst B. 1958. *The Uniting of Europe: Political, Social, and Economic Forces, 1950–57*. Stanford: Stanford University Press.

———. 1961. International integration: The European and universal process. *International Organization* 15:366–92.

Haas, Peter. 1992. Introduction: Epistemic communities and international policy coordination. *International Organization* 46, no. 1: 1–36.

Hall, Peter. 1986. *Governing the Economy: The Politics of State Intervention in Britain and France*. Oxford: Oxford University Press.

Hanson, Brian T. 1998. What happened to Fortress Europe? External trade policy liberalization in the European Union. *International Organization* 52:55–86.

Harding, Christopher. 1993. *European Community Investigations and Sanctions: The Supranational Control of Business Delinquency*. Leicester: Leicester University Press.

Hart, Jeffrey A. 1992. *Rival Capitalists: International Competitiveness in the United States, Japan, and Western Europe*. Ithaca: Cornell University Press.

Hayes-Renshaw, Fiona, and Helen Wallace. 1995. Executive power in the European Union: The function and limits of the Council of Ministers. *Journal of European Public Policy* 2:559–82.

Heclo, Hugh. 1972. Review article: Policy analysis. *British Journal of Political Science* 2:83–108.

Helm, Dieter, and Stephen Smith. 1989. The assessment: Economic integration and the role of the European Community. *Oxford Review of Economic Policy* 5, no. 2: 1–19.

Helpman, Ethan, and Paul Krugman, eds. 1985. *Market Structure and Foreign Trade: Increasing Returns, Imperfect Competition, and the International Economy.* Cambridge: MIT Press.

Helpman, Ethan, and Assaf Razin, eds. 1991. *International Trade and Trade Policy.* Cambridge: MIT Press.

Hoffmann, Stanley. 1966. Obstinate or obsolete: The fate of the nation state and the case of Western Europe. *Daedalus* 95, no. 3: 862–915.

Hölzer, Heinrich. 1990. Merger control. In Peter Montagnon, ed., *European Competition Policy.* London: Royal Institute of International Affairs.

Hosli, Madeleine O. 1993. The admission of the European Free Trade Association states to the European Community. *International Organization* 47, no. 4: 629–43.

House of Commons, Trade and Industry Committee. 1987. *The Motor Components Industry.* Session 1986–1987, Minutes of Evidence. London: HMSO.

House of Lords, Select Committee on the European Community. 1990. *A Single Market for Cars.* Session 1989–90, 22nd Report. London: HMSO.

Hufbauer, Gary C. 1990. An overview. In Gary Hufbauer, ed., *Europe 1992: An American Perspective.* Washington, D.C.: Brookings Institution.

Hufbauer, Gary C., and Jeffrey Schott. 1993. *NAFTA: An Assessment.* Washington, D.C.: Institute for International Economics.

Hülsberg, Werner. 1988. *The German Greens: A Social and Political Profile.* New York: Verso.

Jacobs, Francis, and Richard Corbett. 1990. *The European Parliament.* Boulder: Westview Press.

Jacquemin, Alexis. 1990. Horizontal concentration and European merger policy. *European Economic Review* 34:539–50.

Jones, Daniel T. 1985. The internationalization of the automobile industry. *Journal of General Management* 10, no. 3: 23–44.

Katzenstein, Peter. 1977. Conclusion: Domestic structures and strategies of foreign economic policy. In Peter Katzenstein, ed., *Between Power and Plenty: Foreign Economic Policies of Advanced Industrial States.* Madison: University of Wisconsin Press.

———. 1985. *Small States in World Markets: Industrial Policy in Europe.* Ithaca: Cornell University Press.

Keeley, James F. 1983. Cast in concrete for all time: The negotiation of the auto pact. *Canadian Journal of Political Science* 16, no. 2: 281–98.

Keohane, Robert O. 1984. *After Hegemony: Cooperation and Discord in the World Political Economy.* Princeton: Princeton University Press.

———. 1986. *Neorealism and Its Critics.* New York: Columbia University Press.

Keohane, Robert O., and Stanley Hoffmann. 1991. *The New European Community: Decisionmaking and Institutional Change.* Boulder: Westview Press.

Kim, Charlotte. 1992. CATs and mice: The politics of setting car emission standards. Working Document No. 64. Brussels: Center for European Policy Studies.

Kingdon, John W. 1984. *Agendas, Alternatives, and Public Policy.* Boston: Little, Brown.

Kirman, Alan, and Nathalie Schueller. 1990. Price leadership and discrimination in the European car market. *Journal of Industrial Economics* 39, no. 1: 69–91.

Krämer, Ludwig. 1987. The Single European Act and environment protection: Reflections on several new provisions in Community law. *Common Market Law Review* 24:9–40.

Krasner, Stephen. 1991. Global communications and national power: Life on the Pareto frontier. *World Politics* 43:336–66.

Krause, Lawrence B. 1968. *European Economic Integration and the United States.* Washington, D.C.: Brookings Institution.

Kreuger, Anne O. 1974. The political economy of the rent-seeking society. *American Economic Review* 64, no. 3: 291–303.

Krugman, Paul R. 1979. Increasing returns, monopolistic competition, and international trade. *Journal of International Economics* 9, no. 4: 469–79.

———. 1984. Import protection as export promotion: International competition in the presence of oligopoly and economies of scale. In H. Kierzkowski, ed., *Monopolistic Competition and International Trade.* Oxford: Oxford University Press.

———. 1986. *Strategic Trade Policy and the New International Economics.* Cambridge: MIT Press.

———. 1987. Increasing returns and the theory of international trade. In Truman Bewley, ed., *Advances in Economic Theory, Fifth World Congress.* Cambridge: Cambridge University Press.

———. 1989. Economic integration of Europe: Some conceptual issues. In Alexis Jacquemin and André Sapir, eds., *The European Internal Market: Trade and Competition.* Oxford: Oxford University Press.

———. 1995. The move toward free trade zones. In Phillip King, ed., *International Economics and International Economic Policy: A Reader.* 2d ed. New York: McGraw-Hill.

Krugman, Paul R., and Maurice Obstfeld. 1994. *International Economics: Theory and Practice.* New York: HarperCollins.

Kurth, James. 1979. The political consequences of the product cycle: Industrial history and political outcomes. *International Organization* 33, no. 1: 1–34.

Lauwaars, Richard H. 1988. The "model directive" on technical harmonization. In Roland Bieber et al., eds., *1992: One European Market?* Baden-Baden: Nomos Verlagsgesellschaft.

Laux, James M. 1992. *The European Automobile Industry.* New York: Macmillan.

Law, Christopher. 1991. *Restructuring the Global Automobile Industry: National and Regional Impacts.* London: Routledge.

Lipsey, Richard. 1960. The theory of customs unions: A general survey. *Economic Journal* 70:496–513.

Lodge, Juliet. 1994. *The European Community and the Challenge of the Future.* 2d ed. London: Pinter.

Ludlow, Peter. 1991. The European Commission. In Robert O. Keohane and Stanley Hoffmann, eds., *The New European Community: Decisionmaking and Institutional Change.* Boulder: Westview Press.

McCubbins, Mathew. 1985. The legislative design of regulatory procedure. *American Journal of Political Science* 29:721–48.

McCubbins, Mathew, Roger Noll, and Barry Weingast. 1987. Administrative procedures as instruments of political control. *Journal of Law, Economics and Organization* 3, no. 2: 243–77.

McCubbins, Mathew, and Thomas Schwartz. 1984. Congressional oversight overlooked: Police patrols versus fire alarms. *American Journal of Political Science* 28:167–79.

McLaughlin, A., and G. Gordon. 1994. The rationality of lobbying in Europe: Why are Euro groups so numerous and so weak? Some evidence from the car industry. In Sonia Mazey and Jeremy Richardson, eds., *Lobbying in the European Community.* Oxford: Oxford University Press.

McLeod, J. M. 1992. *The World Motor Industry: Anatomy by Manufacturer.* London: Economist Intelligence Unit, Special Report 2191.

McNamara, Kathleen. 1998. *The Currency of Ideas: Monetary Politics in the European Union.* Ithaca: Cornell University Press.

Magee, Stephen P., William A. Brock, and Leslie Young. 1989. *Black Hole Tariffs and Endogenous Policy Theory.* Cambridge: Cambridge University Press.

Majone, Giandomenico. 1993. The European Community: Between social policy and social regulation. *Journal of Common Market Studies* 31, no. 2: 153–70.

———. 1994. The rise of the regulatory state in Europe. *West European Politics* 17, no. 3: 77–101.

Malot, Maureen Appel. 1993. *Driving Continentally: National Policies and the North American Auto Industry.* Ottawa: Carleton University Press.

Marks, Gary. 1992. Structural policy in the European Community. In Alberta M. Sbragia, ed., *Europolitics: Institutions and Policymaking in the "New" European Community.* Washington, D.C.: Brookings Institution.

Markusen, James A. 1983. Factor movements and commodity trade as complements. *Journal of International Economics* 13:341–56.

Markusen, James A., and Anthony J. Venables. 1988. Trade policy with increasing returns and imperfect competition: Contradictory results from competing assumptions. *Journal of International Economics* 24:299–316.

Martin, Lisa L. 1992. *Coercive Cooperation: Explaining Multilateral Economic Sanctions.* Princeton: Princeton University Press.

———. 1993. International and domestic institutions in the EMU process. *Economics and Politics* 5, no. 2: 125–44.

Mason, Mark. 1994. The political economy of Japanese automobile investment in Europe. In Mark Mason and Dennis Encarnation, eds., *Does Ownership Matter? Japanese Multinationals in Europe.* Oxford: Clarendon Press.

Maxcy, George. 1981. *The Multinational Motor Industry.* London: Croom Helm.

Mazey, Sonia, and Jeremy Richardson, eds. 1994. *Lobbying in the European Community.* Oxford: Oxford University Press.

Mendes, Marques. 1987. *Economic Integration and Growth in Europe.* London: Croom Hill.

Mertens, Yves, and Victor Ginsburgh. 1985. Product differentiation and price discrimination in the E.C.: The case of automobiles. *Journal of Industrial Economics* no. 2: 151–66.

Milgrom, Paul, Douglass North, and Barry Weingast. 1990. The role of institutions in the revival of trade: The law merchant, private judges, and the champagne fairs. *Economics and Politics* 3, no. 1: 1–23.

Miller, Gary J., and Terry M. Moe. 1983. Bureaucrats, legislators, and the size of government. *American Political Science Review* 77:297–322.

Milner, Helen. 1988. *Resisting Protectionism: Global Industries and the Politics of International Trade.* Princeton: Princeton University Press.

Milner, Helen, and David B. Yoffie. 1989. Between free trade and protectionism: Strategic trade policy and a theory of corporate trade demands. *International Organization* 43, no. 2: 239–72.

Milward, Alan S. 1984. *The Reconstruction of Western Europe.* London: Methuen.

———. 1992. *The European Rescue of the Nation State.* London: Routledge.

Moe, Terry M. 1987. An assessment of the positive theory of congressional dominance. *Legislative Studies Quarterly* 12:475–520.

———. 1990. Political institutions: The neglected side of the story. *Journal of Law, Economics and Organization* 6:213–66.

Molle, William. 1990. *The Economics of European Integration: Theory, Practice, and Policy.* Brookfield: Dartmouth.

Moravcsik, Andrew. 1991. Negotiating the Single European Act: National interests and conventional statecraft in the European Community. *International Organization* 45, no. 1: 19–56.

———. 1993. Preferences and power in the European Community: A liberal intergovernmentalist approach. *Journal of Common Market Studies* 31, no. 4: 473–524.

———. 1998. *The Choice for Europe: Social Purpose and State Power from Messina to Maastricht.* Ithaca: Cornell University Press.

Moser, Peter. 1996. The European Parliament as a conditional agenda setter: A critique of Tsebelis (1994). *American Journal of Political Science* 90:834–39.

Mundell, Robert A. 1957. International trade and factor mobility. *American Economic Review* 47:321–35.

MVMA (Motor Vehicle Manufacturers Association of the United States). 1988, 1991, 1992. *World Motor Vehicle Data* (serial). Detroit: MVMA.

Nelson, Douglas. 1988. Endogenous tariff theory: A critical survey. *American Journal of Political Science* 32:796–837.

Neumann, Manfred. 1990. Industrial policy and competition policy. *European Economic Review* 34:562–67.

Nevin, Edward. 1990. *The Economics of Europe.* London: Macmillan.

Niskanen, William. 1971. *Bureaucracy and Representative Government.* Hawthorne: Aldine.

Nugent, Neill. 1994. *The Government and Politics of the European Union.* Durham: Duke University Press.

Oatley, Thomas H. 1997. *Monetary Politics: Exchange Rate Cooperation in the European Union.* Ann Arbor: University of Michigan Press.

OECD (Organization for Economic Cooperation and Development). 1983. *Long Term Outlook for the World Automobile Industry.* Paris: OECD.

———. 1987. COMTAP (Compatible Trade and Production Data Base). Paris: OECD.

Olsen, Mancur. 1965. *The Logic of Collective Action.* Cambridge: Harvard University Press.

Ordeshook, Peter C., and Thomas Schwartz. 1987. Agenda and the control of political outcomes. *American Political Science Review* 81:179–200.

Owen, Nicholas. 1983. *Economies of Scale, Competitiveness, and Trade Patterns within the European Community.* Oxford: Oxford University Press.

Peltzman, Sam. 1976. Toward a more general theory of regulation. *Journal of Law and Economics* 19, no. 2: 211–48.

———. 1980. The growth of government. *Journal of Law and Economics* 23:209–87.

Perrin-Pelletier, François. 1988. 1992: A European market for cars? *Long Range Planning* 21, no. 3: 27–33.

Peters, Guy. 1991. Bureaucratic politics and the institutions of the European Community. In Alberta Sbragia, ed., *Europolitics: Institutions and Policymaking in the New European Community.* Washington, D.C.: Brookings Institution.

Pinder, John. 1988. Enhancing the Community's economic and political capacity: Some consequences of completing the internal market. In Roland Bieber et al., eds., *1992: One European Market?* Baden-Baden: Nomos Verlagsgesellschaft.

———. 1991. *European Community: The Building of a Union.* Oxford: Oxford University Press.

Pollack, Mark. 1997. Delegation, agency, and agenda setting in the European Community. *International Organization* 51:99–135.

Putnam, Robert. 1988. Diplomacy and domestic politics: The logic of two-level games. *International Organization* 43, no. 3: 427–60.

Quattrone, George A., and Amos Tversky. 1988. Contrasting rational and psychological analyses of political choice. *American Political Science Review* 82:719–36.

Quinn, Dennis Patrick. 1988. *Restructuring the Automobile Industry: A Study of Firms and States in Modern Capitalism.* New York: Columbia University Press.

Rapoport, Anatol. 1960. *Fights, Games, and Debates.* Ann Arbor: University of Michigan Press.

Rasmusen, Eric. 1989. *Games and Information: An Introduction to Game Theory.* Cambridge: Basil Blackwell.

Rasmussen, H. 1986. *On Law and Policy in the European Court of Justice.* Boston: Martinus Nijhoff.

Ray, Edward. 1991. Changing patterns of protectionism: The fall in tariffs and the rise in non-tariff barriers. In David Lake and Jeffry Frieden, eds., *International Political Economy: Perspectives on Global Power and Wealth*, 2d ed. New York: St. Martin's Press.

Rehbinder, Eckard, and Richard Stewart. 1985. Legal integration in federal systems: European Community environmental law. *American Journal of Comparative Law* 33, no. 3: 371–443.

Reich, Simon. 1989. Roads to follow: Regulating direct foreign investment. *International Organization* 43, no. 4: 543–84.

———. 1990. *The Fruits of Fascism: Postwar Prosperity in Historical Perspective*. Ithaca: Cornell University Press.

Rhys, D. G. 1992. The motor industry in the 1990s: A decade of change. Unpublished paper.

Richardson, David. 1990. The political economy of strategic trade policy. *International Organization* 44, no. 1: 107–35.

Rogowski, Ronald. 1989. *Commerce and Coalitions: How Trade Affects Domestic Political Alignments*. Princeton: Princeton University Press.

Roos, Daniel, and Robert Altschuler. 1984. *The Future of the Automobile: The Report of MIT's International Automobile Program*. Cambridge: MIT Press.

Ruggie, John. 1983. International regimes, transactions, and change: Embedded liberalism in the postwar economic order. In Stephen Krasner, ed., *International Regimes*. Ithaca: Cornell University Press.

Sadler, D. 1992. Beyond 1992: The evolution of European Community policies towards the automobile industry. *Environment and Planning and Government Policy* 10:229–48.

SAF (Swedish Employers Federation). 1992. *Wages and Total Labour Costs for Workers: International Survey, 1980–1990*. Stockholm: SAF.

Salvadori, Didier. 1991. The automobile industry. In David Mayes, ed., *The European Challenge: Industry's Response to the 1992 Program*. London: Harvester Wheatsheaf.

Sandholtz, Wayne, and John Zysman. 1989. 1992: Recasting the European bargain. *World Politics* 42, no. 1: 95–128.

Scharpf, Fritz. 1988. The joint decision trap: Lessons from German federalism and European integration. *Public Administration* 66:239–78.

Schelling, Thomas C. 1978. *Micromotives and Macrobehavior*. New York: W. W. Norton.

———. 1980. *The Strategy of Conflict*. 2d ed. Cambridge: Harvard University Press.

Shepsle, Kenneth A. 1979. Institutional arrangements and equilibrium in multidimensional voting models. *American Journal of Political Science* 23:27–60.

Shepsle, Kenneth A., and Barry Weingast. 1984. Uncovered sets and sophisticated voting outcomes with implications for agenda control. *American Journal of Political Science* 28:49–74.

Skowronek, Stephen. 1982. *Building a New American State: The Expansion of National Administrative Practices, 1877–1920*. Cambridge: Cambridge University Press.

Slot, Piet Jan. 1990. Procedural aspects of state aids: The guardian of competition versus the subsidy villains? *Common Market Law Review* 27, no. 4: 741–60.

Smith, Alasdair. 1992. Non-tariff barriers in the European car market after 1992. Unpublished paper.

Smith, Alasdair, and Anthony Venables. 1990. Automobiles. In Gary Hufbauer., ed., *Europe 1992: An American Perspective*. Washington, D.C.: Brookings Institution.

———. 1991. Counting the cost of voluntary export restraints in the European car market. In Ethan Helpman and Assaf Razin, eds., *International Trade and Trade Policy*. Cambridge: MIT Press.

Snidal, Duncan. 1986. The game *theory* of international politics. In Kenneth A. Oye, ed., *Cooperation Under Anarchy*. Princeton: Princeton University Press.

Stein, Arthur. 1983. Coordination and collaboration: Regimes in an anarchic world. In Stephen Krasner, ed., *International Regimes*. Ithaca: Cornell University Press.

Stein, Arthur. 1990. *Why Nations Cooperate: Circumstance and Choice in International Relations*. Ithaca: Cornell University Press.

Stephen, Roland. 1994. Investing in a bargain: Power and investment in the European Community. Paper presented at the annual meeting of the American Political Science Association, New York, 1–4 September.

———. 1995. Interests and issue linkage and the power of the European Parliament. Paper presented at the biennial meeting of the European Community Studies Association, Charleston, S.C., 11–14 May.

Stigler, George J. 1971. The theory of economic regulation. *Bell Journal of Economics and Manufacturing Science* 3:3–21.

Stopford, John, and Susan Strange. 1991. *Rival States, Rival Firms: Competition for World Market Shares*. Cambridge: Cambridge University Press.

Strange, Susan. 1986. Supranationals and the state. In John A. Hall, ed., *States in History*. Oxford: Basil Blackwell.

———. 1988. A dissident view. In Roland Bieber et al., eds., *1992: One European Market?* Baden-Baden: Nomos Verlagsgesellschaft.

Streeck, Wolfgang. 1989. Successful adjustment to turbulent markets: The automobile industry. In Peter Katzenstein, ed., *Industry and Politics in West Germany: Toward the Third Republic*. Ithaca: Cornell University Press.

Streeck, Wolfgang, and Phillipe C. Schmitter. 1991. From national corporatism to transnational pluralism: Organized interests in the Single European Market. *Politics and Society* 19, no. 2: 133–64.

Tacet, Daniel, and Gérard Zenoni. 1986. *Renault: Sécret d'État*. Paris: Albin Michel.

Taylor, Paul. 1983. *The Limits of European Integration*. New York: Columbia University Press.

———. 1989. The new dynamics of EC integration in the 1980s. In Juliet Lodge, ed., *The European Community and the Challenge of the Future*. New York: St. Martin's Press.

Thomas, John C. 1992. Whose bargain for Europe? National, sectoral, and firm interests in the Single Market. Paper prepared for the annual meeting of the American Political Science Association, Chicago, September.

Thomas, Kenneth P. 1992. The trade preferences of multinational corporations: The big three and the auto pact. Unpublished paper.

Tsebelis, George. 1990. *Nested Games: Rational Choice in Comparative Politics.* Los Angeles: University of California Press.

———. 1994a. The power of the European Parliament as a conditional agenda setter. *American Political Science Review* 88:128–42.

———. 1994b. Will Maastricht reduce the "democratic deficit"? Unpublished paper.

———. 1996. More on the European Parliament as a conditional agenda setter: Response to Moser. *American Political Science Review* 90:839–44.

Tsoukalis, Loukas. 1993. *The New European Economy: The Politics and Economics of Integration.* Oxford: Oxford University Press.

Tucker, Jonathan. 1988. The international car industry: The shift from protection. *Multinational Business* 4:27–36.

Vandermeersch, Dirk. 1987. The Single European Act and the environmental policy of the European Economic Community. *European Law Review* 12:407–29.

VDA (Verband Der Automobilindustrie). 1991. *Jahresbericht: Auto 90/91.* Frankfurt/Main: VDA.

Venables, Anthony J., and Alasdair Smith. 1986. Trade and industrial policy under imperfect competition. *Economic Policy* 1, no. 3: 622–72.

Verdier, Daniel. 1995. The politics of public aid to private industry: The role of policy networks. *Comparative Political Studies* 28:3–42.

Vigier, Pierre. 1992. La politique communautaire de l'automobile. *Revue du Marché Unique Européen* 3:75–126.

Viner, Jacob. 1950. *The Customs Unions Issue.* New York: Carnegie Endowment for International Peace.

Vogel, David. 1995. *Trading Up: Consumer and Environmental Regulation in a Global Economy.* Cambridge: Harvard University Press.

Volpato, Giuseppe. 1993. L'Internationalezzazzione dell'industria automobilistica italiana. In Archivio Storico Fiat, *L'Industria Italiana nel Mercato Mondiale della fine dell'800 alla metà del 900.* Torino: Fiat Relazione Esterne.

Wallace, William. 1990. *The Dynamics of European Integration.* London: Royal Institute of International Affairs.

Waltz, Kenneth N. 1979. *Theory of International Politics.* New York: Random House.

Weaver, R. Kent. 1989. The politics of blame avoidance. *Journal of Public Policy* 6, no. 4: 371–98.

Weiler, J. H. H. 1991. The transformation of Europe. *Yale Law Review* 100:2403–83.

———. 1993. Journey to an unknown destination: A retrospective and prospective of the European Court of Justice in the arena of political integration. *Journal of Common Market Studies* 31, no. 4: 417–46.

Weingast, B. W., and W. Marshall. 1988. The industrial organization of Congress; or, why legislatures, like firms, are not organized as markets. *Journal of Political Economy* 96:132–63.

Wilks, Stephen. 1984. *Industrial Policy and the Motor Industry.* Manchester: Manchester University Press.

———. 1989. Corporate strategy and state support in the European motor industry. In Leigh Hancher and Michael Moran, eds., *Capitalism, Culture, and Economic Regulation.* Oxford: Clarendon Press.

———. 1992. The metamorphosis of European competition policy. Unpublished paper.

Wilks, Stephen, and Lee McGowan. 1995. Discretion in European merger control: The German regime in context. *Journal of European Public Policy* 2, no. 1: 41–67.

Williamson, Oliver E. 1985. *The Economic Institutions of Capitalism: Firms, Markets, Relational Contracting.* New York: Free Press.

Willis, F. Roy. 1971. *Italy Chooses Europe.* New York: Oxford University Press.

Womack, James T., Daniel T. Jones, and Daniel Roos. 1990. *The Machine That Changed the World.* New York: Rawson Associates.

Yannopoulos, George N. 1990. Foreign direct investment and European integration: The evidence from the early years. *Journal of Common Market Studies* 28, no. 3: 235–59.

Yarborough, Beth V., and Robert M. Yarborough. 1987. Institutions for the governance of opportunism in international trade. *Journal of Law, Economics and Organization* 3, no. 1: 129–40.

Zysman, John. 1982. *Governments, Markets, and Growth: Financial Systems and the Politics of Industrial Change.* Ithaca: Cornell University Press.

Index

ACEA. *See* Association des Constructeurs Européens d'Automobile
adjustment
  difficulties of, 3, 4
  exposure to, 33–35
  firm cooperation, 43
  French auto industry, 60
  Japanese imports, 113
  1992 project, 160
  political costs, 157
  political process, 11
  See also economic integration; Single European Act
agency drift
  European Commission, 175
  incentives, 47
  institutions, 15
  political costs, 156
  See also European Commission
agency slack, 137
agenda setting, 15, 50. *See also* European Parliament (EP)
Alfa-Romeo, 60–61, 66, 166
American Motors Corporation, 60
American multinationals. *See* U.S. multinationals
analytical framework, 17, 170
Andriessen, Frans, 126
ANFIA. *See* Associanzione Nazionale Fra l'Industrie Automobilistiche
anti-dumping, 3

antitrust
  policy outcomes, 25
  powers of the European Commission, 142
  producers and, 2
  rulings, 151
  single-market program, 22
Article 100, 92, 96, 97
Article 235, 92
Articles 85 and 86, 143
Articles 92 and 93, 159
Associanzione Nazionale Fra l'Industrie Automobilistiche (ANFIA), 77
Association des Constructeurs Européens d'Automobile (ACEA), 80, 128, 171
auto dealers, 141, 149
auto emissions
  government and firm cooperation, 18
  harmonization, 21, 40
  regulation in the 1970s, 93
auto industry
  adjustment difficulties, 169
  antitrust rulings, 151
  block exemption, 147
  British, 55
  collusion, 140
  comparative advantage, 33
  competition policy, 146
  competitive position, 127
  cooperative enterprises, 118
  cost of capital, 65

213